social research

An International Quarterly of the Social Sciences

Vol 74 : No 1 : Spring 2007

D1458058

THE NEW SCHOOL
A UNIVERSITY

EDITOR Arien Mack

EDITORIAL BOARD Arjun Appadurai, Alice Crary, Elzbieta Matynia, Corey Robin, Alan Ryan, Charles Tilly, Jamie Walkup

MANAGING EDITOR Cara N. Schlesinger

COPY EDITOR Bill Finan

MANAGING EDITORIAL ASSISTANTS Adam Gannaway, Adam Rothstein

WEB ASSISTANTS John Giunta

COVER Jamie Prokell

BUSINESS & EDITORIAL OFFICE
Social Research, The New School for Social Research, 65 Fifth Avenue–Room 344, New York, NY 10003 <socres@newschool.edu>

SUBSCRIPTIONS

Print + Online: $40 per year individuals, $130 libraries and institutions. Online only: $36 individuals, $120 libraries and institutions. Single print issues available through our office. Agency discounts available. Subscribe online at <www.socres.org> or contact our office.

Social Research is published quarterly by The New School for Social Research, a division of The New School, 65 Fifth Avenue, Room 344, New York, NY 10003. <http://www.socres.org>. E-mail: socres@newschool.edu

Contributions should be no more than 8,000 words and typed double-spaced on 8.5" x 11" paper. Notes and references should be typed as separate documents, double-spaced and according to MLA style. Two copies of the manuscript and a stamped return envelope are required. Articles published in Social Research may not be reprinted without permission.

Reprints of back issues, if still available, may be ordered from Periodicals Service Co., 11 Main St., Germantown, NY 12526. Microfilm or microfiche copies of complete volumes of Social Research may be ordered from Bell & Howell Information and Learning/UMI, P.O. Box 1346, Ann Arbor, MI 48106. Complete volumes may be ordered by regular subscribers and copies of single issues, if out of print, may be ordered by any reader, in either microfilm or in print enlarged from microfilm.

Bernhard DeBoer, Inc., the U.S. bookstore distributor of Social Research, may be contacted at 113 East Centre St., Nutley, New Jersey 07110.

Social Research is indexed in ABC POL SCI, ASSIA, Current Contents / Social & Behavioral Sciences, Public Affairs Information Service (PAIS), Research Alert, Social Sciences Citation Index, Social Scisearch, and United States Political Science Documents.

Copyright 2007 by The New School. All rights reserved. ISSN 0037-783X. ISBN 1-933481-08-0.

Periodicals postage paid at New York, NY and at additional mailing offices.

Postmaster: Send address changes to Social Research, 55 West 13th St., New York, NY 10011

Contents

Difficult Choices

v ARIEN MACK
Editor's Introduction

1 CASS R. SUNSTEIN
Incompletely Theorized Agreements in
Constitutional Law

25 ISAAC LEVI
Identity and Conflict

51 EDNA ULLMANN-MARGALIT
Difficult Choices: To Agonize or Not to Agonize?

79 KENNETH KIPNIS
Forced Abandonment and Euthanasia:
A Question from Katrina

101 JEFF MCMAHAN
Justice and Liability in Organ Allocation

125 DAN W. BROCK
Health Care Resource Prioritization and Rationing:
Why Is It So Difficult?

149 SANFORD LEVINSON
Slavery and the Phenomenology of Torture

169 JONATHAN MOORE
Deciding Humanitarian Intervention

201 MARY B. ANDERSON
To Work, or Not to Work, in "Tainted" Circumstances:
Difficult Choices for Humanitarians

223 C. FRED ALFORD
Whistle-Blower Narratives: The Experience of
Choiceless Choice

NOTES ON CONTRIBUTORS
Inside Back Cover

Arien Mack
Editor's Introduction

A DIFFICULT CHOICE IS A CHOICE THAT IS HARD BECAUSE OF ITS inherent content—whether or not to permit euthanasia, for example. It is a choice that often involves choosing between alternatives, either of which results in sacrificing something one believes in. For example, if we were to allocate an extremely expensive medical treatment on the basis of the likelihood of its success, a sicker person might be denied treatment.

Perhaps human beings have always lived in times that were replete with difficult choices, and perhaps to be fully human, it has always been necessary to confront such choices. Yet somehow it seems that these choices are becoming if not more difficult, then more frequent. If we just consider how our capacity to extend and save lives though biomededical intervention has increased, or how our need to obtain information about possible catastrophic attacks has grown more urgent following 9/11, or if we consider all that we are capable of now that we were not capable of earlier, such as cloning a human organism or communicating with someone anywhere in the world in an instant, the reasons become clear. All of these "advances" bring with them newly difficult choices that simply are added to the stock of earlier, proverbial choices. Moreover, these choice are often choices that are not made by a single individual but rather by groups or governments, and while that too is not new, it seems to be more the case now than earlier. Should we intervene in the Balkans? How do we distribute health care or life-giving organs like kidneys or hearts in an equitable manner when resources are so scarce? And who decides?

These are the kinds of question that motivated this issue. It is an issue in which the authors discuss difficult choices and try to spell out why they are difficult and how such choices might be made. Some of the papers look at a particular difficult choice, like organ allocation or humanitarian intervention, while others deal with more general issues and help to shed light more generally on the nature of difficult choices. Difficult choices will always be difficult but my hope is that this issue will make it easier to think about them more effectively.

Cass R. Sunstein
Incompletely Theorized Agreements in Constitutional Law

IN MANY NATIONS, CITIZENS MUST PROCEED IN THE FACE OF CONFLICT
and disagreement on the most fundamental matters. The existence
of diverse values seems to threaten the very possibility of a constitutional order and social stability. People disagree on rights, on the good
life, on equality and liberty, on the nature and the existence of God.
How can constitutional decisions be feasible in these circumstances?
The problem might seem especially serious for democratic societies,
which aspire to self-governance amidst a great deal of heterogeneity.
In this essay I deal with two issues—constitution-making and constitutional interpretation—in an effort to make some progress on that
question.

My basic suggestion is that people can often agree on constitutional *practices*, and even on constitutional rights, when they cannot
agree on constitutional *theories*. In other words, well-functioning constitutional orders try to solve problems through *incompletely theorized agreements*. Sometimes these agreements involve abstractions, accepted as
such amid severe disagreements on particular cases. Thus people who
disagree on incitement to violence and hate speech can accept a general
free speech principle, and those who argue about same-sex relationships
can accept an abstract antidiscrimination principle. This is an important phenomenon in constitutional law and politics; it makes consti-

tution-making possible. Constitution-makers can agree on abstractions without agreeing on the particular meaning of those abstractions.

But sometimes incompletely theorized agreements involve concrete outcomes rather than abstractions. In hard cases, people can agree that a certain practice is constitutional, or is not constitutional, even when the theories that underlie their judgments sharply diverge. In the day-to-day operation of constitutional practice, incompletely theorized agreements on certain rules and doctrines help to ensure a sense of what the law is, even amid large-scale disagreements about what, particularly, accounts for those rules and doctrines.

This latter phenomenon suggests a general strategy for handling some of the most difficult decisions. When people disagree or are uncertain about an abstract issue—Is equality more important than liberty? Does free will exist? Is utilitarianism right? Does punishment have retributive aims?—they can often make progress by moving to a level of greater particularity. They attempt a *conceptual descent*. This phenomenon has an especially notable feature: it enlists silence, on certain basic questions, as a device for producing convergence despite disagreement, uncertainty, limits of time and capacity, and heterogeneity. In short, silence can be a constructive force. Incompletely theorized agreements are an important source of successful constitutionalism and social stability; they also provide a way for people to demonstrate mutual respect.

Consider some examples. People may believe that it is important to protect religious liberty while having quite diverse theories about why this is so. Some people may stress what they see as the need for social peace; others may think that religious liberty reflects a principle of equality and a recognition of human dignity; others may invoke utilitarian considerations; still others may think that religious liberty is itself a theological command. Similarly, people may invoke many different grounds for their shared belief that the Constitution should ensure an independent judiciary. Some may think that judicial independence helps ensure against tyranny; others may believe that it makes government more democratic; still others may think that it leads to greater efficiency in economic terms.

The agreement on particulars is incompletely theorized in the sense that the relevant participants are clear on the practice or the result without agreeing on the most general theory that accounts for it. Often people can agree that a rule—protecting political dissenters, allowing workers to practice their religion—makes sense without entirely agreeing on the foundations of their belief. They may accept an outcome—affirming the right to marry for heterosexual couples, protecting sexually explicit art, banning racial segregation—without understanding or converging on an ultimate ground for that acceptance. Often people can agree not merely on the outcome, but also on a rationale offering low-level or mid-level principles on its behalf. But what ultimately accounts for the outcome, in terms of a full-scale theory of the right or the good, is left unexplained.

There is an extreme case of incomplete theorization, offered when disagreement is especially intense: *full particularity*. This phenomenon occurs when people agree on a result without agreeing on any kind of supporting rationale. They announce what they want to do without offering a reason for doing it. Any rationale—any reason—is by definition more abstract than the result that it supports. Sometimes people do not offer reasons at all, because they do not know what those reasons are, or because they cannot agree on reasons, or because they fear that the reasons that they have would turn out, on reflection, to be inadequate and hence to be misused in the future. This is an important phenomenon in Anglo-American law. Juries usually do not offer reasons for outcomes, and negotiators sometimes conclude that something should happen without saying why it should happen. I will not emphasize this limiting case here, and shall focus instead on outcomes accompanied by low-level or mid-level principles.

My emphasis on incompletely theorized agreements is intended partly as descriptive. These agreements are a pervasive phenomenon in constitution-making and constitutional law. Such agreements are crucial to the effort to make effective decisions amidst intense disagreement. But I mean to make some points about constitutionalism amid pluralism as well. In short, there are special virtues to avoiding large-scale theoretical conflicts. Incompletely theorized agreements can operate as foundations for both rules and analogies, and such agreements are especially well suited to the limits of many diverse institutions, including legislators and courts. Incompletely theorized agreements have their place in the private sector as well. They can be found in university faculties, in the workplace, and even within families. At the same time, there are many puzzles about the limits of incomplete theorization, and about the relationship between incomplete theorization and self-consciously traditionalist approaches to constitutional law and social life in general.

HOW PEOPLE CONVERGE

It seems clear that outside of law, people may agree on a *correct* outcome even though they do not have a theory to account for their judgments. You may know that dropped objects fall, that bee stings hurt, that hot air rises, and that snow melts without knowing exactly why these facts are true. The same is true for morality, both in general and insofar as it bears on constitutional law. You may know that slavery is wrong, that government may not stop political protests, that every person should have just one vote, and that it is bad for government to take your land unless it pays for it without knowing exactly or entirely why these things are so. Moral judgments may be right or true even if they are reached by people who lack a full account of those judgments (though moral reasoners may well do better if they try to offer such an account, a point to which I will return). The same is true for law, constitutional and otherwise. A judge may know that if government punishes religious behavior, it has acted unlawfully, without having a full account of why this principle has been accepted as law. We may thus offer an epistemological point: people can know *that* X is true without entirely knowing *why* X is true.

There is a political point as well. Sometimes people can agree on individual judgments even if they disagree on general theory. In American constitutional law, for example, diverse judges may agree that *Roe v. Wade* (410 U.S. 113, 1973),[1] protecting the right to choose abortion, should not be overruled, though the reasons that lead each of them to that conclusion sharply diverge. Some people think that the court should respect its own precedents; others think that *Roe* was rightly decided as a way of protecting women's equality; others think that the case was rightly decided as a way of protecting privacy; others think that the decision reflects an appropriate judgment about the social role of religion; still others think that restrictions on abortion are unlikely to protect fetuses in the world, and so the decision is good for pragmatic or consequentialist reasons. We can find incompletely theorized political agreements on particular outcomes in many areas of law and politics—on both sides of disputes over national security, on both sides of discrimination controversies, both sides of disputes over criminal justice, both sides of disputes over taxation.

Within the United States, there are incompletely theorized agreements within the Republican Party and among Republican-appointed judges. There are similar agreements within the Democratic Party and among Democratic-appointed judges. Political parties are held together by incomplete theorization; when such parties fracture, or fall apart, it is sometimes because theorization must become more complete. Some of the most interesting agreements can be found not within but across the parties. In the United States, Republicans and Democrats agree on a great deal, not necessarily because they accept the same foundational commitments, but because people of diverse commitments can converge on the same practices and even principles.

RULES AND ANALOGIES

Rules and analogies are the two most important methods for resolving constitutional disputes without obtaining agreement on fundamental principles. Both of these devices—keys to public law in many nations—attempt to promote a major goal of a heterogeneous society: *to make it possible to obtain agreement where agreement is necessary, and to make it unnecessary to obtain agreement where agreement is impossible.*

People can often agree on what constitutional rules are even when they agree on very little else. Their substantive disagreements, however intense, are usually irrelevant to their judgments about the meaning and the binding quality of those rules.[2] And in the face of persistent disagreement or uncertainty about what justice and morality require, people can reason about particular constitutional cases by reference to analogies. They point to cases in which the legal judgments are firm. They proceed from those firm judgments to the more difficult ones. In fact this is how ordinary people tend to think.

We might consider in this regard Supreme Court Justice Stephen Breyer's discussion of one of the key compromises reached by the seven members of the United States Sentencing Commission (Breyer, 1988: 14-19). As Breyer describes it, a central issue was how to proceed in the face of highly disparate philosophical premises about the goals of criminal punishment. Some people asked the commission to follow an approach to punishment based on "just deserts"—an approach that would rank criminal conduct in terms of severity. But different commissioners had very different views about how different crimes should be ranked. In these circumstances, Justice Breyer reports, there could be an odd form of deliberation in which criminal punishments became more and more irrationally severe, because some commission-ers would insist that the crime under consideration was worse than the previously ranked crimes. In any case, agreement on a rational system would be unlikely to follow from efforts by the seven commissioners to rank crimes in terms of severity.

Other people urged the commission to use a model of deter-rence. There were, however, major problems with this approach. No good empirical evidence links all possible variations in punishment to prevention of crime. In any case, the seven members of the commission were highly unlikely to agree that deterrence provides an adequate account of the aims of criminal sentencing. To many people, it is contro-versial to suggest that deterrence is the sole or even principal goal of punishment. An approach based on deterrence seemed no better than an approach based on just deserts.

In these circumstances, what route did the commission follow? In fact, the commission abandoned large theories altogether. It adopted no general view about the appropriate aims of criminal sentencing. Instead, the commission abandoned high theory and adopted a rule— one founded on precedent: "It decided to base the Guidelines primarily upon typical, or average, actual past practice." Consciously articulated explanations, not based on high theory, were used to support particular departures from the past. The decision to adopt this approach must have been based on a belief that the typical or average practice contained sense rather than nonsense—a belief that can be supported by reference to the frequent "wisdom of crowds."[3]

Justice Breyer sees this effort as a necessary means of obtaining agreement and rationality within a diverse, multimember body charged with avoiding unjustifiably wide variations in sentencing. Thus his more colorful oral presentation: "Why didn't the Commission sit down and really go and rationalize this thing and not just take history? The short answer to that is: we couldn't. We couldn't because there are such good arguments all over the place pointing in opposite directions. . . . Try listing all the crimes that there are in rank order of punishable merit . . . Then collect results from your friends and see if they all match. I will tell you they don't" (Rosen, 1994: 19, 25).

The example suggests a more general point. Through both analogies and rules, it is often possible for participants in constitutional law to converge on both abstract principles and particular outcomes without resolving large-scale issues of the right or the good. Indeed, the Universal Declaration of Human Rights was produced through a process akin to that described by Justice Breyer, with a refusal to engage high theory and instead an effort to build on widespread understandings (see Glendon, 2001). The basic enterprise operated by surveying the behavior of most nations, and by building a "universal declaration" on the basis of shared practices. A philosophers' group, involved in the project, "began its work by sending a questionnaire to statesmen and scholars around the world" (Glendon, 2001: 51).

At a key stage, the people involved in drafting the declaration produced "a list of forty-eight items that represented . . . the common core of" a wide range of documents and proposals, including judgments from "Arabic, British, Canadian, Chinese, French, pre-Nazi German, Italian, Latin American, Polish, Soviet Russian and Spanish" nations and cultures (Glendon, 2001: 57). The Universal Declaration of Human Rights emerged from this process. Thus Jacques Maritain, a philosopher closely involved in the Universal Declaration, famously said, "Yes, we agree about the rights, but on condition no one asks us why" (Glendon, 2001: 77). The general point is that a judgment in favor of a set of rights can emerge across disagreement or uncertainty about the foundations of those rights.

FEATURES OF ANALOGY

Analogical thinking is pervasive in law and in everyday life. In ordinary discussions of political and legal questions, people proceed not by reference to first principles or ambitious theories but analogically. You think that racial hate speech is not protected by the first amendment; does this mean that government can silence political extremists? A familiar argumentative technique is to show inconsistency between people's claim about case X in light of their views on case Y. The goal is to reveal hypocrisy or confusion, or to force the claimant to show how the apparently deep commitment on the case about which the discussants agree can be squared with the claimant's view about a case on which they disagree.

In analogical thinking as I understand it here, deep theories about the good or the right are not deployed. In constitutional law, such theories are not usually invoked on behalf of one or another result. On the other hand, analogizers cannot possibly reason from one particular to another particular without saying something at least a little abstract (Dworkin, 2006). They must invoke a reason of principle or policy to the effect that case A was decided rightly *for a reason*, and they must say that that reason applies, or does not apply, in case B. This method of proceeding is ideally suited to a legal system consisting of numerous judges who disagree on first principles and who must take most decided cases as fixed points from which to proceed. For the same reason, those outside of law often think analogically in difficult cases.

Consider some examples. We know that an employer may not fire an employee for agreeing to perform jury duty; it is said to "follow" that an employer is banned from firing an employee for refusing to commit perjury. Turning to a constitutional issue, we know that a speech by a member of the Ku Klux Klan, advocating racial hatred, cannot be regulated unless it is likely to incite and directed to inciting imminent lawless action (see *Brandenburg v. Ohio*, 395 U.S. 444, 1969); it is said to follow that the government cannot forbid members of the Nazi Party to march in Skokie, Illinois. We know that there is no constitutional right to welfare, medical care, or housing (see *Dandridge v. Williams* , 397 U.S. 471, 1970); it is said to follow that there is no constitutional right to government protection against domestic violence.

From a brief glance at these cases, we can get a sense of the characteristic form of analogical thought in law. The process appears to work in five simple steps: 1) Some fact pattern A—the "source" case—has certain characteristics; call them X, Y, and Z. 2) Fact pattern B—the "target" case—has characteristic X, Y, and Q, or characteristics X, Y, Z, and Q. 3) A is treated a certain way in law. 4) Some principle, created or discovered in the process of thinking through A, B, and their interrelations, explains why A is treated the way that it is. 5) Because of what it shares in common with A, B should be treated the same way. It is covered by the same principle.

Some people think that analogical reasoning is really a form of deduction; but this is a mistake. To be sure, analogical reasoning cannot proceed without identification of a governing idea—a principle, a standard, or a rule—to account for the results in the source and target cases. This is the crucial step 4 above. But the governing idea is not given in advance and applied to the new case. Instead, analogical reasoning helps identify the governing idea and is indispensable to its acceptance; we do not know what the idea is until we have assessed the cases. Analogy and disanalogy are created or discovered through the process of comparing cases, as people discern a principle that makes sense of their considered judgments. They did not know, in advance, to what principle they might become committed. In this sense, there is a relationship between analogical reasoning, as it operates in law, and Rawls' understanding of the search for reflective equilibrium (see Rawls, 1971; on the relationship, see Sunstein, 1996).

Analogical reasoning in constitutional law usually operates without anything like a deep or comprehensive theory that would account for the particular outcomes it yields. The judgments that underlie convictions about the relevant case are incompletely theorized. Of course, there is a continuum from the most particularistic and low-level principles to the deepest and most general. It is also true that those engaged in analogical reasoning might have to be more ambitious than they like in order to think well about hard cases. I suggest only that analogizers in constitutional law try to avoid those approaches that come close to the deeply theorized or the foundational. Agreement amidst heterogeneity is possible for that reason.

It might be asked at this point: Why is agreement so important, in constitutionalism or elsewhere? The fact that people can obtain an agreement of this sort—about the value and meaning of a right or about the existence of a sound analogy—is no guarantee of a good outcome. Perhaps the Sentencing Commission incorporated judgments that were based on ignorance, confusion, or prejudice. Some of the same things can be said about analogies. People in positions of authority may agree that a ban on same-sex marriages is constitutionally acceptable because it is analogous to a ban on marriages between uncles and nieces; but the analogy may be misconceived, because there are relevant differences between the two cases, and because the similarities are far from decisive. The fact that people agree that some constitutional case A is analogous to case B does not mean that case A *or* case B is rightly decided. Perhaps case A should not be taken for granted. Perhaps case A should not be selected as the relevant foundation for analogical thinking; perhaps case Z is more pertinent. Perhaps case B is not really like case A. Problems with analogies and low-level thinking might lead us to be more ambitious. We may well be pushed in the direction of general theory—and toward broader and perhaps more controversial claims—precisely because analogical reasoners offer an inadequate and incompletely theorized account of relevant similarities or relevant differences.

All this should be sufficient to show that the virtues of decisions by rule and by analogy are partial. But no system of politics and law is likely to be either just or efficient if it dispenses with rules and analogies. In fact, it is not likely even to be feasible.

CONSTITUTIONS, CASES, AND INCOMPLETELY THEORIZED AGREEMENTS

Incompletely theorized agreements play a pervasive role in constitutional law and in society generally. It is quite rare for a person or group completely to theorize any subject—that is, to accept both a general theory and a series of steps connecting that theory to concrete conclusions. Thus we often have an incompletely theorized agreement on a general principle—incompletely theorized in the sense that people who accept the principle need not agree on what it entails in particular cases. This is the sense emphasized by American Supreme Court Justice Oliver Wendell Holmes in his great aphorism, "General principles do not decide concrete cases" (*Lochner v. New York*, 198 U.S. 48, 69, 1908, Holmes, J., dissenting). The agreement is incompletely theorized in the sense that it is incompletely specified. Much of the key work must be done by others, often through case-by-case judgments, specifying the abstraction at the point of application.

Consider the cases of Poland, Iraq, and South Africa, where constitutional provisions include many abstract provisions on whose concrete specification there has been sharp dispute. Constitutional provisions usually protect such rights as "freedom of speech," "religious liberty," and "equality under the law," and citizens agree on those abstractions in the midst of sharp dispute about what these provisions really entail. Much lawmaking also becomes possible only because of this phenomenon. And when agreement on a written constitution is difficult or impossible, it is because it is hard to obtain consensus on the governing abstractions. Consider the case of Israel, which lacks a written constitution because citizens have been unable to agree about basic principles, even if they are pitched at a high level of abstraction.

Observers of democratic constitutionalism might place particular emphasis on a different kind of phenomenon, of special interest for constitutional law in courts: incompletely theorized agreements on particular outcomes, accompanied by agreements on the narrow or low-level principles that account for them. There is no algorithm by which to distinguish between a high-level theory and one that operates at an intermediate or lower level. We might consider, as conspicuous examples of high-level theories, Kantianism and utilitarianism, and see illustrations in the many distinguished (academic) efforts to understand such areas as tort law, contract law, free speech, and the law of equality as undergirded by highly abstract theories of the right or the good. By contrast, we might think of low-level principles as including most of the ordinary material of low-level constitutional justification or constitutional "doctrine" —the general class of principles and justifications that courts tend to offer. These principles and justifications are not said to derive from any particular large theories of the right or the good, have ambiguous relations to large theories, and are compatible with more than one such theory.

By the term "low-level principles," I refer to something relative, not absolute; I mean to do the same thing with the terms "theories" and "abstractions" (which I use interchangeably). In this setting, the notions "low-level," "high," and "abstract" are best understood in comparative terms, like the terms "big" and "old" and "unusual." Thus the "clear and present" danger standard for regulation of speech in American law is a relative abstraction when compared with the claim that government may not stop a terrorist's speech counseling violence on the Internet, or that members of the Nazi Party may march in Skokie, Illinois. But the "clear and present" danger idea is relatively particular when compared with the claim that nations should adopt the constitutional abstraction "freedom of speech." The term "freedom of speech" is a relative abstraction when measured against the claim that campaign finance laws are acceptable, but the same term is less abstract than the grounds that justify free speech, as in, for example, the principle of personal autonomy or the idea of an unrestricted marketplace of ideas.

In analogical reasoning, incompletely theorized agreements are omnipresent. In the law of discrimination, for example, many people think that sex discrimination is "like" race discrimination, and should be treated similarly, even if they lack or cannot agree on a general theory of when discrimination is unacceptable. In the law of free speech, many people agree that a ban on speech by a Communist or a terrorist is "like" a ban on speech by a member of a fascist political party, and should be treated similarly—even if they lack or cannot agree on a general theory about the foundations of the free speech principle.

INCOMPLETE THEORIZATION AND THE CONSTRUCTIVE USES OF SILENCE

What might be said on behalf of incompletely theorized agreements about the content of a Constitution, or incompletely theorized judgments about particular constitutional cases? Some people think of incomplete theorization as quite unfortunate—as embarrassing, or reflective of some important problem, or a failure of nerve, or even philistine. When people theorize, by raising the level of abstraction, they do so to reveal bias, or confusion, or inconsistency. Surely participants in politics and constitutional law should not abandon this effort.

There is important truth in these usual thoughts; it would not be sensible to celebrate theoretical modesty at all times and in all contexts. Sometimes participants in constitutional law and politics have sufficient information, and sufficient agreement, to be very ambitious. Sometimes they have to reason ambitiously in order to resolve cases. To the extent that the theoretical capacities of judges, or others, are infallible, theoretical ambition is nothing to lament. But in the face of human fallibility, they help make constitutions and constitutional law possible; they even help make social life possible. Silence—on something that may prove false, obtuse, or excessively contentious—can help minimize conflict, allow the present to learn from the future, and save a great deal of time and expense. What is said and resolved may be no more important than what is left out. There are four points here.

The first and most obvious point is that incompletely theorized agreements about constitutional principles and cases may be necessary for social stability. They are well suited to a world—and especially a legal world—containing social disagreement on large-scale issues. Stability would be difficult to obtain if fundamental disagreements broke out in every case of public or private dispute. In the nations of Eastern Europe, stable constitution-making has been possible only because the meaning of the document's broad terms has not been specified in advance.

Second, incompletely theorized agreements can promote two goals of a constitutional democracy and a liberal legal system: to enable people to live together, and to permit them to show each other a measure of reciprocity and mutual respect. The use of low-level principles or rules allows judges on multimember bodies and even citizens generally to find a common way of life without producing unnecessary antagonism. At the same time, incompletely theorized agreements allow people to show each other a high degree of mutual respect, civility, reciprocity, or even charity. Frequently, ordinary people disagree in some deep way on an issue—conflicts in the Middle East, pornography, same-sex marriages, the war on terror—and sometimes they agree not to discuss that issue much, as a way of deferring to each other's strong convictions and showing a measure of reciprocity and respect (even if they do not at all respect the particular conviction that is at stake). If reciprocity and mutual respect are desirable, it follows that public officials or judges, perhaps even more than ordinary people, should not challenge their fellow citizens' deepest and most defining commitments, at least if those commitments are reasonable and if there is no need for them to do so. Indeed, we can see a kind of political charity in the refusal to contest those commitments when life can proceed without any such contest.

To be sure, some fundamental commitments are appropriately challenged in the legal system or within other multimember bodies. Some such commitments are ruled off-limits by the Constitution itself. Many provisions involving basic rights have this function. Of course it is not always disrespectful to disagree with someone in a fundamental way; on the contrary, such disagreements may sometimes reflect profound respect. When defining commitments are based on demonstrable errors of fact or logic, it is appropriate to contest them. So too when those commitments are rooted in a rejection of the basic dignity of all human beings, or when it is necessary to undertake the contest to resolve a genuine problem. But many cases can be resolved in an incompletely theorized way, and this is the ordinary stuff of constitutional law; that is what I am emphasizing here.

The third point is that for arbiters of social controversies, incompletely theorized agreements have the crucial function of reducing the political cost of enduring disagreements. If participants in constitutional law disavow large-scale theories, then losers in particular cases lose much less. They lose a decision, but not the world. They may win on another occasion. Their own theory has not been rejected or ruled inadmissible. When the authoritative rationale for the result is disconnected from abstract theories of the good or the right, the losers can submit to legal obligations, even if reluctantly, without being forced to renounce their largest ideals.

Fourth, and finally, incompletely theorized agreements are especially valuable when a society seeks moral evolution and even progress over time. Consider the area of equality, where considerable change has occurred in the past and will inevitably occur in the future. A completely theorized judgment would be unable to accommodate changes in facts or values. If a culture really did attain a theoretical end-state, it would become rigid and calcified; we would know what we thought about everything. Unless the complete theorization were error-free, this would disserve posterity. Hence, incompletely theorized agreements are a key to debates over equality in both law and politics, with issues being raised about whether discrimination on the basis of sexual orientation, age, disability, and other characteristics are analogous to discrimination on the basis of race; such agreements have the important advantage of allowing a large degree of openness to new facts and perspectives.

At one point, we might think that same-sex relations are akin to incest; at another point, we might find the analogy bizarre. Of course, a completely theorized judgment would have many virtues if it were correct. But at any particular moment in time, this is an unlikely prospect for human beings, not excluding judges in constitutional disputes, or those entrusted with the task of creating constitutional provisions.

Compare practical reasoning in ordinary life. At a certain time, you may well refuse to make decisions that seem foundational in character—about, for example, whether to get married within the next year, or whether to have two, three, or four children, or whether to live in San Francisco or New York. Part of the reason for this refusal is knowledge that your understandings of both facts and values may well change. Indeed, your identity may itself change in important and relevant ways, and for this reason a set of firm commitments in advance—something like a fully theorized conception of your life course—would make no sense. Legal systems and nations are not altogether different.

BURKE AND HIS RATIONALIST ADVERSARIES

Those who emphasize incompletely theorized agreements owe an evident debt to Edmund Burke, who was, in a sense, the great theorist of incomplete theorization. I do not attempt anything like an exegesis of Burke, an exceedingly complex figure, in this space, but let us turn briefly to Burke himself and in particular to his great essay on the French Revolution, in which he rejected the revolutionary temperament because of its theoretical ambition (Burke, 1999).

Burke's key claim is that the "science of constructing a commonwealth, or reforming it, is, like every other experimental science, not to be taught a priori" (Burke, 1999: 442). To make this argument, Burke opposes theories and abstractions, developed by individual minds, to traditions, built up by many minds over long periods. In his most vivid passage, Burke writes:

> The science of government being therefore so practical in itself, and intended for such practical purposes, a matter which requires experience, and even more experience than any person can gain in his whole life, however sagacious and observing he may be, it is with infinite caution than any man ought to venture upon pulling down an edifice which has answered in any tolerable degree, for ages the

common purposes of society, or on building it up again, without having models and patterns of approved utility before his eyes (Burke, 1999: 451).

It is for this reason that Burke describes the "spirit of innovation" as "the result of a selfish temper and confined views" (Burke, 1999: 428) and offers the term "prejudice" as one of enthusiastic approval, noting that "instead of casting away all our old prejudices, we cherish them to a very considerable degree" (Burke, 1999: 451). Emphasizing the critical importance of stability, Burke adds a reference to "the evils of inconstancy and versatility, ten thousand times worse than those of obstinacy and the blindest prejudice" (Burke, 1999: 451). Burke's sharpest distinction, then, is between established practices and individual reason. He contends that reasonable citizens, aware of their own limitations, will effectively delegate decision-making authority to their own traditions. "We are afraid to put men to live and trade each on his own private stock of reason" simply "because we suspect that this stock in each man is small, and that the individuals would do better to avail themselves of the general bank and capital of nations, and of ages. Many of our men of speculation, instead of exploding general prejudices, employ their sagacity to discover the latent wisdom which prevails in them" (Burke, 1999: 451).

Burke was enthusiastic about reasoning by analogy, and it is easy to imagine an unambivalently Burkean advocate of incompletely theorized agreements. But Burke's enthusiasm for traditions is contentious, and for good reason. In the aftermath of apartheid, should South Africa have built carefully, and in a tradition-bound way, on its own past? Or should it have adopted a constitution on the basis of some kind of account of human liberty and equality? Social practices, and constitution-making, can be incompletely theorized while also being anti-Burkean. The South African constitution itself includes stirring and tradition-rejecting ideals of various kinds, and those ideals can be accepted from many different foundations. In constitutional adjudication, judges who believe in incompletely theorized agreements might require government to come up with a reason for its practice—and insist that a tradition, or a longstanding practice, is not itself a reason.

In constitutional law, we can imagine fierce contests between Burkeans and their more rationalist adversaries, even if both camps are willing to march under the banner of incomplete theorization (see Sunstein, 2006). Those contests cannot be resolved in the abstract; everything depends on the nature of the relevant traditions and the competence of those who propose to subject them to critical scrutiny. My central point is that Burkeans are committed to incompletely theorized agreements, but those who believe in such agreements need not be Burkeans. The American constitutional tradition generally requires reasons, even if low-level ones, and hence Burkeanism seems self-defeating for the United States, because it cannot easily be fit with American traditions.

CONCEPTUAL ASCENTS FOR CONSTITUTIONAL LAW?

Borrowing from Henry Sidgwick's writings on ethical method (Sidgwick, 1966: 96-104), a critic of incompletely theorized agreements might respond that constitutional law should frequently use ambitious theories.[4] For example, there is often good reason for people interested in constitutional rights to raise the level of abstraction and ultimately to resort to large-scale theory. Concrete judgments about particular cases can prove inadequate for morality or constitutional law. Sometimes people do not have clear intuitions about how cases should come out. Sometimes their intuitions are insufficiently reflective. Sometimes seemingly similar cases provoke different reactions, and it is necessary to raise the level of theoretical ambition to explain whether those different reactions are justified, or to show that the seemingly similar cases are different after all. Sometimes people simply disagree.

By looking at broader principles, we may be able to mediate the disagreement. In any case there is a problem of explaining our considered judgments about particular cases in order to see whether they are not just a product of accident or error. When modest judges join an opinion that is incompletely theorized, they must rely on a reason or a principle, justifying one outcome rather than another. The opinion must itself refer to a reason or principle; it cannot just announce a victor. Perhaps the low-level principle is wrong because it fails to fit with other cases, or because it is not defensible as a matter of (legally relevant) political morality.

In short, the incompletely theorized agreement may be nothing to celebrate. If a judge is reasoning well, he should have before him a range of other cases, C through Z, in which the principle is tested against others and refined. At least if he is a distinguished judge, he will experience a kind of "conceptual ascent" in which the more or less isolated and small low-level principle is finally made part of a more general theory. Perhaps this would be a paralyzing task, and perhaps our judge need not often attempt it. But perhaps it is an appropriate model for understanding law and an appropriate aspiration for evaluating judicial and political outcomes. On one view, judges who insist on staying at a low level of theoretical ambition are philistines, even ostriches.

There is some truth in this response. At least if they have time and competence, moral and constitutional reasoners thinking about basic rights should try to achieve vertical and horizontal consistency, not just the local pockets of coherence offered by incompletely theorized agreements. In democratic processes, it is appropriate and sometimes indispensable to challenge existing practice in abstract terms. But this challenge to incompletely theorized agreements, should not be taken for more than it is worth. Any interest in conceptual ascent must take account of the distinctive characteristics of the arena in which real-world constitutional-makers and judges must do their work.

As I have noted, incompletely theorized agreements have many virtues, including the promotion of stability, the reduction of costs of disagreement, and the demonstration of humility and mutual respect. All this can be critical to successful constitution-making in pluralistic societies. These points bear on constitutional disputes as well. In a well-functioning constitutional democracy, judges are especially reluctant to invoke philosophical abstractions as a basis for invalidating the outcomes of electoral processes. They are reluctant because they know that they may misunderstand the relevant philosophical arguments and they seek to show respect to the diverse citizens in their nation. A conceptual ascent might be appealing in the abstract, but if those who ascend will blunder, they might stay close to the ground.

There are many lurking questions. How, exactly, do moral and political judgments bear on the content of law in general and constitutional law in particular? What is the relation between provisional or considered judgments about particulars and corresponding judgments about abstractions? Sometimes people interested in constitutional law write as if abstract theoretical judgments, or abstract theories, have a kind of reality and hardness that particular judgments lack, or as if abstract theories provide the answers to examination questions that particular judgments, frail as they are, may pass or fail. On this view, theories are searchlights that illuminate particular judgments and show them for what they really are. But we might think instead that there is no special magic in theories or abstractions, and that theories are simply the (humanly constructed) means by which people make sense of the judgments that constitute their ethical, legal, and political worlds. The abstract deserves no priority over the particular; neither should be treated as foundational. A (poor or crude) abstract theory may simply be a confused way of trying to make sense of our considered judgments about particular constitutional cases, which may be better than the theory.

INCOMPLETELY THEORIZED AGREEMENTS AND DISAGREEMENT

Incompletely theorized agreements have many virtues; but their virtues are partial. Stability, for example, is brought about by such agreements, and stability is usually desirable; but a constitutional system that is stable and unjust should probably be made less stable. Consider two qualifications to what has been said thus far. Some cases cannot be decided *at all* without introducing a fair amount in the way of theory. Some constitutional cases cannot be decided *well* without introducing more ambitious theory. If a good theory (involving, for example, the right to free speech) is available, and if judges can be persuaded that the theory is good, there should be no taboo on its judicial acceptance. Theoretical depth can hardly be rejected in the abstract.

What of disagreement? The discussion thus far has focused on the need for convergence. There is indeed such a need; but it is only part of the picture. In law, as in politics, disagreement can be a productive and creative force, revealing error, showing gaps, moving deliberation and results in good directions. The American constitutional order has placed a high premium on "government by discussion," and when the process is working well, this is true for the judiciary as well as for other institutions. Agreements may be a product of coercion, subtle or not, or of a failure of imagination.

Constitutional disagreements have many legitimate sources. Two of these sources are especially important. First, people may share general commitments but disagree on particular outcomes. Second, people's disagreements on general principles may produce disagreement over particular outcomes and low-level propositions as well. People who think that an autonomy principle accounts for freedom of speech may also think that the government cannot regulate truthful, nondeceptive commercial advertising—whereas people who think that freedom of speech is basically a democratic idea, and is focused on political speech, may have no interest in protecting commercial advertising at all. Constitutional theorizing can have a salutary function in part because it tests low-level principles by reference to more ambitious claims. Disagreements can be productive by virtue of this process of testing.

Certainly if everyone having a reasonable general view converges on a particular (by hypothesis reasonable) judgment, nothing is amiss. But if an agreement is incompletely theorized, there is a risk that everyone who participates in the agreement is mistaken, and hence that the outcome is mistaken. There is also a risk that someone who is reasonable has not participated, and that if that person were included, the agreement would break down. Over time, incompletely theorized agreements should be subject to scrutiny and critique, at least in democratic arenas, and sometimes in courtrooms as well. That process may result in more ambitious thinking than constitutional law ordinarily entails.

Nor is social consensus a consideration that outweighs everything else. Usually it would be much better to have a just outcome, rejected by many people, than an unjust outcome with which all or most agree. A just constitution is more important than an agreed-upon constitution. Consensus or agreement is important largely because of its connection with stability, itself a valuable but far from overriding social goal. As Thomas Jefferson wrote, a degree of turbulence is productive in a democracy.[5] It may well be right to make an unjust constitutional order a lot less stable. We have seen that incompletely theorized agreements, even if stable and broadly supported, may conceal or reflect injustice. Certainly agreements should be more fully theorized when the relevant theory is plainly right and people can be shown that it is right, or when the invocation of the theory is necessary to decide cases. None of this is inconsistent with what I have claimed here.

It would be foolish to say that no general theory about constitutional law or rights can produce agreement, even more foolish to deny that some general theories deserve support, and most foolish of all to say that incompletely theorized agreements warrant respect whatever their content. What seems plausible is something no less important for its modesty: except in unusual situations, and for multiple reasons, general theories are an unlikely foundation for constitutional-making and constitutional law. For fallible human beings, caution and humility about theoretical claims are appropriate, at least when multiple theories can lead in the same direction. This more modest set of claims helps us to appreciate incompletely theorized agreements as important phenomena with their own special virtues.

Incompletely theorized agreements thus help illuminate an enduring constitutional and indeed social puzzle: how members of diverse societies can work together on terms of mutual respect amid sharp disagreements about both the right and the good. If there is a solution to this puzzle, incompletely theorized agreements are a good place to start.

NOTES

1. On the refusal to overrule Roe, see *Planned Parenthood v. Casey*, 112 S. Ct. 2791 (1992).
2. Ronald Dworkin (1985) rightly suggests that disputes over meaning are sometimes produced by disputes over underlying principles. I am suggesting only that most of the time, disputes over principles are accompanied by agreement over meaning. I do not attempt here to explore disagreements about interpretation, though the basic themes certainly bear on that topic.
3. For a popular treatment, see Surowiecki (2005); a more technical account, with reference to the Condorcet Jury Theorem, can be found in Sunstein (2006).
4. This is the tendency in Dworkin (1985).
5. Thus Jefferson said that turbulence is "productive of good. It prevents the degeneracy of government, and nourishes a general attention to . . . public affairs. I hold . . . that a little rebellion now and then is a good thing" (Letter to Madison in Peterson, 1975).

REFERENCES

Breyer, Stephen. "The Federal Sentencing Guidelines and the Key Compromises Upon Which They Rest." *Hofstra Law Review* 17 (1988).

Burke, Edmund. "Reflections on the Revolution in France." *The Portable Edmund Burke*. Ed. Isaac Kramnick. New York: Penguin Books, 1999: 416-451.

Dworkin, Ronald. *Law's Empire*. Cambridge: Harvard University Press, 1985.

———. *Justice in Robes*. Cambridge: Harvard University Press, 2006.

Glendon, Mary Ann. *A World Made Anew*. New York: Random House, 2001.

Peterson, Merrill D., ed. *The Portable Thomas Jefferson*. New York: Viking Press, 1975.

Rawls, John. *A Theory of Justice*. Cambridge: Belknap Press, 1971.

Rosen, Jeffrey. "Breyer Restraint." *The New Republic* (July 11, 1994).

Sidgwick, Henry. *The Methods of Ethics*. 7th ed. New York: Dover Publications, 1966.

Sunstein, Cass R. *Legal Reasoning and Political Conflict*. New York: Oxford University Press, 1996.

———. *One Case At A Time*. Cambridge: Harvard University Press, 1999.

Sunstein, Cass R. "Burkean Minimalism." *Michigan Law Review* 105 (2006).

Sunstein, Cass R. *Infotopia: How Many Minds Produce Knowledge*. New York: Oxford University Press, 2006.

Surowiecki, James. *The Wisdom of Crowds*. New York: Doubleday, 2005.

Isaac Levi
Identity and Conflict

IDENTITY AND VALUES

AMARTYA SEN WISELY REMINDS US OF A FAMILIAR FACT: ALL AGENTS carry many different "identities." X may be a US citizen, a Democrat, a secular humanist, a father, a husband, a grandfather, bureaucrat, and a great many other things.[1]

As Sen recognizes, to say that all agents carry many different identities should not be equated with the banal observation that each of us possesses many different characteristics at a given time and over time. An agent identifies only with some of the groups with whom the agent shares traits in common. These are the groups who have an influence "on what we value and how we behave" (Sen, 2006: 20).

Sen has long been a critic of attitudes among economists concerned with explaining and predicting behavior in terms of self-interest even if such interest is generous enough to include interest in the welfare of others or interest in promoting the goals of others. The values promoted by decisionmakers can vary. They may become affiliated with institutions, ethnic or religious groups, with their country, profession, their families in ways that run counter to their personal goals no matter how altruistic the latter may or may not be. They may conform to the requirements of some moral code or code of honor. Doing any one of these things may entail considerable self-sacrifice. We need not insist on a view as to how widespread this behavior is in order to acknowledge that such behavior counts for a considerable portion of both routine and deliberate behavior. According to Sen, having an identity is an affiliation with a group and commitment to a code of conduct or system of value commitments associated with the affiliation.

Sen points out that the classical model of rational economic man may be described as urging a monomaniacal insistence on a single affiliation. Rational X affiliates with the group (typically a unit set) committed to promoting X's self-interest. Affiliating with the value commitments of a single group is a feature rational economic man shares in common with fundamentalist Christians, Muslims, and Jews of the more fanatical varieties who express loyalty exclusively to their religious groups or to the God who is the alleged object of adoration.

According to Sen, most of us have many affiliations. In some contexts, some are more salient than others. Even where loyalty to several affiliations is called for, it is often feasible to gratify the demands of all of them. Where it is not feasible, the need to prioritize the several identities can lead to conflict within a single individual or group or to violent struggle between groups. Sen denies that violent struggle is inevitable. He contends, however, that recognition of the multiple affiliations that agents have presents an opportunity to replace violent struggle with deliberate choice of resolutions of conflict based on reasoned deliberation where the conflicting demands of competing identities are weighed and evaluated.

This is not an excessively optimistic view of identity politics. Sen does not predict that agents with multiple affiliations will seize the opportunities for avoiding violent struggle and choosing the path of reasoned deliberation. He points out that the many identities that agents have is an *opportunity* for exercising reasoned choice. And he seeks to encourage the exercise of such opportunities. But he does not predict that agents will take advantage of these opportunities.

Some aspects of Sen's admirable attitude call for closer scrutiny. One way of "seeing oneself" is, as Sen points out, through an appeal to history and background. It is not the only way, but it is one way. However, it is far from clear that this way of seeing oneself entails devotion to any particular code of conduct or network of value commitments. No doubt one's upbringing inculcates certain values. But one can retain identification with one's family, ethnicity, and background without endorsing those values. I was brought up to be a moderately observant Jew and a

social research

65 FIFTH AVENUE · ROOM 344, NEW YORK, NY 10003

PLEASE ENTER MY SUBSCRIPTION TO *SOCIAL RESEARCH*, STARTING WITH THE CURRENT ISSUE.

(These rates are for print only. For print + online or online only, please subscribe at www.socres.org.)

☐ **ONE YEAR**	Individual subscribers $36	Institutions $120
☐ **TWO YEARS**	Individual subscribers $60	Institutions $210
☐ **THREE YEARS**	Individual subscribers $80	Institutions $300

Foreign subscribers add $20 postage per year.
Agents and booksellers take 15% off institutional rates only.

☐ CHECK ENCLOSED   ☐ BILL MY VISA/MASTERCARD

CARD NUMBER/EXPIRATION _____

SIGNATURE _____

NAME _____

STREET _____

CITY _____ STATE _____ ZIP _____

TEL.: 212.229.5776x1 • FAX: 212.229.5476   74:1

Zionist. I am now a nonbeliever without any particular attachment to Jewish religious practice or the state of Israel. Although there are Jews who would allege that I am no longer Jewish, others would insist otherwise and allege that I indulge in self-hate. I regard myself as Jewish and so would most of my acquaintances, whether Jewish or not, who think about it. I do not see any of the value commitments to which I subscribe as being particularly connected with this identity. Perhaps my affection for my extended family is caught up in this, but I doubt it. In having family connections, I am no different than others who have different ethnic or religious affiliation. It may be argued that there is a difference in culture involved, in style or aesthetic sensibility. But if there is, it is not very significant. Yet, I would resist the allegation that I am not Jewish. If there were another outburst of Nazi style anti-Semitism I would, like Henri Bergson, voluntarily wear the Jewish star. Perhaps, that is what my Jewish identity amounts to in the way of a code of conduct.

That is not to say that other Jews do not have stronger networks of value commitments that they associate with their identification as Jews. But that makes the point I mean to emphasize. Identifying with a group does not, in many cases, entail a unique system of value commitments and, indeed, may not entail any or any very significant value commitments at all. Moreover, the identification may remain constant even though the value commitments change over time.

For this reason, I am inclined to engage in what Sen calls "identity disregard." No doubt some groups are defined by the value commitments their members support. An agent who belongs to such a group has an identity that supports fairly substantive value commitments. But this is far from true in every case. I doubt that it is true in the case of embracing a Muslim identity anymore than it is in the case of adopting a Jewish identity. I do not mean to dismiss the importance of having value commitments and even systems of value commitments that are not focused on promoting self-interest or one's own goals. But I submit that identifying with a group is neither necessary nor sufficient for having such value commitments

VALUE COMMITMENTS[2]

Deliberation, whether it concerns the purchase of a grass whip at some hardware store or the decision to marry Betty Jane, to join the Marines, or to vote in the next election, concerns a choice among options as recognized by the deliberating agent. Hence, it inevitably involves a comparison among the options with respect to which are better than which. The decisionmaker may not be in a position to provide a complete ranking of the options recognized as available. And even when a complete ranking can be constructed, the agent may not impute a numerical value or utility to the options.

Sometimes such incompleteness is a feature of the agent's commitment as to how to evaluate the options. Sometimes, however, it reflects a failure on the part of the agent to fulfill his or her commitments. We should not confuse value commitments with the performances that qualify as attempts to fulfill these commitments. Failure to make complete comparisons of the available options may be due to failures of performance even when the agent is committed to such comparisons. Remedy for such failures calls for therapy, moral exhortation, and efforts to elicit the agent's attitudes from assessments as to how the decisionmaker would choose in various hypothetical circumstances as well as how the decisionmaker chooses in empirically observed situations.

But often enough failures to make complete comparisons of the available options are an expression of clearheaded doubt. The agent endorses value commitments that recognize more than one way of evaluating the available options to be permissible to use in making a decision. X may wish to protect American workers by preventing the immigration of individuals willing to work for paltry wages while deploring the xenophobia that suffuses the debate over immigration. Recognition of several different ways of evaluating the available immigration policy grounds a principled doubt concerning what is to be done. When X is in such doubt, X fails to regard ranking policies guided by the concern to protect American workers as impermissible and fails to rule out rankings guided by hostility to xenophobia. Both types of evaluations may be judged to be permissible even though there may be no way to choose from the available options that is optimal according to both. According to X's "all things considered" judgment, there is no best option among those available. There is no complete ranking representing X's all things considered judgment. Yet, X is neither confused nor irrational. X has a "real and living doubt" of the sort that provokes inquiry according to Peirce and Dewey. Therapy is not warranted.

Although value commitments may be formulated in many ways, specifying a scope and a constraint constitutes a useful way to do so.

The prototype for this formulation is found in one way of characterizing laws of nature. Newton's second law states that all physical bodies (bodies located in space and time and possessing mass) move in conformity with $F = kma$. This law is characterized by identifying a domain of application D (physical bodies) and a formula or "law" F ($F = kma$) and asserting that everything in the domain D satisfies the formula F.

Value commitments may be formulated in a similar way. A value commitment is a prescription specifying that the evaluation of any decision problem within the scope S is subject to the constraints C. Thus, the claim that it is wrong to break a promise may be recast as follows: in any context where there is a choice between keeping and breaking a promise, keeping the promise is to be valued more than breaking it. Because there may be several alternative ways to keep a promise, the decisionmaker may recognize several ways of evaluating the options as permissible. The constraints of the value commitment may not rule out ranking keeping a promise with good cheer over doing so grudgingly or vice versa. Endorsing a value commitment need not secure a complete ordering of the options in the decision problem covered by the value commitment.

I leave open how the scope S is to be formulated except to say that the domain should be a set of decision problems of some kind. The constraints should be constraints on the way in which the relevant possible consequences of options in decision problems in S are evaluated as better or worse.[3] I assume that the most specific coherent and relevant representation of the evaluation of the consequences of a set of options is by means of a utility function.

Whatever the constraints may be, in any specific context of choice the constraints will be satisfied by some utility functions over the consequences and violated by others. The set of utility functions that are satisfied is the set of *permissible* utility functions according to the value commitment.[4] This set of permissible utility functions for the set O of consequences of options in A open to the decisionmaker is called the *Extended Value Structure EV(O)* for the set O.[5]

In the case of promise keeping as construed above, the domain included all cases where the set A included a case of promise breaking and a case of promise keeping. The consequences in this case may be equated with the options themselves. This can happen sometimes in contexts of decision making under certainty where the decisionmaker is certain of the consequences of implementing the various options conditional on their being implemented. The extended value structure is the set of all permissible utility functions over the consequences of the several options.

When the decision problem is one that the decisionmaker is certain what the consequences of each available option will be, each permissible utility function over the consequences is also a permissible expected utility function over the options. So the set of permissible expected utility functions belonging to the value structure $V(A)$ of the set of options in A is the same as the set of permissible utility functions in the extended value structure $EV(O)$ for the set O of possible consequences of options in A.

This mode of representation is needlessly complicated if we are going to consider only decision making under certainty. But in typical situations, there is some uncertainty as to what the consequences of a given option in A might be. To ignore such complications is to indulge in superficial thinking. The proposals made here seek to provide a general way of accommodating various kinds of complexity. I do not mean to dwell on the complexities in this essay; but in order to speak in a relatively general way, it is necessary to make reference to some complications.

In decision making under uncertainty, derivation of permissible expected utility functions in V(A) requires appeal to judgments of subjective or credal probabilities for the consequences of each option in A conditional on that option being implemented. The decisionmaker may not have made up his or her mind as to which system of numerically determinate probabilities is permissible and may be in a credal state B recognizing members of a convex set of probabilities to be permissible. The value structure V(A) is derived from the credal state B and the extended value structure EV(O) by pairing each element of V(A) with an element of B and computing the expected utility.

The credal state B is derived from the decisionmaker's *confirmational commitment C* and *state of full belief K*. The extended value structure is derived from the decisionmaker's *value commitment* (and when necessary state of full belief K). Our concern here is with the value commitment. But this short sketch should indicate how value commitments are related to their function in guiding the decisionmaker's decisions (see Levi, 1999 for a brief account of these ideas).

In the subsequent discussion, I shall suppose that the decisionmaker faces a choice that either the consequences of each option are known for sure or if there is uncertainty, there is exactly one permissible probability function so that probabilities are determinate. The ramifications of my remarks for more complex cases will not be altered substantially by this simplification.

In cases of the sort envisaged, value commitments impose constraints on value structures that are determined by the constraints imposed directly on extended value structures and the uniquely permissible credal probability function. In the subsequent discussion, therefore, the often important differences between the way that value commitments constrain value structures as compared to extended value structures will be overlooked.

SYSTEMS OF VALUE COMMITMENTS AND THEIR MODIFICATION

In the sense to which I have just gestured, a given agent X may endorse many different value commitments covering a wide variety of different decision problems. Sometimes such value commitments cannot be jointly implemented. X may be committed to keeping X's promises and to feeding X's family. A situation may arise where the options are such that X cannot satisfy the constraints appropriate to the two kinds of decision problem.

Such a situation implies not only conflict between X's value commitments but inconsistency in X's full beliefs (Levi, 1986: 7). X's commitment to promise keeping and to feeding X's family presupposes that satisfying both can be implemented. Logically possible scenarios where joint satisfaction is not feasible are ruled out as not serious possibilities. When X recognizes that joint satisfaction is not feasible, X faces an inconsistency in full beliefs from which he or she should retreat. So X must modify his full beliefs.

But that is not all. Once X recognizes that X is confronting a situation where the scope of X's value commitment to promise keeping and the scope of X's value commitment to feeding X's family both apply, X faces another incoherence. The constraints of the two value commitments cannot be jointly satisfied. X should alter X's system of value commitments in order to escape from this form of rational incoherence.

X faces three options for doing so: 1) restrict the scope of the commitment to promise keeping so as not to cover the problematic situation and retain the scope of the commitment to feed X's family, 2) retain the commitment to promise keeping and restrict the scope of the commitment to feed X's family so as not to cover the problematic situation, or 3) restrict the scope of both commitments.

If option 3 is taken, presumably X will retain the constraint from the injunction to keep promises for those cases of choice where there is no conflict with feeding X's family. Similarly, the obligation to feed X's family will be endorsed in those cases where there is no conflict with promise keeping. X will also need to provide a constraint on permissible utility functions to cover the problematic cases where conflict arises. I have suggested elsewhere that X should initially recognize as permissible all utility functions that are permissible according to one or the other initial value commitments. In addition, X should recognize as permissible all potential compromises between any pair of utility functions as represented by the convex hull of the two extended value structures on offer. If this extended value structure is deemed too indeterminate, inquiry aimed at reducing the indeterminacy may be undertaken.

IDENTITY AND SYSTEMS OF VALUE COMMITMENTS

As I have characterized value commitments, agents will generally endorse many distinct value commitments covering different types of decision problems. And just as agents seek to systematize their beliefs about the world with the aid of explanatorily comprehensive theories, so too they seek to organize their value commitments into systems they judge to "make sense."[6]

I have already argued that it is neither necessary nor sufficient to identify with a group to endorse a value commitment or system of value commitments associated with a group. In this respect I advocate "identity neglect." But there may be some stronger sense of identification associated with the organization of a set of value commitments into a system. In this stronger sense, identity neglect may no longer be appropriate.

The 613 commandments of Jehovah constitute a set of value commitments regulating all sorts of activities rendered systematic because they are injunctions imposed on the Hebrews by God. The systematization is fashioned out of beliefs as to what is true (that God enjoined the 613 commandments) and a value commitment to obey the will of God. Someone who is not an Israelite might adopt these beliefs and this value commitment without undertaking to conform to the 613 commandments because these commandments are imposed on the Israelites. However, only if the person identifies himself or herself as belonging to the children of Israel will the beliefs of fact and the value commitment entail an obligation to conform to these commandments.

For the Israelite to give up one of the commandments (which can be reformulated as a value commitment) would entail modifying the systematization—perhaps by calling into question whether conformity to the value commitment was enjoined by God or whether one ought to obey God's commandments. The agent X might come to doubt that he or she is an Israelite so that even if thesis that God enjoined the commandment remains a full belief and that God ought to be obeyed remains unquestioned, the agent calls into question the truth of the claim that he or she is an Israelite and can, therefore, call into question whether X is obliged to obey the 613 commandments without irrationality. Or, even if X does not doubt the fact that X is an Israelite as a factual claim, X judges that X has control over whether X remains an Israelite and chooses to leave the community. Any one of these modifications incurs a cost to X that constitutes a deterrent to modification.

Among the possible ways of giving up one of the commandments specified are two that are related to X's identity. One calls for X to give up the full belief that X is an Israelite. In so doing, X is denying that, as a matter of fact, X is an Israelite. X is denying a factual identification with the children of Israel.

But even if X is convinced that he is an Israelite, he or she may decide to opt out of the Israelite community and thereby cease being committed to maintaining conformity with the 613 commandments. X cannot thereby deny the fact that X was an Israelite or that X may continue to be truly described as being an Israelite. Nonetheless, X judges that it is up to him or her to decide whether to remain loyal to the Israelites or to disassociate him or herself from them. Call identification in this sense *commitment identity*.

Akeel Bilgrami claims that "identities in politics in the *subjective* sense of identity come from deep *value commitments* that individual or groups have to their religions, or their nationalities, their race their gender, and so forth" (Bilgrami, 2004: 183). I take it that Bilgrami is thinking of identity in the sense in which an agent chooses to associate or disassociate oneself from a group. By referring to value commitments to a group, Bilgrami seems to have in mind reference to a group that figures in the scope specification of a value commitment in the sense in which I am proposing to understand this notion. That is to say, the decisionmaker undertakes the value commitment or system of value commitments associated with the group in question by that agent or refuses to give up the commitments if they are already undertaken.

It may be objected that the notion of identification just mentioned does not cover the notion articulated by Patrick Henry when he declared "My country right or wrong!" But this is not so. The constraint imposed by a commitment to support the decisions taken by one's "country" is far from clear. But minor adjustments might clarify the constraint imposed. The scope of the commitment also involves obscurity. Does it cover the decisions of all citizens or merely "patriotic" citizens? Here too minor adjustments can rescue some clarity. Some value commitments are simply obscure.

Thus, in the sense of identification (commitment identification) I am taking as an elaboration of Bilgrami's idea: to identify with a group is to embrace a value commitment or system of value commitments whose scope covers agents who are members of that group.

Returning to Sen's contention that we all have many identities, can Sen's notion of identity be equated with the one just elaborated? I think it can. As Sen himself acknowledges, it is not enough to point out that each of us has many different characteristics to sustain his thesis that we have many identities. Nonetheless, he is right to maintain this view. Each of us identifies with many different groups that support diverse commitments. X can identify with the Muslims, be a member of the American Bar Association, belong to the PTA in some school in Ann Arbor, etc.

Bilgrami does not think this is quite right. He does not deny that agents can have multiple identities in the weak commitment sense according to which an identity is the type of affiliation that is associated with endorsement of a system of value commitments. But he thinks there is a stronger notion of identity that it is important to understand.

> The notion of identity can be characterized in terms of what I . . . called an agent's most "fundamental commitments." These are desires that she most identifies with.

How are these to be characterized? It is not enough to repeat that these are the desires that are highly reinforced because those will be too many to deliver anything so focused as the notion of identity. To the extent that we believe in the notion of identity, we will have to do better and specify desires that have an even greater centrality in our psychological economy. These are specified in counterfactual terms. *A desire is a fundamental commitment if one wants it fulfilled even were one not to have the desire.* In case this sounds too abstract, it can be indexed to times a desire is a fundamental commitment at a given time, if at that time one wants if fulfilled at a future time, even if one believes that at the future time one may not have that desire. This temporal elaboration of the counterfactual will be crucial to my argument against the classical liberal picture. For now an intuitive sense of such a commitment can be given by an example. Many of our desires are not fundamental commitments in this sense, but a few indeed are. Take, for example, the fact that certain sections of the Iranian government are explicitly arguing that increasingly modernizing influences around them may well have the effect in the future that they will lose their desire to live by Islamic tenets, nevertheless they now want their future to be one where they are in fact living by Islamic tenets, even if they do not have the desire to do so then (and they are in fact arguing that they should entrench things so that that can happen) (Bilgrami, 1999: 172).

Bilgrami thinks this formulation has "a right to be seen as rigorously reflecting our identity-shaping commitments for they reveal our deepest self-conception in a way that vague existentialist rhetoric about authenticity fails to do" (1999: 172). In my judgment the criterion has no substantial bite. If X right now wants to play pinochle every Thursday for the rest of his life and has the opportunity to guarantee that he will do so even if he might lose interest next week, it would be entirely rational for X to impose X's current will on X's future self if he can and as long as the cost of exercising the opportunity is not excessive. Indeed, if there are no costs, X is *obliged* as a rational agent to exercise the opportunity. The fundamentalist Muslim reported by Bilgrami would be irrational not to protect his current Islamic interests at a later time when his ardor will wane as long as he can do so cost free. And if the costs are not too excessive he should also be prepared to do it. This is no more and no less than what any rational agent should do to promote his or her long-term interests against undermining in the future when this can be done cost free or sufficiently cheaply. Thus, any value commitment or set of value commitments to which X subscribes at *t* that enjoins a certain code of behavior or the satisfaction of a certain set of conditions either at all times or at specific times in the future is held "in the mode of Ulysses and Sirens." Systems of value commitments that have a significant future horizon are very common. The types of value commitments that are ruled out are commitments to styles of clothing or food or modes of entertainment that may have a short time horizon.

There are, of course, differences between value commitments with long time horizons. The difference between such commitments concerns how much X is prepared to pay or sacrifice to prevent X's future self from overturning values to which X is currently committed under the often belief contravening presupposition that X has the opportunity and resources to engage in such preventative measures. But this difference is quite like differences in value commitments (regardless of time horizon) that can come into conflict with the interest of others. The amount of effort and resources X is willing to expend on preventing Y from preventing X from pursuing X's value commitments can vary quite widely.

Bilgrami is trying to provide a characterization of identification or affiliation with a group in some sense stronger than weak or mere affiliation. In the weak sense, Sen is perfectly correct to suggest that we all have many social or political identities. When the systems of value commitments associated with these identities conflict in the sense that they cannot be jointly implemented, agents can engage in rational deliberation involving the weighing of the competing interests in order to reach a reasoned decision without loss of integrity. When agents identified with groups in the strong sense come into conflict, reasoned resolution without loss of integrity is allegedly far more difficult. I have just suggested that his appeal to Ulysses and the Sirens singles out value commitments with long time horizons and that the possibilities for conflict occasioned by endorsing such conflicts are quite symmetric with possibilities of conflict between value commitments of different agents whether the value conflicts have long or short time horizons. I fail to see how Bilgrami's proposal characterizes identification in a sense that makes reasoned resolution without loss of integrity unusually difficult.

What if the weight is given to one of the identities exclusively? Can reasoned deliberation for the resolution of differences take place without loss of identity?

Sometimes the conflicts arising in value commitments arise within the set of value commitments associated with a single group. Resolving such conflicts will involve changes like those described as 1, 2, and 3 earlier in the discussion. In such cases, the identity-value commitment pair initially adopted must change. But in such cases, no resolution will require abandoning the group with whom the agent is identified. It involves instead a modification of the value commitments associated with the group. No one need lose his or her weak commitment identity.

But when an agent who plays different roles confronts a situation where the demands made by value commitments associated with different group affiliations cannot be jointly implemented, a different predicament arises. The agent faced with such a conflict between identity A and identity B can (a*) abandon identity A and retain B, (b*) abandon identity B and retain A, or (c*) identify with the group that is the union of A and B and treat the conflict as one between value commitments belonging to a single group. According to this third alternative, a resolution is constructed as follows: keep the value commitments associated with A and those associated with B as they were as long as they do not conflict. Those that do conflict are replaced by the potential compromises between the permissible evaluations according to A and to B.

When confronted with a predicament like the choice between (a*), (b*), and (c*), one of the two identities (more precisely, one of the two identity-value commitment pairs) has to be abandoned and, perhaps, both. One might say that in case (c*), identities A and B are preserved for problems where the value commitments do not conflict but this cannot be said for problems where they do. In those cases, it is clear that identities A and B are abandoned for an identity that is the union of A and B. Such situations differ from predicaments where the problem faced is one where only value commitments associated with one identity are invoked, or where value commitments associated with both identities apply coherently without conflict.

In conflicts between the value commitments associated with A and with B, the need to change at least one weak commitment identity may or may not be seen by the participants in the dispute to be threats to their integrity. Those who take their integrity to be threatened identify with one of the two groups in a stronger sense than weak commitment identification, just as Bilgrami suggests. But the strong sense is not characterized by a Ulysses and the Sirens type model. I propose the following as an improvement.

> Agent X strongly commitment-identifies at time t with group A if X weakly commitment-identifies with A and at t would refuse to abandon this identity were X to face at t a value conflict where X must abandon identification with group A or with some other group with which X is also weakly identified.

Sen writes: "Given our inescapably plural identities, we have to decide on the relative importance of our different associations and affiliations in any particular context" (Sen, 2006: xiii). As long as the plural identities are not strong commitment identities, Sen is surely right.

X cannot, however, coherently embrace more than one strong commitment identity at the same time. X can have other associations and affiliations. X may have priorities for some over others, depending on context. However, in every context where conflict arises between the group with which X has a strong commitment identity, all weight must be given to the strong commitment identity. X cannot be kidded out of it without losing X's integrity.

If this is right, it becomes unclear why exclusive affiliation with a single group would be objectionable if abandoning that group for another did not compromise X's integrity—that is, as long as commitment identification was in the weak but not the strong sense. I have little doubt that few if any individuals have exclusive affiliations in the weak sense but there is no difficulty in conceiving of such individuals.

This does not undermine Sen's rejection of exclusive affiliation with a single group as long as the singular affiliation is a commitment identification in the strong sense. Indeed, to reject singular affiliation with strong commitment identity is to disallow strong commitment identity altogether. Sen is thus in favor of strong commitment identity neglect.

We can see that Sen's understanding of identification is ambiguous. He objects to identity neglect and singular commitment. Sen should oppose weak commitment identity neglect but he should not oppose singular weak identity commitment. On the other hand, he should urge strong commitment identity neglect while objecting to singular strong identity commitment. More crucially, strong commitment identity cannot be rejected on the basis of the uncontentious assumption that we all have many weak commitment identities supplemented by minimal principles of reason.

Rejecting strong commitment identification is taking a stand against a form of zealotry. Anyone who refuses to open one's mind under any circumstances to the system of value commitments associated with an alternative affiliation to the one with which one has affiliated is an uncompromising partisan and qualifies, according to English usage, as a zealot.

Nonetheless, an agent who has a strong commitment identification with some group can appear quite open minded. A zealot can play many different roles as long as the value commitments associated with these roles do not conflict with the value commitments of the group with whom the zealot is strongly commitment identified. Thus a zealot can appear to be a paragon of reasonableness in many of his or her activities. In particular a zealot can coherently appear open-minded in addressing value conflicts internal to the system of value commitments associated with the group with which the zealot is strongly commitment identified.

Bilgrami thinks such conflicts can create serious difficulty for the zealot. This need not be so. Internal conflicts among the value commitments associated with the zealot's strong identity can call for the modification of the system without leading to the abandonment of the affiliation to the group. *Pace* Bilgrami, a zealous fundamentalist Muslim can allow for modification of his or her value commitments without abandoning his or her strong commitment identification. Perhaps, the fundamentalist Muslim is committed, as in Bilgrami's example (2004: 186) to censorship of blasphemy and other values that support free speech. The fundamentalist who recognized this might modify his or her support of free speech to make an exception of censorship of blasphemy. The fundamentalist could make this change in his or her initial value commitments without renouncing his or her affiliation with Islam.

The situation parallels that of a lover of freedom and human rights who, in the face of the events of September 11, is prepared to allow for the use of torture and other violations of the Geneva Conventions because of the allegedly exceptional circumstances involved in facing the threat of terrorism. This person may not think that he has betrayed the community of advocates of civil liberties.

What the zealot (including our fundamentalist Muslim) cannot abide is abandonment of his or her system of value commitments by abandoning his or her affiliation with the group currently associated with that system. But the possibility of being confronted with the demand for such an abandonment is no difficulty for the zealot. It is the zealot's readiness with a response to such an eventuality (namely, never to give up his or her strong commitment identity) that defines his or her zealotry.

When zealous X and an agent Y (who may or may not be a zealot) share affiliation with the same group but differ in the systems of value commitments they associate with the group, it is possible for them to engage in reasoned deliberation rather than warfare in order to settle the disputes that may arise. But if zealot X and Y (who again need not be zealot) belong to different groups with different associated systems of value commitments, reasoned deliberation and inquiry is no longer an option. In that confrontation, a nonzealot Y could surrender his or her affiliation and embrace the group to whom X belongs. Alternatively, X can adopt an attitude of contemptuous toleration of differences—an attitude that Y can repay in kind. Or Y, whether Y is a zealot or not, refuses to concede to X and X fails to adopt an attitude of contemptuous toleration toward Y. Violent confrontation may then ensue.

To be sure, parties to a dispute who are not zealots may also come to blows or turn to other unpleasant alternatives to reasoned inquiry. The peculiarity of disputes with zealots is that they cannot succumb to reasoned deliberation and inquiry and remain true to their strong commitment identity.

Zealotry, in short, is a serious social disease. Like incapacity to think rationally, it cannot be eliminated even in principle by marshalling the results of inquiry. Zealots may meet all the requirements demanded by minimal rationality. But they refuse to engage in critical discussion and inquiry with others regarding issues that threaten their strong commitment identification. From the point of someone seeking to engage in earnest inquiry with them, it makes little difference that they can engage in such inquiry if they desire where the individual whose intellectual abilities are stretched beyond their limits is incapable of doing so. Conflict with zealots resembles conflict with those who are rationally deranged. The conflict cannot be addressed by trying to reason with those who promote strong commitment identification. Containment and eradication (humanely and peaceably if possible) are the chief remedies.

It may seem that I have exiled zealots such as religious fundamentalists from the community of rational thinkers on the grounds that their views are inaccessible to inquiry and rational criticism. That is a half truth. Their *views* are not inaccessible to inquiry and rational criticism. *They* are. Someone could embrace the same doctrines, but without zealotry.

IDENTITY OF RESPECT

There is another type of identification or affiliation with a group that merits some consideration. It is far less pernicious than the strong commitment identity associated with zealotry. Indeed, many find it a comfortable way of proceeding.

One version of liberalism takes the position that if Y dissents from the view endorsed by liberal X, liberal X ought automatically to move to a position of suspense between X's initial belief and the belief of the dissenter Y. That is to say, X is obliged not only to tolerate Y's view but to afford it the kind of respect that moving to a position of doubt expresses. This brand of liberalism is justly ridiculed as promoting the politics and morality of the empty mind (Levi, 1997, chap. 12).

An alternative vision holds that if Y dissents from X's view, X ought to open up X's mind to Y if a good case can be made for doing so. What then constitutes a good case for abandoning firm convictions in order to be open to the view of a dissenter?

One type of good case looks to the merits of the values espoused by the dissenter—for example, if the dissenter advocates extending a liberty to a larger category of individuals, it may be pointed out to X, who already favors extending the liberty to the largest group of individuals who resemble current rights holders in whatever the relevant respects may be, that it is an open question as to whether there is a relevant difference between the candidate category and current rights holders.

An alternative mind-opening strategy appeals to the authority or virtue of the dissenter. X displays a certain respect for the opinions of Y not by adopting them on Y's say-so but by being willing to seriously entertain them and explore their merits in comparison with X's initial views in a non-question-begging manner. No dictate of practical reason requires X and Y to open up their minds to each other in such a manner. Yet, if Y and X have mutual trust and respect for the opinions of the other, it makes sense for them to consider each other's views seriously if they are in conflict.

Often members of certain groups take it to be incumbent upon themselves to exhibit such trust and respect for the views of other members of the same group. Indeed, group identification often takes the form of such trust and respect. This is the way members of the class of '89 at Washtub U are supposed to treat each other. Identification or affiliation with a group of this kind coheres with but does not entail either weak or strong commitment identification. An agent can identify with several groups in this sense or only one.

> X *respect-identifies* with group A if and only if X respects
> the beliefs and values of members of group A even if they
> disagree with X's own.

The form of liberalism that counsels listening to every dissenter quickly collapses into empty-mindedness. But respect-identifying with a more narrowly identified group does not have this property and may, depending on the group with whom one respect-identifies, be an entirely legitimate form of belief or value change. Scholarship and scientific inquiry could not proceed without relying on authorities and experts whose dissent from our views occasions critical review of our views. To be sure, some practices of respect-identification may represent instances of the "old boys" network that feminists and other outsiders deplore. Discriminating between good and bad forms of respect identification calls for care and intelligence.

CORRIGIBILISM, ZEALOTRY, AND RELATIVISM.

The authority of the mandarins of epistemology to the contrary notwithstanding, an agent does not need a justification for current beliefs but only for changes in belief. This is so both when the change involves expanding one's beliefs by adding new information and contracting by giving up convictions one currently endorses. A parallel view ought to apply to judgments of value as well as to beliefs. This view implies that an agent ought not to come to doubt his or her own views because someone differs—unless a good case can be made for respecting the dissenter or the dissenter's views. Elaborating on this point requires entering into detailed epistemological elaborations that I cannot undertake here. Even so, it is safe to say that some form of respect-identification will need to be a feature of such an epistemology. This epistemology presupposes the revisability (corrigibility) of current beliefs and values. Such corrigibility does not entail uncertainty or doubt concerning these current beliefs and values. Corrigibilism does not entail fallibilism—the doctrine that insists that an agent ought to acknowledge that his current full beliefs might be false. Such a fallibilism is incoherent. The function of the agent's full beliefs is to serve as a standard for distinguishing between conjectures and hypotheses that are currently open to doubt and those claims that are not currently subject to any real and living doubt.

Advocates of such a corrigibilist epistemology must take a stand against zealotry. Zealots engage in a form of strong commitment identification that precludes modifying some of their value commitments without betraying their identity. To this extent, the zealot is committed to treating his or her value commitments as unrevisable. Such incorrigibilism precludes having respect for the views of those who dissent. As long as the zealot is a zealot, he or she cannot engage in a non-question-begging inquiry to settle differences relevant to his or her commitment identity. This is the best reason I can think of for siding with Sen's hostility to what I have called strong commitment-identification politics.[7]

The zealot's refusal to engage in non-question-begging inquiry is, as long as it is in force, an obstacle to any prospect of resolving the zealot's differences with his liberal critics. The zealot has good reason for the refusal—if one is needed. If he or she does not refuse, his or her integrity is compromised.

The refusal throws up roadblocks in the path of inquiry, and that is anathema to the corrigibilist. It provides the corrigibilist or liberal with an excellent reason (should he or she need one at all) for refusing to open up his or her mind to the zealot's view. To open up to the value commitment of the zealot including the strong commitment identity is quite as much a betrayal of corrigibilism as is the zealot's opening up to the corrigibilist a betrayal of his or her strong commitment identification.

The standards of minimal rationality to which all rational agents are committed cannot be wheeled in to support breaking the impasse between the corribigibilist and the zealot.[8] Using the jargon made fashionable by Williams (1981) as construed by Bilgrami (2004), external reasons for breaking the impasse do not exist. Moreover, the agent committed to corrigibilism cannot appeal to reasons "internal" to the zealot to persuade the zealot to move to a position of suspense concerning the disputed issues. Bilgrami rightly turns his back on appeals to external reasons to settle such disputes. He thinks, nonetheless, that appeals to internal reasons can be brought to bear. In my judgment, his appeal does not succeed.

By his own description of the road to resolution, no matter how coherent one or both of the parties to the dispute is in their values, historical circumstance can inject conflict into these values. The Muslim who advocates censorship of blasphemy may come to prize freedom to preach the virtues of Islam in a fundamentalist Christian community in which he or she has settled even though such preaching is blasphemy in that community. The liberal may then appeal to this latter consideration, which has become an internal reason for supporting protections against blasphemy for the Muslim, to undermine the Muslim's support for censorship of blasphemy.

Bilgrami (2004: 186) concedes that his model can succeed only if the Muslim is conflicted between reasons for and against censorship. The conflict need not be blatant initially but implicit in the commitments of the Muslim. And it may be a conflict that is produced by changes in the Muslim's life situation. Bilgrami thinks most agents are inconsistent in this sense (although he would not put it in this way).

If this is so, the agent should retreat from inconsistency as soon as he or she recognizes it. In Bilgrami's example, the Muslim can either abandon his advocacy of censorship of blasphemy, his support for protections against persecution for blasphemy, or move to a position of suspense. But by hypothesis our fundamentalist Muslim has a strong commitment identity to the Muslim values, including censorship of blasphemy. If conflict is made explicit to him, he would rank loyalty to Islam as he sees it above support for protections from prosecution for blasphemy and also above suspense. All things considered, he would have an internal reason to abandon his reasons against censorship of blasphemy in escaping from inconsistency.

Bilgrami is, of course, right that as long as the agent remains in the inconsistent state, he or he endorses reasons for and against conflict. But the reasons of relevance here concern how to retreat from inconsistency. And the fundamentalist has every reason to give up the considerations arguing against censorship. That is to say, this is so as long as the fundamentalist has a strong commitment identification to his or her brand of Islam.

Bilgrami's approach can succeed only if the zealot is not so zealous after all. And if he is not so zealous, Sen's appeal to the circumstance that the not-so-zealous zealot has multiple commitment identities in the weak sense should be enough to provide a liberal interlocutor with an opportunity to engage in non-question-begging inquiry with him or her.

Sen and other opponents of strong commitment identification or zealotry disagree with the zealot concerning what constitutes good reasons for changing one's mind. I would argue (and have done so elsewhere) that such "good reasons" are inevitably value laden—even in the context of justifying changes concerning matters of fact (Levi, 1967, 1980). If the zealot is seriously committed to strong commitment identification, the corrigibilist must abandon his or her preferred approach to confronting those with whom the corrigibilist disagrees.

In spite of this, there is an important kernel of truth in Bilgrami's view. Bilgrami thinks that his "liberal" (or my corrigibilist) can adopt as a "default" the view that the zealot might succumb and change his or her views so that he might be won over to liberalism by invoking internal reasons. This seems to me to be just right.

The fundamentalist Muslim, we have learned, may not be what he seems to be: a devotee of strong commitment identification with Islam. In that case, it may after all be possible to engage in joint inquiry with the fundamentalist on disputed issues. Of course, the fundamentalist may be the real article in which case joint inquiry is fruitless. But the liberal, like Charles Peirce's scientist, ought not to place roadblocks in the path of inquiry. He should initially adopt the hopeful view that joint inquiry can be pursued with profit. Only if this path proves disappointing should he reconsider and conclude that an impasse has been reached. The optimism here is not based on some metaphysics but on a hope that is driven by corrigibilist values.

NOTES

1 Thanks are due to Akeel Bilgrami for discussions that helped clarify my thoughts about the topics discussed here.

2. The material on value commitments is based on Levi (1986, chap. 2).

3. This does not entail utilitarianism or any variety of consequentialism except the most trivial. Implementing one of the options in a given choice situation may be considered a consequence of the implementation. See Levi (1997, chap. 4) for a review of various varieties of consequentialism.

4. I require as a constraint of rationality on all value commitments that the set of permissible utility functions should be convex—that is, if u is a permissible utility function and u' is another, $\alpha u + (1-\alpha)u'$ is also permissible. The convexity requirement is a controversial issue that cannot be discussed here. Some aspects of this controversy are discussed in Seidenfeld, Kadane, and Schervish (1989) and Levi (1990, 1999). Further issues are discussed in unpublished work by Seidenfeld, Kadane and Schervish. Value Structures and Extended Value Structures are considered in Levi (1986).

5. Each option a_i determines a subset O_i of O. I require this set O_i to be *basic*. That is to say, refining an o_{ij} of O_i into alternatives $q_{ij_1}, q_{ij_2}, \ldots, q_{ij_k}$ is an irrelevant refinement of the consequences according to the agent's value commitments. Every permissible utility function in $EV(O)$ assigns a utility to a member of the refinement equal to the utility of the unrefined o_{ij}. In this sense, the consequence descriptions in O represent everything the agent cares about in the context of the given decision problem.

6. Although I think that any satisfactory account of explanation in science should incorporate the idea that an explanation involves an appeal to laws specifying a scope and maintaining that anything belonging to the scope satisfies the requirements articulated by a formula, this condition is a weak necessary condition on explanation. For the rest, satisfactory explanation depends on the research program of the inquirer or community of inquirers and, hence, on value commitments. The value commitment is relevant in contexts where the inquirer finds his or her beliefs challenged and needs to contract his or her state of full belief. In such cases, the evaluation of contraction strategies may seek to minimize loss of explanatory value as specified by the inquirer's value commitments. Similarly, systems of value commitments that "make sense" reflect a concern for systematic organization in accord with the requirements of some standard set by another value commitment. When systems of value commitments are to be modified, one might well seek to minimize the loss of systematicity according to the given standard. I doubt that there any very strong necessary conditions on such making sense and surely none that may be elevated to requirements of rationality.

Akeel Bilgrami has introduced a notion of "reinforcement" (1999) that serves as part of the engine by means of which contingent events can engender conflicts in values that in turn become the occasion for modifying value commitments.

7. The difficulty is not that zealots are absolutely certain of their views. Anyone—including corrigibilists—is entitled to have full beliefs (that is, be absolutely certain) of substantive theses. Corrigibilists insist, however, that such convictions are revisable. The zealot's commitment to strong commitment identification entails refusal to betray the group with which he or she commitment identifies. As long as this commitment remains operative, zealots must regard these commitments as immune to legitimate revision.

8. Bilgrami (2004: 175) invokes the jargon made fashionable by Williams (1981). An external reason is a reason that "all rational people are supposed to accept, not because of any substantive values they hold but because these external reasons precisely make no appeal to other

substantive values of theirs; they make appeal only to their capacity to think rationally." Internal reasons do invoke substantive values. In these terms, I claim that the corrigibilist cannot appeal to reasons internal to the zealot to persuade the zealot to move to a position of suspense concerning the disputed issue. Bilgrami, as we shall see, disagrees.

REFERENCES

Bilgrami, A. "Secular Liberalism and the Moral Psychology of Identity." *Multiculturalism, Liberalism, and Democracy.* Eds. Rajeev Bhargava, Amiya Bagchi, and S. Sundaram. Oxford: Oxford University Press India, 1999.

———. "Secularism and Relativism." *Boundary 2* 31:2 (2004): 173-96.

———. "Identity," *International Encyclopedia of the Social Sciences.* Ed. D. Sills. New York: Macmillan, 1968.

Levi, I. *Gambling with Truth.* New York: Knopf, 1967. Reissued in paper by MIT Press in 1973.

———. *The Enterprise of Knowledge.* Cambridge: MIT Press, 1980. Reissued in paper, 1983.

———. *Hard Choices.* Cambridge: Cambridge University Press, 1986.

———. "Consensus and Pareto Unanimity." *The Journal of Philosophy* 87 (1990): 481-492.

———. *The Covenant of Reason.* Cambridge: Cambridge University Press, 1997.

———. "Value Commitments, Value Conflict, and the Separability of Belief and Value." *Philosophy of Science* 66 (1999): 509-33.

Seidenfeld, T., J. Kadane, and M. Schervish. "On the Shared Preferences of Two Bayesian Decision Makers." *The Journal of Philosophy* 86 (1989): 225-44.

Sen, A. K. *Identity and Violence.* New York: Norton, 2006.

Williams, B. *Moral Luck.* Cambridge: Cambridge University Press, 1981.

Edna Ullmann-Margalit
Difficult Choices: To Agonize or Not to Agonize?

"AGONY OF DOUBT"

"WHAT A DIFFICULT CHOICE," A FRIEND SMILINGLY COMMENTS AS SHE faces the well-endowed dessert counter at a party.* Having heard the traffic report on the radio in the morning, I may find it difficult to choose which route to take, as I learn that all routes to my destination are likely to be congested. A relative tells me that the formal act of signing the final papers committing his aging parent to an institution was one of the most difficult choices he experienced. Reflecting on the legal and medical professions, the comment is sometimes heard that in choosing either of them one must be prepared to face many difficult choices in one's professional career; so, too, with regard to being a politician or a statesman.

In the summer of 2006, Israel went to war against Hezbollah in Lebanon. The Israeli cabinet, led by the prime minister, took the decision to go to war within a few hours after a border skirmish in which three soldiers were killed and two soldiers were kidnapped by Hezbollah. Some two months later, after the war ended with ambiguous results, pressure mounted on the Israeli government to appoint a commission of inquiry into the conduct of the war. Prime Minister Ehud Olmert agonized for about two weeks before finally reaching the decision about which format of commission, from a menu of several options, he was going to approve.

In what follows, I shall be concerned to explore what makes choices difficult above and beyond the difficulty of expected-value calculation. I shall consider a choice difficult to the extent that it poses a special, noncalculative challenge to the choosing agent, either in virtue of certain characteristics of the choice itself or of the agent facing it. From the point of view of the psychologist, the description of Olmert's behavior clearly indicates that the choice to appoint a state commission of inquiry (rather than, say, a judicial commission) was to the prime minister more difficult than the choice to go to war. The longer it takes to reach the decision, says the psychologist's formula, the more difficult the choice reveals itself to be.

Let us try to make sense of Olmert's choices, in light of the psychologist's formula relating the difficulty of the choice directly to the time it takes. One possible conclusion from applying the psychologist's formula here is that the intuitively suggestive link between the difficulty of the choice and the momentousness of the outcome should be questioned: even though the choice to go to war was clearly the more momentous one, the choice of the format of inquiry appears to have been the more difficult one. Another possible conclusion is that a choice whose outcome is likely directly to affect the agent's own life and career is more difficult than a choice whose outcome is likely directly to affect the lives of many people other than the agent's—even when the effect on the lives of the many might be momentous.

Yet another way to react to the attempt to apply the psychologist's formula to Olmert's case is to say that Olmert's situation shows the formula to be wrong: some difficult choices are made quickly. Rather than the speed of the choice attesting to its nondifficulty, it may attest to some other feature of the choice situation or, sometimes, to the perversity of the agent making the choice. We may recognize that the decision about the format of inquiry took longer for the prime minister to make than the decision about going to war, but reject the notion that the former is, as such, a more difficult decision than the latter.

Consider in this connection the well-known phenomenon, popularly referred to as one of Parkinson's laws, that the time spent by committees over a decision is inversely related to the cost of the project to be decided on. Ordinary committee members tend to have particular views and to feel strongly about issues they are familiar with, at the same time that they feel alienated from important, expensive, and unfamiliar items. Overwhelmed, people feel uncomfortable discussing big items: they tend to rely on experts' advice and they want the vote over quickly. A parliamentary committee is likely, for example, to spend much more time on a proposal for new parking arrangements than over a proposal for a multimillion dollar nuclear facility.[1]

We may at this point want to go beyond the simplistic positive formula relating the difficulty of the choice with the time spent on it, and to ask normative questions. Harking back to the depiction of difficult choices as those that pose a special challenge to the choosing person, is it acceptable to us that the choice to go to war is less difficult than the choice of the format of inquiry? Can it be right? Or does the time difference in reaching the decisions possibly reflect more about the personality of the choosing agent than about the nature of the choices involved?

A preliminary distinction suggests itself: *a difficult choice versus a choice difficult for agent A.* The distinction is between choices that are difficult, in and of themselves, and choices that particular agents have difficulties coping with (while others may not). In dealing with the first sort, the focus is on an analysis of types of choice situations; in dealing with the second the focus is on an analysis of personality types and—possibly—of personality disorders.

Clearly, the two classes of choices are not, as a matter of empirical fact, coextensive: not everyone has difficulty dealing with difficult choices, and not every choice that someone finds difficult merits being considered a difficult choice per se. At the same time, these two classes cannot be disjoint. We would like to be able to assert that certain choices are intrinsically difficult and that people facing them do, should agonize over them.

Whether the task of providing a list of necessary and sufficient conditions for this sort of cases makes sense, remains an open question. But it seems that we all recognize some of their characteristic and salient features. Irrespective of whether they are complex or difficult to calculate, difficult choices typically involve consequences of significant moment either to the life of the person making the choice or to the lives of others; also, they typically have a moral dimension that might involve a clash of values. A person taking a difficult choice lightly and making it quickly is amiss: we feel justified in being judgmental of such a person. Having said that we note, however, that the longer time spent over the choice is not a characterizing feature of difficult choices; rather, it is a symptom thereof.

Taking our time over a difficult choice and agonizing over it is not always an option. There are cases in which the speed with which the decision has to be made is in the nature of the decision itself. Under the heading "A Man Down, a Train Arriving, and a Stranger Makes a Choice," Cara Buckley of the *New York Times* (January 3, 2007) tells the story of 50-year-old Wesley Autrey, who was waiting for the downtown local at 137th Street and Broadway in Manhattan. He saw a man stumbling to the platform edge and falling to the tracks, between the two rails. "The headlights of the No. 1 train appeared. 'I had to make a split-second decision,' Mr. Autrey said. So he made one, and leapt."

The question whether brave Mr. Autrey made a difficult choice in a split second or acted from instinct must remain moot. But consider a story in which an excruciatingly difficult choice was squarely faced and made under the severest time limitation—a story which, in Israel, is as well known as it is traumatic. On February 21, 1973, a Libyan Arab airliner on a regularly scheduled flight from Tripoli to Cairo left Tripoli, but lost its course over northern Egypt, entering Israeli airspace of Sinai at 13:54. After failed attempts at communication by Israeli F-4s, the plane changed course and started to descend. Suddenly, it turned back toward the west and increased altitude, as if trying to escape. Warning shots were fired. By now, the Israelis had assessed as high the risk that the plane was on a terrorist mission and they decided it must not escape. The plane was shot down at 14:08, resulting in the loss of 108 out of 113 people on board.

The incident lasted 14 minutes, from start to finish. In the duration, the entire top echelon of the Israeli air force was involved; moreover, it was later revealed that the Libyan plane had been shot down with the personal authorization of the Israeli chief of staff. The risk of shooting down a passenger-carrying civilian plane was recognized and assessed, but the risk of an airborne terrorist attack was assessed as higher.

In subsequent debriefings and interviews, some of the officers involved described this as one of the most difficult choices they ever had to make in their lives. This is surely an extreme case of a difficult choice in the sense of a difficult-to-calculate one under conditions of acute uncertainty and constraints of time, to which are added the further elements of momentousness and the moral dimension of the life-or-death aspect of the decision. And in the event, it was a case in which an expected-utility calculation was applied and did prevail.

Cases of severe time limitation notwithstanding, taking our time over a difficult choice and agonizing over it is no guarantee that the choice will be correct, whatever meaning we wish to assign to "correct" here; it is no guarantee that we shall not regret the choice later, either. But it seems that we have a strong sense, albeit vague in its details, that the process of agonizing—in the classical sense of "agony of doubt"— over a difficult choice is normatively indispensable.

What such a process consists of goes beyond a calculative exercise of possible outcomes and their payoffs. It involves the activation of empathic imagination: an attempt to envision each of the possible outcomes, to see oneself—and others—in each of them and to go through all of their implications, including their emotional ones. (Think of the example, brought at the outset, of the decision to commit an aging parent to a home.) A difficult choice seems to entail that we owe such a process to ourselves and sometimes to others as well, and that going through it increases the chances that the decision we finally make will be correct, and will have left us more mature and better able to learn from our own experience and from our own mistakes.

RATIONAL CHOICE AND DIFFICULT CHOICES

Rational choice theorists do not concern themselves with reaction time or, indeed, with any other aspect of the phenomenology of decision making. Within rational choice theory there is no room for the question "What makes a choice difficult for A" (beyond the possible computational burden). But there must be room within rational choice theory for the question "What makes a choice difficult." How, then, does it deal with this question?

As a first approximation, it seems fair to say that within rational choice theory, no choice is *in principle* difficult. The chooser's object is to maximize some value, say (expected) utility—and the rest is calculative, practical detail. Of course, some information may be missing or uncertain, probabilities may be unknown, and the actual calculation may at times be complex and arduous—think, for example, of choices concerning insurance, or pension plans. But otherwise, no difficulty is in principle involved.

Yet, certain types of choice situations do present a principled, as distinct from practical, challenge to the rational choice approach. I shall now proceed to survey a list of categories illustrating various prototypes of such choices within the framework of rational choice theory.

Picking

▸ Which can of Coke shall I select?
▸ Being a hungry ass, which of the two identical bales of hay shall I take?

These questions exemplify cases in which we are strictly indifferent with regard to the alternatives before us because our preferences over the alternatives are completely symmetrical. To the extent that we take choosing to be choosing for a reason, and choosing for a reason to presuppose preferences, it looks like we have to conclude that in such cases choosing is precluded. As Leibniz put it in his *Theodicy,* "In things which are absolutely indifferent there can be no choice . . . since choice must have some reason or principle" (Leibniz, 1951: 148-9).

Leibniz believed that in the absence of sufficient reason, choice is precluded. Algazel, Dante, Montaigne, Spinoza, and other philosophers who had occasion to discuss the issue we nowadays refer to as the problem of Buridan's ass, also denied the possibility of picking (Ullmann-Margalit and Morgenbesser, 1977, notes 3 and 14 and accompanying text). "I entirely grant," says Spinoza, "that if a man were placed in such a state of equilibrium [like the ass of Buridanus] he would perish of hunger and thirst, supposing he perceived nothing but hunger and thirst, and the food and drink which were equidistant from him. If you ask me whether such a man would not be thought as ass rather than a man, I reply that I do not know" (Spinoza, 1937: 102). That is to say, where there is no preference there can be no choice, and where there is no choice there must be inaction and therefore the agent—whether man or ass—is destined to starve to death.

Several philosophers down the ages maintained that, whether or not choice without preference is a theoretical possibility, it is not a practical possibility: real indifference between alternatives, they believe, never occurs and hence no picking situations exist in practice. "Nothing is presented to us," says Montaigne, "wherein there is not some difference, how light so ever it be; and that either to the sight, or to the feeling, there is ever some choice, which tempts and draws us to it, though imperceptible and not to be distinguished" (de Montaigne, 1965: 333).

The psychologist Kurt Lewin developed a "field theory" to deal with psychological conflict (Lewin, 1935, 1951). Conceptualizing difficult choices as choices under conflict, his theory was the reigning dogma for decision making in the decades before the rise of rational choice theory. Generations of psychology students, as well as students in other fields interested in questions of choice and decision, grew up on Lewin's conflict theory and its conceptual tools and vocabulary.

One instance of psychological conflict, according to Lewin, is the case of "plus-plus" conflict, where the person stands midway between two "positive valences." Using as an example the choice confronting a man trying to decide between two television programs that he expects to be equally enjoyable, Lewin posits that in fact the simple plus-plus conflict will resolve within a short time: "The equilibrium of the forces is unstable, since any slight change in the relative attractiveness of the two regions will drive the person off the exact center and toward one or the other of the goals. . . . So, for example, the TV viewer who has selected Channel 2 over Channel 4 is unlikely to be driven back toward Channel 4 if the program lives up to his positive expectations" (Levinger, 1957: 331-2).

Notably, as a psychologist Lewin was also interested in the corresponding negative case, namely the minus-minus case. From his point of view, this case is not entirely symmetrical to the positive one. Here a person is envisaged standing between two negative valences of equal strength—a case of "Buridan's ass between two skunks." (The phrase was coined by the eminently quotable Kenneth Boulding.) Lewin sees this conflict as unstable since the person will tend to dissolve the equilibrium of forces by moving out of the conflict zone altogether—an option not regularly considered within rational choice theory. When faced rather than avoided, however, a minus-minus conflict leads to less rapid resolution than the plus-plus one, since an approach to either of the regions leads to stronger forces driving the person in the opposite direction. Where barriers exist which prevent exit, the equilibrium will be stable and the conflict unresolved. Still, "if the negative valences in the minus-minus conflict situation are sufficiently strong, the person will turn against the barriers in his attempts to escape" (333).

Rational choice theory uses the preference relation as its major building block. Being a partial ordering, the relation "person P prefers alternative *a* over alternative *b*" requires complementation. The equivalence relation of indifference is therefore a necessary component in the system. Moreover, the phenomenon of multiple equilibria brings the notion of picking—that is, choice without preference—to the fore, and does not let rational choice theorists ignore the existence of picking situations or remain indifferent to indifference. It is noteworthy however, that for nonpsychologically oriented rational choice theorists, the difference between a "plus-plus" case (that is, indifference between two good alternatives) and a "minus-minus" case (that is, indifference between two bad alternatives) makes no difference: they are indifferent to it.

Rational choice theory does not accept Leibniz's (et al.) view that picking locks the agent into an impasse, nor does it have any use for Lewin's theory of plus-plus or minus-minus conflict. At the same time, beyond counseling one to minimize the sum of decision costs and error costs by just picking, it does not itself have much of insight to offer on the issue of how to deal with picking situations. While picking thus presents a principled difficulty of sorts to rational choice theory, it should not be concluded however that cases of picking count as cases of difficult choices within that theory. After all, picking situations do not typically involve consequences of significant moment, nor do such situations typically involve a clash of values or require inordinate amounts of time to handle. On the contrary, to the extent that one may generalize about them, the generalization will likely be that picking cases typically involves "small decisions" of the can of Coke variety.[2]

Big Decisions

▸ Shall I marry Ann?
▸ Shall I quit my job as a high-tech executive and become a Buddhist monk?

These questions exemplify big decisions. As a first approximation, I characterize a big decision as personal and transformative: a decision taken at a major crossroad of one's life and likely to transform one's future self in a significant way. Decisions such as whether to marry, to migrate, or to leave the corporate world in order to become an artist might be examples.[3]

Big decisions in the sense meant here are points of no return. In making a big decision, one is embarking upon a road that is one way only, leaving burning bridges behind. Also constitutive of the concept of a big decision is the aspect of awareness: the person facing it is conscious of its being such and is open-eyed about it. A big decision thus involves alternatives that are likely to change one's beliefs and desires (or utilities) and are perceived as such by the person making the decision, in real time. Inasmuch as one's beliefs and desires shape the "rational core" of the rational decision maker, we may say that a person making a big decision emerges from it as a different person.

By transforming the sets of one's core beliefs and desires, a big decision brings about a personality shift that alters the person's cognitive and evaluative systems. There is no continuity in his personality identity and hence there is a problem about his being consistent in his choices. While New Person's new sets of beliefs and desires may well be internally consistent, inconsistency now exists between New Person's system of beliefs and desires, taken as a whole, and Old Person's system taken as a whole.

So the notion of the big decision as here expounded poses another difficulty to rational choice theory. Given that the rationality of decision making and of choice is predicated on the continuity of personality identity over time,[4] big decisions raise the problem of how to assess their rationality, involving as they do choices that straddle two discontinuous personalities. Note however that the problem as posed relates to the theoretical, not to the practical, aspect of big decisions qua rational choices. It does not question the decisionmaker's actual ability to make a choice, or his subsequent ability to assess himself as happy or unhappy with his choice. (I say more on the practical aspect of coping with big decisions at the end.)

In addition to the difficulty they pose for rational choice theory, big decisions often count as cases of difficult choices within that theory. Relevant considerations here are, first, that big decisions by definition involve consequences of significant moment to the decisionmaker's own life and, second, that they obviously demand from the decisionmaker that he take his time in making them in more than a calculative sense.

Big decisions as so far described are self-affecting personal decisions. One may also consider big decisions that are other-regarding, such that have a transformative effect upon the lives of others. Other-regarding big decisions are typically taken in virtue of one's official position or institutional role; for example, a statesman's (such as Olmert's) decision to go to war—or indeed to stop a war. Truman's decision to use the atom bomb at Hiroshima is a dramatic case in point exemplifying big decisions of this sort, one that may be considered paradigmatic of difficult choices. Or consider the headline proclaiming not long ago in the *Los Angeles Times*, "Pope Benedict Faces 'Difficult Choice' In Determining Whether to Recommend Condoms as HIV Prevention Method" (Boulay, 2006).[5]

Note, however, that to the extent that we consider these choices difficult, we do so because we recognize that these choices involve consequences of significant moment for the lives of a huge number of people, and because they have an urgent moral dimension to them. These choices, agonizingly difficult as they may be, do not pose a theoretical difficulty to rational choice theory as such. Unlike the self-regarding big decisions discussed earlier, they do not involve points of discontinuity in the personality identity of the persons making them.

Multidimensional choices

▸ Shall I spend my week's vacation in Paris or in Venice?
▸ Shall I go on a ski vacation or buy a new laptop computer?

These questions exemplify multidimensional choices. The problem with these choices arises if and when the alternatives they present cannot be put on a single scale and cannot be compared along a single dimension. For example, when deciding which apartment to buy, is a spare bedroom more important than a shorter commute to work? Are better schools in the area more important than a sun balcony or lack of noise from the street?

When many considerations have to be taken into account and somehow properly weighted, the choice is difficult. The difficulty increases the more dimensions there are and the higher the stakes.

Multidimensional choices bring home to us the importance of finding out what we really care about. They force us to focus on what our "true" priorities, or preferences, are.

Faced with such a choice we may sometimes realize that the notion that all we have to do is to discover our preexisting preferences is a myth: deliberation may not be enough and we may have to make up our preferences by fiat—or look for *force majeure*. Raz observes that not only does one care about which option to choose even when the options are incommensurable, but one can indeed agonize over incommensurable options, if the reasons on either side are deep and important (Raz, 1986: 332). In choice situations in which the alternatives are not commensurate, it is not an easy or a straightforward matter to follow rational choice theory's exhortation to maximize value.

Multidimensional choices are difficult choices in theory, and often in practice too. On the level of theory, one complication is that they sometimes invite systematically intransitive choices. "Intransitivity often occurs when a subject forces choices between inherently incompatible alternatives. The idea is that each alternative invokes 'responses' on several different 'attribute' scales and that, although each scale itself may be transitive, their amalgamation need not be" (Luce and Raiffa, 1967: 25). This phenomenon takes place on the level of individual choice as well with regard to group choice.[6] Cycles of intransitive choices, whether vicious or not, have been amply documented, classified, studied, and analyzed. Indeed, the observation—sometimes referred to as Condorcet's paradox—that the requirement of transitivity is inconsistent with the majority-vote rule was made already in the eighteenth century. Moreover, such cycles can occur where the context "is transparent and the decisionmaker is reflective" (Bar-Hillel and Margalit, 1988: 119), where the violation of the consistency requirement is not attributable to factors such as cognitive limitations, emotional interferences, taste-change over time, etc.

On the practical level, some evidence suggests that people are in fact more casual and cavalier in the way they handle their difficult multidimensional choices than in the way they handle their less difficult ones.[7] In a series of studies reported recently in *Science* (Dijksterhuis, Bos, and Nordgren, 2006), researchers found that people who spend a lot of time consciously weighing the pros and cons of a decision with many considerations often do not choose wisely. The researchers conclude that the best strategy is to gather all of the relevant information and then put the decision out of mind for a while. Their advice for anyone who is struggling to make a difficult decision: stop thinking about it. When the time comes to decide, go with what feels right.

According to the psychologist Ap Dijksterhuis, who led the research, the unconscious appears to do a better job of weighing the factors of a multidimensional decision and arriving at a sound conclusion than the conscious mind. In an ordinary, conscious decision-making process, people can pay attention to only a limited amount of information at once. They focus on just a few factors and are thus in danger of losing the bigger picture. Also, people often tend to weigh some factors too heavily, and discount others that may be important. For difficult choices, then, "once you have done a certain amount of thinking to gather relevant information, further thinking is counterproductive. Instead, busy yourself with other tasks, and let your unconscious work on the problem" (Cook, 2006).[8]

Dilemmas

▸ If I work, I shall have no free time; and if I am idle, I shall have no money. What shall I do?
▸ If I abort the fetus, a life will be lost; if I do not abort the fetus, my life will be ruined. What shall I do?

These questions exemplify classical dilemmas. Meant to capture the situation of "damned if I do and damned if I don't," these cases present a person with a situation in which she is obliged to choose one of two options (the two "horns of the dilemma"). Each option leads to a state of affairs that is undesirable to her; hence the problem. A classic dilemma is traditionally portrayed as answerable with a counterdilemma in which both options lead to states of affairs that are desirable to the agent; the problem, or difficulty, being that the agent cannot choose both, and so whatever she does she ends up having to give up something that she is reluctant to give up. The counterdilemma in our first case is "If I work, I earn money; and if I am idle, I enjoy myself."[9]

On a closer look, the multidimensional cases can also be presented as dilemmas of this sort. On the one hand, I can focus on the upside of each option that my budget allows (I will enjoy the advantages of a laptop computer or I will enjoy the vacation). On the other hand, however, I can focus on the downside of having to give up the other option, given that my budget allows me to purchase only one (I will not have a laptop computer or I will not have a vacation).

This means that the dilemma, along with its counterdilemma, is perhaps merely a clever rhetorical way of presenting multidimensional choices. If so, then the difficulty inherent in the multidimensional choices is not in principle different from the difficulty inherent in dilemmas. The main nonprincipled difference between the two types of cases is that the options in a dilemma are meant to be exclusive and exhaustive—I cannot avoid doing one or the other and I cannot do both—whereas in ordinary multidimensional choices this is not usually the case.

Returning to Lewin's depiction of choice in terms of conflict theory, we note that what he refers to as "plus-plus conflict" is to him a conceptual simplification of a dilemma. He takes the usual choice situation to be such that attaining one goal entails sacrificing the other: although neither TV program may be particularly good, tuning in on one does mean missing the other. Since almost any choice between attractive goals has also a few negative features, Lewin subsumes the plus-plus conflict under his more general and complex case of "double plus-minus conflict."[10]

We may still ask whether it is the upside or the downside version (the "half-full cup" or the "half-empty cup") of this kind of choice situation that is more difficult. Noting that the difference between the versions boils down to a framing issue, the answer to this question would seem to depend on the personality of the choosing agent and on the psychological biases she is prone to rather than on the choice situation as such. In other words, the agent may experience one version of this dilemma as more difficult, in the sense of more taunting or agonizing, than the other version, but this does not reflect on the choice situation itself. It is likely that the degree to which the agent is prone to regret might have some effect on the degree to which she experiences the upside version of the problem as more, or less, difficult than its downside version; Kahneman and Tuersky's *Prospect Theory* (1979) is of particular relevance here.

Still, their facetious rhetorical aspect notwithstanding, some dilemmas seem to have an irreducible element of *gravitas*. The example of the abortion dilemma above may be a case in point; this may also be true for President Truman's atomic dilemma. As a further example we may consider the dilemma faced by Lillian Hellman and others who were summoned to testify before the House Committee on Un-American Activities in the 1950s.[11] In this kind of case, there is a very real sense in which the person who has to make the choice is damned whatever he or she does. I suppose the serious dilemmas I am concerned to delineate are correctly depicted by saying that they have a tragic element to them. They involve a situation of a moral trial where the decision-maker becomes a courageous hero facing hostile, relentless fate. With no possibility of redemption, the best one can hope for in these situations is the retention of one's human dignity.

These choices are truly difficult ones. One cannot take them lightly, descriptively speaking or normatively speaking. Moreover, such options force the choosing persons to come to terms with and to articulate their own priorities in domains where people normally do not have priorities and where they would rather evade articulating them. Perhaps the most difficult aspect of such a dilemma is the fact that, while making the choice one is aware that one will have to bear responsibility for it and go on living with its consequences.

At the extreme, there are horror dilemmas, real or fictional, like "Sophie's Choice." No right or good or optimal choice exists in such situations, not even a tolerable or acceptable choice. Whichever choice one makes, one is going to feel guilt and remorse (rather than regret) for the rest of one's life. The responsibility for having condemned one's child to death, for example, is not something a normal person can be expected to live with. In the original story, the choice Sophie is forced to make is part of an evil setup of torture and abuse. This may indeed be a characteristic feature of such dilemmas: that in a serious sense the choice situations they present are embedded in a larger, man-made scheme of abuse.

DOCTORS DECISIONS, JUDGES' DECISIONS, AND "HARD CASES"

Consider the case of a doctor who faces a terminally ill patient and has to determine a course of treatment. Suppose radiation and chemo-therapy may somewhat prolong the patient's life but they have bad side effects, which reduce the patient's quality of life for the duration; also, these treatments are expensive. Alternatively, painkillers and other drugs may improve the patient's quality of life but hasten the end. With some further elaboration of details, this looks like a classic case of a multidimensional choice. Is it a prototypical case of a difficult choice?

Whatever the answer, with the help of the Hippocratic oath the medical profession has taken care to eliminate the multidimensional-ity from such decision situations. Presumably for rule-consequentialist related reasons, it has taken an institutional metadecision to disregard all dimensions of medical decisions of this kind except one, namely, the prolongation of life. Doctors are supposed to use all the infor-mation whey can obtain and the best of the technology available to them in order to postpone the cessation of their patient's life. They are not supposed to maximize more than just this variable. In prac-tice, of course, matters might get complicated for a variety of reasons, and doctors often agonize over their decisions concerning courses of treatment. But in principle these decisions are explicitly meant not to constitute cases of difficult choices.

Switching to the legal arena, we note that at the end of a criminal trial, the trial judge (or jury) has to come up with a verdict of guilt or innocence. Is this a situation of making a choice between two options? And, if so, might this be a prototypical case of a difficult choice?

In the somewhat trivial sense in which the situation calls for the judge to make up her mind, we might say that she has to choose. When seen from the point of view of the law, however, this is not strictly a decision-making situation and therefore it is not a case of a difficult choice—however much anguish the judge may experience. It is, rather, a situation in which the judge is called upon to draw the right conclusion from the totality of facts found and evidence entered in the case before her. The judge, in this case, is much like a scientist who labors to draw the right conclusion from the facts that he has collected and from the experiments that he has conducted: they both draw conclusions; neither is making a choice.

But even if they are both engaged in the business of drawing conclusions, there is also an important difference between the respective tasks of the judge and the scientist. Crudely put, what constrains the scientist in drawing his conclusion is nothing but logic, whereas the judge is constrained by the law—by legislation and precedent. In other words, the judge has to determine what conclusion the law dictates, given the body of evidence; she has to find out how the law applies to the circumstances in hand. Rather than making a choice as to what is just, she has to determine what follows. In principle, the rules governing the institution of criminal justice are meant to ensure that there is a right answer, and the role of the judge is to find it. Coming up with the right answer might be a difficult matter, but this is a different story from the difficulty of making a decision.

Similarly, in noncriminal and other cases, judges sometimes have to balance competing rights and come up with the answer as to which is weightier. They may for example recognize that the state has a compelling interest in providing public education for young children at the same time as they recognize the right of parents to direct the upbringing and education of their children (*Pierce v. Society of Sisters,* 1925). The process of striking the correct balance may be difficult, time-consuming, and even anguishing. But legal fiction has it that, ultimately, judges find it; they do not make it up.

A somewhat different twist on this situation occurs with respect to what some legal theorists call *hard cases*. A "hard case" refers to a situation when no settled rule dictates a decision either way: when a particular lawsuit cannot be brought under a clear rule of law. In such cases, the judge has discretion to decide either way. The contested question among legal theorists is whether, faced with a hard case, the judge is to invent new rights retrospectively (as argued by legal positivists), or the judge's duty is to discover the preexisting rights of the parties and thereby discover which party has the right to win the case (Dworkin, 1978: 81-130). Dworkin's example is the *Spartan Steel* case from 1973. "The defendant's employees had broken an electrical cable belonging to a power company that supplied power to the plaintiff, and the plaintiff's factory was shut down while the cable was repaired. The court had to decide whether to allow the plaintiff recovery for economic loss following negligent damage to someone else's property."

Do hard cases present difficult choices? Whether judges have, as a matter of fact, more difficulty in deciding hard cases than in other cases is an empirical question about which I am not aware that relevant data exists. I can however see an argument for thinking that a hard case constitutes, conceptually, a more difficult choice than an ordinary judicial decision. The argument is that, in principle, hard cases present the judges with a two-tier decisional problem. First, the judge has to do a search: she has to go through the procedure of looking for a suitable rule of law under which the case might be brought. Only after the search ends in failure and the judge determines that no such rule of law exists can she proceed to the next stage of either generating or unearthing the right solution to the problem. The question remains moot whether or not such *more difficult* choices indeed constitute *difficult* choices, as distinct from merely more complex or demanding ones.

WAYS OF COPING

Escape and Reduction

A major tenet of liberal ethics holds that the good life is a freely chosen one, in which people develop their unique capacities as part of a plan of life. Central to autonomous personhood is the thesis that people ought to be free to choose their own projects, personal relationships, and ways of life. Liberal thinkers like Joseph Raz and Amy Gutmann, and free-market economists like Milton Friedman, extol the virtues of the large menu of options of ways of life, from which people should be free to choose their own. The liberal conception of human beings, then, rests on a web of intimate and intricate connections between the notions of rationality, autonomy, and freedom to choose.

There is another side to this coin, however. It is that people often find choosing, as such, difficult. People often dislike making decisions and are reluctant to face them; sometimes they will give much to avoid having to choose altogether. The picture that naturally emerges from rational choice theory, of people as decision-making animals constantly making choices to maximize interest, does not accurately capture the human condition.

Walter Kaufmann (1973) speaks of *decidophobia*, conceptualizing it as the fear of autonomy. Erich Fromm speaks of the Escape from Freedom: "Can freedom become a burden, too heavy for man to bear, something he tries to escape from?" (Fromm, 1969: 4). He outlined three major escape mechanisms that people might use to alleviate from themselves the burden of freedom and choice: authoritarianism, destructiveness, and automaton conformity. Fromm's analysis of the mechanism of authoritarianism, in terms of a person allowing oneself to be controlled by another, became especially well known and influential.

While Fromm related his analysis in particular to the appeal of fascism, its current relevance is largely to the born-again phenomenon within the world's leading religions. A major aspect in the life of the born-again is the surrender of their personal autonomy to the rabbi, to the mullah, or to whoever is their religious authority. The desire to remove the freedom of choice by submitting that freedom to someone else came to be recognized as the contradictory complement to humanity's longing for freedom and self-governance.

People resort to a variety of devices in their attempt to cope with what, to them, are difficult choices. If they do not escape, they may contrive to transform a difficult choice to a nondifficult, or less difficult, one. The reduction of multidimensionality to a single dimension of choice is a paramount method, one manifestation of which is the case of the medical profession discussed above. A critique sometimes voiced of the discipline of economics says that economists teach their students to ignore all aspects of the complexity of economic decisions and focus solely on the maximization of profit (Rubinstein, 2006).

If it is not the reduction of the number of dimensions a choice involves, sometimes the reduction of the number of alternatives from which to choose is the adopted method. In the daily life of observant Jews the number of alternatives from which to choose—whether in food, form of dress, which newspaper to read, who to marry, what educational institution to send one's child to and so on—is drastically shrunk in comparison with the number of alternatives faced by nonobservant individuals. The reason, above and beyond the voluntary submission of the observant person to the authority of the rabbis, is the multiplicity of prohibitions applying to practically every choice situation.

Second-Order Decisions

Ordinary people and social institutions are often reluctant to make on-the-spot decisions. They want to reduce the burdens of making choices in an attempt to minimize the difficulty associated with choice. They are reluctant to calculate the costs and benefits of alternative courses of action in particular cases; moreover, they are aware of their own shortcomings and they know that they may err. Individuals, as well as institutions, may therefore resort to second-order strategies for reducing the burdens of, and risk of error in, first-order decisions. In other words, they adopt simplifying strategies well before on-the-spot decisions must be made, attempting to minimize the sum of the costs of choice and the costs of error. Some of these strategies have the effect of giving over one's first-order, on-the-spot choices to an automatic device that proceeds to make the relevant choice without one's intervention.

The costs of choice are the costs of coming to closure on some action or set of actions. They are of diverse kinds: time, money, unpopularity, anxiety, boredom, agitation, anticipated ex-post regret or remorse, feelings of responsibility for harm done to self or others, injury to self-perception, guilt, or shame. The costs of error relate to achieving suboptimal outcomes, whatever the criteria for deciding what is optimal. These costs are assessed by examining the number, the magnitude, and the kinds of possible mistakes. The anticipated costs constitute an important motivation for the adoption of "second-order decisions," meaning decisions about an appropriate strategy for avoiding decisions or for reducing the difficulties associated with making them. Sometimes, second-order strategies are a response to motivational difficulties rather than to cognitive problems; people try, for example, to counteract their own tendencies toward impulsiveness, myopia, and unrealistic optimism (Weinstein. 1987).

A second-order decision is made when people choose one from among several possible strategies: when they adopt a firm rule or a softer presumption; when they create standards and follow routines; when they delegate authority to others; when they take small reversible steps; when they pick rather than choose.[12]

People frequently adopt rules, presumptions, or self-conscious routines to guide decisions that they know might be too difficult or costly to make, or might be made incorrectly because of their own motivational problems. I might decide, for example, that I shall turn down all invitations for out-of-town travel in the month of September, or you might adopt a presumption against going to any weddings or funerals unless they involve close family members, or our friend might make up her mind that at dinner parties, she will drink whatever the host is drinking. Bureaucracies and institutions often adopt rules and routines in the form of "standard operating procedures." They do so from the need to avoid situations in which low-level officials are called upon to apply discretion and make on-the-spot difficult choices. In a way the notion of *casus belli* can be seen in this light as a second-order decision. Suppose the type of provocation that a country considers legitimate cause for war is decided upon and made public ahead of time. Then, if the provocation occurs, going to war is meant to be almost an automatic matter, not requiring an arduous decision-making process. (This could have been the case with Olmert's decision to go to war, but was not.)

In cases involving self-control problems, the adoption ahead of time of second-order devices may be particularly important because of the particular difficulty associated with the numerous on-the-spot choices (Schelling, 1984). Thus, a person might adopt a rule: cigarettes only after dinner; no gambling, ever; chocolate cake only on holidays; alcohol only at parties when everyone else is drinking. Or a presumption might work better—for example, a presumption against chocolate cake, with the possibility of rebuttal on special occasions, when celebration is in the air and the cake looks particularly good. Rules, presumptions, and routines of this kind are sometimes chosen self-consciously and as an exercise of will, but often they are, or become, so familiar and simple that they appear to the agent not to be choices at all and hence not to be difficult.

Why might an agent pick rather than choose? When would small steps be best? At the individual level, it can be obvious that when you are in equipoise, you might as well pick; it simply is not worthwhile to go through the process of choosing, with its high cognitive or emotional costs. The result can be picking in both low-stakes (cereal choices) and high-stakes (employment opportunities) settings. Picking can even be said to operate as a kind of delegation, where the object of the delegation is "fate," and the agent loses the sense of responsibility that might accompany an all-things-considered choice. Thus, some people sort out difficult choices by resorting to a chance device (like flipping a coin).[13]

Anglo-American judges often proceed case-by-case as a way of minimizing the burdens of decision and the consequences of error.

If, for example, a court in a case involving an asserted right to physician-assisted suicide is likely to have too little information, and if it attempted to generate a rule that would cover all imaginable situations in which that right might be exercised, the case would take a very long time to decide. Perhaps the burdens of decision would be prohibitive. Such a court may have a great deal of difficulty in reaching closure on broad rules. Small steps are a natural result. Incremental decisions are a good way of responding to the particular problem of bounded rationality created by ignorance of possible adverse effects.

The "right to die" example illustrates the complications encountered by multimember institutions in which there is the need to reach a degree of consensus. Consider, too, a legislature that might find it difficult to specify the appropriate approach to global warming, given the problems posed by disagreement, varying intensity of preference, and aggregation issues. The result may be the strategy of small steps; sometimes the strategy of delegation is chosen.

An institution facing political pressures may have a distinctive reason to adopt a particular kind of second-order decision, one that will deflect responsibility for choice. A monarch is relieved of responsibility for unpopular but indispensable decisions if he can point to a separate institution that is charged with the relevant duty.[14] In modern states, the existence of an independent central bank is often justified on a similar ground. In the United States, the fact that the Federal Reserve Board is unelected is an advantage.[15] There are analogues in business, in workplaces, and even in families.

Sometimes the second-order decisions that individuals or institutions make in order to reduce the burdens of later decisions in particular cases are themselves costly. A special willingness to expend a great deal of effort to generate rules seems to exist when planning and fair notice are important, and when it is anticipated ahead of time that a large number of decisions will be made (Kaplow, 1992).

A person facing a "big decision" in the sense expounded earlier may obviously experience it as a difficult choice. Infrequent and exceptional as such decisions are, big decisions hardly lend themselves to being relieved by the devising of second-order strategies; our own past-experience or the experience of others can offer little help either. One mechanism of coping with the difficulty posed by a big decision is self-deception—namely, pretending that it is an ordinary-size decision (or a series of such). Another way of coping is by subtly framing it in such a way that one of the alternatives up for choice appears to us as compelling and imposed on us by *force majeur*. On the level of theory, we recognize that big decisions test the limits of rational-choice theory; on the practical level, however, we try cope with and to extricate ourselves from them as best we can.

NOTES

* I am grateful to Daniel Kahneman, Gil Kalai, Avishai Margalit and Cass R. Sunstein for very helpful conversations and comments.

1. Parkinson theorized that when the costs go way beyond the incomes of those deciding they switch off, but when the amounts are closer to those they are used to in their own lives, they are more willing to debate.

2. For more on the smallness of picking see Ullmann-Margalit and Morgenbesser (1977: esp. 783-5) and Ullmann-Margalit (2006: 157-8).

3. For more on big decisions, see Ullmann-Margalit (2006).

4. The best known philosophical discussion of the connection between rationality and the idea of stability of personal identity over time is Parfit (1986, chap. XIV). However, he speaks of personal identity whereas for the purposes of the present discussion it is preferable to speak of personality identity. For more on this distinction, see Margalit (2004: 46 ff).

5. The article explains: "Pope Benedict XVI faces a difficult choice: preserving the Roman Catholic Church's traditional ban on contraception or shifting to a relative 'yes-sometimes' policy that gives us an effective weapon against AIDS but opens up church policy on contraception, abortion and infallibility to new challenges."

6. Note however that, the "attempt to distinguish between group choice and individual choice is complicated by the fact that some

choices cannot be crisply classified into one or the other" (Bar-Hillel and Margalit, 1988: 121). Consider such cases as: a benevolent dictator who makes a decision on behalf of a group; a group of experts (doctors, say) making a decision on behalf of an individual; an individual who bases his or her decision on the (pair-wise) choices others would have made—based, for example, on consumer-guidance publications; and more. An analogy also exists between the attempts of a group to integrate the rankings given by each of its members into an overall group ranking, and the attempt of an individual to integrate the rankings on each of a number of dimensions into an overall ranking of the alternatives (Bar-Hillel and Margalit, 1988: 125).

7. Regarding the ways people handle their difficult financial decisions— for example, their retirement plans—see Sunstein and Thaler (2003).

8. The above summary of Dijksterhuis et al.'s research owes to this report by Cook.

9. The classical sophist dilemma is "If I say what is just, men will hate me; and if I say what is unjust, the gods will hate me"—the counter-dilemma being "If I say what is just, the gods will love me; and if I say what is unjust, men will love me."

10. In the typical plus-minus case, according to Lewin, the person "vacillates around a point where the plus forces are strong enough to hold him but not strong enough to overcome the growing minus forces" (Levinger, 1957: 333-4).

11. A valuable discussion of difficult choices in Schick (1997) uses Lillian's Hellman's case as a leading example.

12. For more on second-order decisions see Sunstein and Ullmann-Margalit (1999). See in particular the discussion about when one or another of the available strategies will be chosen, when one or another makes best sense, and how both rational and boundedly rational persons and institutions might go about making the relevant choices.

13. Flipping a coin may have a different function, though. Consider: "Whenever you're called on to make up you mind / And you're hampered by not having any, / The best way to solve the dilemma,

you'll find / Is simply by spinning a penny. / No—not so that chance shall decide the affair / While you're passively standing there moping / But the moment the penny is up in the air, / You suddenly know what you're hoping" (Hein, 1982: 38). I am indebted to Thomas Schelling for this reference.

14. This is an important kind of *enabling constraint*; for more see Holmes (1996).

15. Independent central banks can be advantageous for a country also for the different, though not entirely unrelated, consideration of "time inconsistency": a central bank worries about making decisions for the greater good in the long run, not about keeping elected politicians in office and popular.

REFERENCES

Bar-Hillel, Maya, and Avishai Margalit. "How Vicious Are Cycles of Intransitive Choice?" *Theory and Decision* 24 (1988).

Boulay, Peter. "Pope Benedict Faces 'Difficult Choice' in Determining Whether to Recommend Condoms as HIV Prevention Method." *Los Angeles Times,* November 6, 2006.

Cook, Gareth. "Thought for Thinkers: 'Follow Your Gut,'" *Boston Globe,* February 17, 2006.

Dijksterhuis, Ap, Maarten W. Bos, Loran F. Nordgren, and Rick B. van Baaren. "On Making the Right Choice: The Deliberation-without-Attention Effect." *Science* 311:5763 (February 2006): 1005-1007.

Dworkin, Ronald. *Taking Rights Seriously.* Cambridge: Harvard University Press, 1978.

Fromm, Erich. *Escape from Freedom.* New York: Henry Holt and Company, 1969.

Hein, Piet. "A Psychological Tip." *Grooks.* Cogpenhagen: Borgens Forlag, 1982.

Holmes, Stephen. *Passions and Constraint.* Chicago: University of Chicago Press, 1996.

Kahneman, Daniel, and Amos Tuersky. "Prospect Theory: An Analysis of Decision under Risk." *Econometrica* 47 (1979): 263-291.

Kaplow, Louis. "Rules and Standards: An Economic Analysis." *Duke Law Journal* 42 (1992): 189-221.

Kaufmann, Walter. *Without Guilt and Justice: From Decidophobia to Autonomy*. New York: Peter H. Wyeden, 1973.

Leibniz, Gottfried Wilhelm. *Theodicy*. Trans. E. M. Huggard. London: Routledge and Kegan Paul, 1951.

Levinger, George. "Kurt Lewin's Approach to Conflict and Its Resolution: A Review with Some Extensions." *Journal of Conflict Resolution* 1:4 (1957).

Lewin, Kurt. *Dynamic Theory of Personality*. New York: McGraw-Hill Book Co., 1935.

———. *Field Theory in Social Science*. Ed. D. Cartwright. New York: Harper & Bros, 1951.

Luce, R. Duncan, and Howard Raiffa. *Games and Decisions*. New York: John Wiley and Sons, 1967.

Margalit, Avishai. *The Ethics of Memory*. Cambridge and London: Harvard University Press, 2004.

de Montaigne, Michel Equem. *Essays*. Vol. 2. Trans. John Florio. London: J. M. Dent and Sons, 1965.

Parfit, Derek. *Reasons and Persons*. Oxford: Oxford University Press, 1986.

Raz, Joseph. *The Morality of Freedom*. Oxford: Clarendon Press, 1986.

Rubinstein, Ariel. "A Sceptic's Comment on the Study of Economics." *The Economic Journal* 116 (2006): C1-C9.

Schelling, Thomas. "Self-Command in Practice, in Policy, and in a Theory of Rational Choice." *American Economic Review* 74 (1984): 1-22.

Schick, Frederic. *Making Choices*. New York: Cambridge University Press, 1997.

Spinoza, Benedict. *Ethics*. 4th ed. Trans. W. Hale White. London: Oxford University Press, 1937.

Sunstein, Cass R., and Richard H. Thaler. "Libertarian Paternalism Is Not an Oxymoron." *AEI-Brookings Joint Center Working Paper* 03-2 (2003).

Sunstein, Cass R., and Edna Ullmann-Margalit. "Second-Order Decisions." *Ethics* 110 (1999): 5-31.

Ullmann-Margalit, Edna. "Big Decisions: Opting, Converting, Drifting."

Political Philosophy. Ed. Anthony O'Hear. Cambridge: Cambridge University Press, 2006: 157-172.

Ullmann-Margalit, Edna, and Sidney Morgenbesser. "Picking and Choosing." *Social Research* 44:4 (1977): 119-145.

Weinstein, Neil. "Unrealistic Optimism about Susceptibility to Health Problems." *Journal of Behavioral Medicine* 10 (1987): 481-512.

Kenneth Kipnis
Forced Abandonment and Euthanasia: A Question from Katrina

INTRODUCTION*

I DO NOT KNOW WHAT HAPPENED ON THE SEVENTH FLOOR OF MEMORIAL
Medical Center (MMC) during the darkest hours of the New Orleans
catastrophe.[1] We do know that, in addition to staff, patients and family
members, hundreds of others had sought shelter in the hospital as
hurricane Katrina approached Louisiana on Sunday, August 28, 2005. By
Monday afternoon the storm had passed but the levee walls along the
city's canals had begun to fail. A foul mixture of waters from the New
Orleans sewer system and Lake Pontchartrain was coursing through
the streets, eventually reaching the low-lying area where the hospital
stood, inundating the lower floors of its buildings and submerging the
cars in the hospital's parking lot. From the outside, MMC had become
an island. On the inside, the electricity and plumbing were failing.
The staff would have no lighting, no elevators, no toilets, no running
water, no overhead pagers, no refrigeration, no air conditioning, no
telephones, no ventilation, and no powered medical devices. The flood
had crippled the hospital's capacity to provide standard medical care
for its patients and, with perhaps 2,000 patients and refugees crowded
together, Memorial Medical Center may have become a health hazard.
Notwithstanding this, the staff continued to care for patients, moving
those they could to the roof of a nearby parking garage, where they
might be evacuated by helicopters, or to the second floor, where they
might board water craft.[2]

As the days passed, many of those in the hospital were able to leave. But many hundreds remained, including the sickest patients who could not be moved, and the staff who were staying on to care for them until help arrived. There had been assurances of a timely rescue. But early Thursday morning—three days after the hurricane—it was announced that those still in the hospital would be on their own (Deichmann, 2006: 110). There would be no rescue by federal, state, or local government agencies. Dr. Richard Deichmann, the hospital's chief of medicine, described the effect:

> It was a phenomenal blow to hear that nobody was coming to get us. The worst thing for us was always waiting for someone to come and get us and then never showing up. There was this feeling of betrayal all the time. That freezes your ability to do things. And that is what happened Wednesday and Thursday (Meitrodt, 2006).

Some clinicians may have concluded, perhaps reasonably, that both they and their patients had been abandoned.

After days of enervating heat, darkness, and sickening stench, some clinicians are said to have ended the lives of some patients before leaving the hospital themselves. No living patients were left behind. Alleging that there had been homicides, Louisiana's attorney general subsequently ordered the arrest of a doctor and two nurses.

It is unclear, at this writing, how many indictments there will be. It is too early to make a confident judgment about what the conditions were at MMC between its isolation in Katrina's floodwaters and the final evacuation by Tenet, the corporation that owned the hospital and that sent helicopters for the last survivors. Nor is it now possible to say who did what during the crisis and what they believed and intended at the time. Journalists have given us a preliminary account, the courts may follow with further evidence, and historians will eventually have the last word. But we may never know the full story.

Despite the obscurity of the actions and circumstances, Katrina has posed a new question that complicates our thinking about caring for patients at the end of life. Can the conditions in a collapsing health care delivery system ever excuse euthanasia? The focus here is on the ethical norms that should govern health care professionals working *in extremis*. There is a need for responsible standards that, in fairness, should be honored by practitioners and respected both by the law and by society. What might those standards be?

In the pages that follow, I will, first, review some of the current thinking about the causation of death in the clinical setting, looking at some familiar standards from law and ethics. I will then consider the permissibility of euthanasia, focusing initially on what I will call the argument from "intractable suffering," perhaps the strongest and most common justification. I will also survey objections to that argument.

With that as background, I will go on to look at disaster medicine and a different reason for withholding and withdrawing life support. When, following mass casualties, medical resources are in short supply, it becomes justifiable to withhold them from seriously injured patients, allowing them to die even though, on an ordinary day, clinicians would act aggressively to save them. In this context, I will consider an issue that has received comparatively little attention in mainstream bioethics: battlefield euthanasia. Circumstances that may be unheard of in civilian medical care are tragically more familiar in military medicine. I will show that conditions arising on the battlefield can mirror conditions that could have arisen during Katrina. Building on that discussion, I will develop and defend a professional standard for assessing the conduct of health care professionals who are, in this way, *in extremis*. If not a wholly new line of thought, the narrow defense of euthanasia that is offered here is at least one that has largely gone unnoticed in the bioethics literature. The argument from "forced abandonment" (as I shall call it) sidesteps some objections to the argument from intractable suffering.

So there will be no misunderstanding, the pages that follow are not intended as a defense of what health care professionals did in Louisiana. As has been emphasized, we do not know what that was. Current accounts of the events in question are neither comprehensive nor consistent with each other and, indeed, it would not be a surprise to discover that some elements of my narrative are incorrect. But the argument of this paper does not turn on the accuracy of its account of the Katrina catastrophe. This inquiry is a more abstract one. Are there conditions that, had they been present in New Orleans (or anywhere else), would have excused ending the lives of patients, conditions under which both law and professional ethics should withhold condemnation? The answer offered here is yes. Where it is impossible to evacuate patients and dangerous and medically futile to remain with them, clinicians may have to choose between abandonment and euthanasia. There may be no third option. I will argue that physicians who choose euthanasia under these conditions should be excused from ethical and legal responsibility for misconduct. It would be wrong to blame them for what they have done.

The distinction between justifying and excusing conditions is central to what follows. When an act is justified, it is not a wrong at all: "I didn't file a tax return because the law says I am not supposed to. Not filing a return was the right thing to do." However when a wrongful act is excusable, the agent should not be blamed or punished for it: "I didn't file a tax return because I was gravely ill at the time. While I should have filed, it would be wrong to fault me for having failed to do so." Section II of this essay explores a common justification for one type of euthanasia. In contrast, Section III defends the excusability of another type.

EUTHANASIA AND THE MEDICAL CAUSATION OF DEATH
Euthanasia

The Greek roots of the term "euthanasia" denote "good death." Though it is common to think of death as unequivocally bad—it is, after all, our most severe punishment—it is easy to distinguish between dying processes that are mercifully tolerable and others that are agonizing beyond endurance. During the events that have become known as 9/11, scores of people who were trapped in the World Trade Center leaped from windows to escape the heat and smoke, some holding hands with others as they fell. Knowing their lives had come to an end, it is likely they were choosing deaths that were better than the ones they would suffer if they remained inside. Though it was tragic that so many died in this way, it does not appear to have been publicly argued that it was wrong for them to have ended their lives as they did.

Euthanasia requires a second person's involvement. Sometimes called "mercy killings," these acts are carried out by one person for the benefit of another. Again, the everyday inclination is to think that, except for self-defense and a few other cases where killing is justified or excused, it is a grave wrong to cause the foreseeable death of another human being, to harm another in that comprehensive way. But one can imagine oneself struggling through the heat and smoke to reach a window high in the World Trade Center. A coworker who uses a wheelchair is also there, but unable to get past the debris and into the air outside. She asks for your assistance.[3]

Euthanasia, as an ethical problem, has traditionally engendered debate on whether and, if so, when, killing another person can be justified or excused on the grounds that the person killed is benefited rather than harmed. Except in some European countries, euthanasia is a crime. Those who end the lives of the intractably suffering, even when they are following urgent requests, can expect to be charged with homicide. Should the law be changed to permit some beneficent killings?

Clearing the Ground

In examining euthanasia, three issues characteristically muddy the waters. First, "euthanasia" was the euphemism the Nazis used to sanitize their early extermination of those they deemed defective. The program quickly evolved to kill millions: Jews, Roma, homosexuals, communists, and so on. Treated as vermin, those who were involuntarily and secretly gassed in the concentration camps were not killed beneficently. Indeed "involuntary" euthanasia—"beneficently" killing another against his or her will—seems a contradiction in terms. While some fear that loosening the law of homicide will send us down the slippery slope to holocaust, such prognostications must be examined with care.

The second issue concerns what some still call "passive euthanasia": the discontinuation of life-prolonging measures, often the removal of a ventilator (a mechanical breathing device). When a patient or an authorized proxy withdraws consent to treatment, then the doctor, no longer at liberty to continue, can lawfully withdraw life support, causing death. It is sometimes urged that these patients die from their underlying diseases rather than from the doctor's action. But if death is a foreseeable consequence, then the clinical removal of a ventilator kills a patient (Brock, 1993) just as surely as the removal of a regulator kills a deeply submerged scuba diver. The law of homicide already includes this special exception for doctors, and much of the ethical and legal discussion of death and dying turns on the patient's legal and ethical power to refuse treatment, often through an advance directive and/or a legally authorized representative. While suffering can sometimes be averted by withdrawing life-support, this strategy is often unavailable and, moreover, the deaths caused by abating treatment may not be as tolerable as those that are induced. Nonetheless, it is nearly everywhere unlawful to administer medications for that purpose. Should this be changed?

Life-supporting treatment can also be withdrawn on the grounds that it no longer constitutes a benefit for the patient or, while it may be beneficial in some ways (prolonging life for a few additional days for example), the treatment is disproportionally harmful in other ways (painful or costly, for example). Doctors may be permitted to withdraw life support, causing death, on the grounds that continuing treatment would either be futile or harmful on balance: that is, not "medically indicated." Here as well death is caused by the withdrawal of treatment.

The third issue has to do with physician-assisted dying, now legalized in Oregon. In this case a doctor provides the means to end life: commonly a prescription with special instructions. Note that the doctor does not take the final life-ending step. While the reasons given for physician assistance are somewhat similar to the arguments for euthanasia (considered in Section II), I shall not explore them here.

I will now examine the active causation of death when it is done for the benefit of the one killed. Should the law of homicide be amended to permit some beneficent killings? I will consider two types of case where the defense of euthanasia is perhaps the strongest. The more familiar one arises in connection with intractable suffering. The argument from intractable suffering, together with some objections, will be explored in Section II. The second argument, in Section III, arises in connection with forced abandonment. It is, if perhaps not a novel argument, at least one that is less familiar. It is proposed that this second argument is sound and that, legally and ethically, such acts of euthanasia ought to be excused.

THE ARGUMENT FROM INTRACTABLE SUFFERING
The Standard Argument

Suffering commonly affects patients with a progressive illness—metastatic cancer, multiple sclerosis, Huntington's disease, for example. As Hippocrates put it, they are or soon will be "overmastered" by disease. While much of the euthanasia literature focuses on pain, the suffering brought on by severe illness comes in many flavors: dizziness, diarrhea, disfigurement, itching, insomnia, incontinence, exhaustion, strains upon relationships, shortness of breath, anxiety, cognitive impairment and dementia, debt, depression, disabilities of all kinds, dependency, loss of control, nausea, offensive odors, and the loss of dignity that can accompany these. Such conditions are familiar to those who provide hospice care. Sometimes—but not always—symptoms can be managed while preserving positive elements that give value and richness to a waning life: talking with loved ones, listening to music, enjoying a sunset. But residual abilities too can succumb, even as a patient retains sensitivities that can make life intolerable.

One strategy is "terminal sedation." Doctors can render a patient unconscious while withholding nutrition and hydration: death ensues in a matter of days. But not every patient would prefer such "care" to a timely passing. There is a broadly understood difference between having a life and being alive in the biological sense. It is the former— the life one has—that is often paramount for a patient. As with those trapped on 9/11, that life can come to an end before death occurs.

When a human life deteriorates to the point where one reasonably desires to end it, the argument for the permissibility of euthanasia can turn on autonomy: the ethical and legal power, within civic constraints, to chart the course of one's own life, especially in areas where the stakes that others have in the choice are not as great as one's own. The root political idea is that, provided there are no sound and proportional countervailing reasons, adults should enjoy the freedom to make their own decisions.[4] The presumption ought properly to be in favor of liberty: here the liberty of informed, suffering, competent individuals to choose the manner and time of their death. In the face of intractable suffering and an expressed and settled preference for death, there are strong arguments 1) that voluntary euthanasia should be permitted in these cases and 2) that it is cruel to prohibit or condemn charitable assistance to those who are relevantly similar to the 9/11 coworker in her wheelchair. Those who act out of courageous compassion in these cases are surely not the criminals we have in mind when we build prisons. Accordingly, public policy should regulate, but not prohibit, voluntary euthanasia.

The Objections

Objections to the argument from intractable suffering focus on the proviso that there be "no sound and proportional countervailing reasons." Here it is useful to distinguish between "yellow light" objections, urging caution, and "red light" objections, admonishing one to stop. While the former express concerns about the possibility of adverse consequences, the latter hold that euthanasia is impermissible on its face.

Many are the yellow-light objections. There is the alleged slippery slope down which we can slide to holocaust. Further, compassionate homicide might erode the professional commitments of physicians as well as our trust in doctors. (That might be a reason for barring the involvement of physicians.) There are the fears that patients will be depressed or pressured at the time of decision, that they may have been misdiagnosed, that haste in ending patients' lives can prevent possible recoveries, that relatives and health care providers will conspire to end the lives of the ill, and that protective measures will be unequal to the task of preventing carelessness and misconduct. These objections can be definitively assessed only when we have determined what protective measures we are talking about and how these have worked in practice. Here we can usefully study the Oregon record, as it becomes available, and the experience of the Dutch, the Belgians, and the Swiss. Unlike the Nazis, we can require our protocols to be implemented in the light of day. And even if some adverse consequences should occur following legalization, these would have to be measured carefully against the adverse consequences of prohibition.

Prematurity is a concern that permeates many of the yellow light objections: worries that life-ending decisions will be unnecessarily rushed. If only there were enough time to reconfirm the diagnosis, to labor with patients about their decisions, to try out other strategies for alleviating discomfort or for stopping the progress of the disease, to await new treatments that might suddenly become available, to rule out depression or undue pressures on the part of friends and relatives. . . . *If only there were enough time*, then many (most? all?) patients who now seem only *too* ready to let go of their lives might decide to hold on instead. Physicians have weighty duties to prevent the deaths of their patients or, failing that, to see them through the burdens of the dying process. When the death of another is a foreseen consequence, one wants to be sure there are no better options. Perhaps no one can ever be sure enough. There is here a venerable ideal of a certain type of therapeutic partnership between the vulnerable patient and the steadfast clinician. Even if a dying person is pleading for the relief that only death can promise, a clinician who kills a patient arguably betrays his or her commitment to that alliance.

Many of the red light objections emerge from within discrete religious traditions. These sectarian counterarguments often proceed from a premise that human life is, in some way, sacred, not to be discarded or taken; that euthanasia is, at bottom, a mortal sin. But in a pluralist society, the considerations that settle public issues ought to be ones that can, at least in principle, persuade any reasonable person: not just those who have embraced some preferred sectarian view.[5] So if, for example, the closely related idea of human dignity can be given a secular interpretation—one that is both broadly persuasive and sufficiently weighty—and if the favored understanding of that idea mandates the continuation of medical care while precluding euthanasia, then it may be reasonable to keep the law of homicide as it is (Sulmasy, 1994). Such arguments would have to be examined in detail (Dworkin, 1994: 68-101, 179-217).

No position is taken here on whether the argument from intractable suffering is sound or whether any of the listed objections constitute effective refutations. I now proceed to the second argument.

THE ARGUMENT FROM FORCED ABANDONMENT
Disaster Triage

In a disaster, there may not be enough to go around. The number of patients who present at a hospital can significantly exceed its carrying capacity and, moreover, it may not be possible to transfer them to other regional medical centers. Plane crashes, explosions, epidemics, and the release of toxic gas: all of these (and others) can overwhelm the resources of a community's hospitals.

Hospitals everywhere practice specialized procedures for these events. Disaster triage is the distinctive sorting method used in patient intake. Clinicians must narrow their attentions to patients who will probably live if treated but probably die if untreated. Using colored tags and rapid assessment techniques, they will set aside patients without life-threatening injuries (the "walking wounded") and those who will likely die despite treatment. Patients in this last group—sometimes termed "expectant" and identified with black tags—are not abandoned.

They receive ongoing comfort care (pain medications) and medical reassessments, especially if they unexpectedly survive the period of scarcity. On an ordinary day, the patients who are set aside to die would usually be treated aggressively, and many might survive. What would be a serious wound in a hospital with an untapped surge capacity can become a fatal injury in a hospital coping with disaster.

These queuing procedures are intended to save the maximum number of lives. Because there is not enough to go around, it is imperative to avoid waste. Resources are wasted when they are expended on patients who are likely to die even if they receive treatment (the black-tagged, most severely injured) or likely to live even if treatment is withheld (the walking wounded, the least severely injured). But resources will be efficiently used if clinicians prioritize those who will live if treated but die if untreated, the group in the middle. And, within that subset, those who are both closest to death and most easily treated will receive medical attention first.

Notice that the reason for withholding life-prolonging treatment from black-tagged patients has nothing to do with intractable suffering nor with any decision these patients have made about having had enough. There is a dramatic shift in these situations from an individualized doctor-patient relationship to something more like a public health perspective, with attention refocused on the group rather than on the individuals making it up. Compassion and individualized commitment, so much the pride of everyday clinical practice, can cost lives during a disaster. A skilled emergency physician will complete a physical assessment in no more than 90 seconds. The colored tag is attached and it is on to the next patient. The goal is to have saved, at the end of the day, the maximum number of lives.

Catastrophe and Battlefield Euthanasia

In a *medical disaster*, the resources of a health care setting are overwhelmed. Triage helps to solve the problem. In contrast, a *medical catastrophe* occurs when a health care delivery system collapses (Kipnis, 2003: 95-107). The hospital (or any setting where medical care has been provided) has somehow become hazardous to the point where all must relocate to safety. Though this may or may not have occurred at Memorial Medical Center, there are scenarios where this condition would be met. Here are three.

1. An earthquake and ongoing aftershocks have caused structural damage and are threatening to topple occupied sections of a now burning hospital.
2. Biological, chemical, or radiological agents have contaminated the buildings even while the clinical staff are unprepared to protect themselves.
3. A deadly epidemic is fueling riots by angry mobs who believe that essential supplies are being hoarded inside.

In all three cases, clinicians and patients are present in the hospital and, for different reasons, it is not safe for them to remain.

The argument from forced abandonment arises against the background of a medical catastrophe: the collapse of a health care delivery system. It becomes applicable when, in addition, it is impossible to evacuate black-tagged patients and impossible to remain with them. While rare, such conditions are more familiar in battlefield medicine. In his World War II personal narrative, *The Road Past Mandalay*, John Masters recounts one such episode (Masters, 1979: 277-78). Commanding a British unit in Burma, he and 2,000 of his men are being forced to retreat by a fresher and better-equipped Japanese force. A doctor has summoned him.

> The stretchers lay in the path itself, and in each stretcher lay a soldier of 111 Brigade. The first man was quite naked and a shell had removed the entire contents of his stomach. Between his chest and pelvis there was a bloody hollow, behind it his spine. Another had no legs and no hips, his trunk ending just below the waist. A third had no left arm, shoulder or breast, all torn away in one piece. . . .

Nineteen men lay there. A few conscious. At least, their eyes moved, but without light in them.

The doctor said, "I've got another thirty on ahead, who can be saved, if we can carry them. . . . These men have no chance. . . . None can last another two hours, at the outside."

I said aloud, "Very well. I don't want them to see any Japanese." . . . Shells and bombs burst on the slope above and bullets clattered and whined overhead.

"Do you think I want to do it?" the doctor cried in helpless anger. . . . "We can't spare any more morphia."

"Give it to those whose eyes are open," I said. "Get the stretcher bearers on at once. Five minutes."

He nodded and I went back up to the ridge, for the last time. One by one, carbine shots exploded curtly behind me. I put my hands to my ears but nothing could shut out the sound.

There are several features that are worth noticing in this description.

1. There is, in the background, a medical disaster. The 19 men who can no longer be saved have, in effect, been black-tagged but not abandoned. They are receiving narcotics and, with difficulty, are being evacuated. The medical objective is to save as many lives as possible and to insure that even the most severely injured receive care and attention that is appropriate under the circumstances.
2. The moving British unit is attempting to carry out an organized retreat from an attacking Japanese force. Their lives depend on the execution of this difficult maneuver. Whatever semblance of a clinic that existed before the retreat began, nothing is left of it now. A medical catastrophe has occurred.
3. It appears to be impossible to evacuate the black-tagged patients without risking the lives of 30 less severely wounded soldiers. One

supposes that further casualties would be expected if the retreat were interrupted.

4. It is not possible for the doctor to remain behind with the black-tagged patients. Were he to do this, it would be a culpable abandonment of the other wounded soldiers in the unit. He would likely be captured or killed by the advancing Japanese and he has weighty duties not to let either of these happen.

5. It appears to be unacceptable to abandon the black-tagged patients to capture by the Japanese. Perhaps it is believed that they will be mistreated; or that they will not be provided with appropriate medical attention during their remaining hours; or that, grievously wounded and left alone to die, they will endure deaths that human beings should be spared, if possible, by those caring for them. The officer may also appreciate what he would be required to do with Japanese wounded were the situation reversed.

6. Though neither the doctor nor the officer says so, it is evident that the issue is whether to euthanize the gravely injured soldiers before moving on. It is striking that the two men *are not deliberating*. Their common purpose seems rather *to confirm the inevitability of a profoundly unwelcome choice*.

The Question from Katrina

I can now address the question with which we began: Can the conditions in a collapsing health care delivery system ever excuse euthanasia? As on the battlefield, health care professionals and their patients, during massive civilian disasters like Katrina, can also be compelled to evacuate. Should it prove impossible to relocate the black-tagged patients, health care professionals will have only three choices: they can remain with their patients, they can leave them behind, or they can euthanize them before leaving themselves (Swann, 1987).

The first option, remaining with the black-tagged patients, tests the commitments of physicians, nurses, and others. While the obligations that clinicians have to their patients are weighty, it would be hard to defend the proposition that they are absolute: to be honored regardless of the costs to the caregivers and to others with competing claims. To be sure, the continuing presence of health care professionals may extend somewhat the lives of dying patients, may make the dying process more endurable, and may express a community's commitment to respect the dignity of those in the greatest need. But whatever the sources and the weight of the duty to remain with patients, it is an open question what burdens health care providers must shoulder to fulfill this professional obligation, and what expectations others (clinician's families, other patients) must forfeit. A catastrophic collapse of a health care system can require doctors and nurses to work without proper equipment in uncontrolled environments; without adequate food, water, or sleep; and amid hazards that threaten their own lives and health. What they can accomplish by remaining may be precious little and far less than what they might do elsewhere. At some point they may have done everything required of them.

There appear to be two distinct justifications for setting a limit to the obligation to remain with patients where leaving them would constitute abandonment. In the first place are *unreasonable personal burdens* that health care professionals and their families would have to take on were they to remain. Family members and others may also suffer significant derivative loss. In the second place are *competing professional obligations*. As with the doctor in the Burma narrative, other patients may have weightier claims than the black-tagged patients. In a disaster, allocation rightly shifts resources to where they can do the most good. Accordingly, any decision to remain with victims who are beyond saving may violate weightier obligations to attend to salvageable patients in urgent need of vital care. For these reasons, I will assume in what follows that the prohibition on abandoning patients cannot be absolute.

One other consideration is worth mentioning. Consider the risks routinely taken by firefighters, soldiers, and police officers. Notice that the community helps them do their jobs in reasonable safety. Firefighters receive breathing equipment and protective clothing. The burden of remaining at one's station despite hazards does not fall solely on their shoulders. Society must support essential services if it is to expect men and women to act heroically when the need arises. Now whatever the social obligation of firefighters to enter burning buildings, it is arguably diminished when a community fails to provide protective equipment and other forms of support. Likewise, if a community expects health care professionals to remain steadfast during a catastrophe, it must be prepared to support them through the darkest hours so they can keep at their work while protecting themselves. But when health care professionals are abandoned by the communities they serve, the duty to brave hazards may be attenuated.

If, as I have argued, there is a line delimiting where there is no duty to remain, and if it is reasonable to judge that it has been crossed, health care professionals could conclude that they were at liberty to leave. But having chosen to leave, clinicians would then face a second dilemma: either abandon the black-tagged patients to die unmedicated and unattended, or euthanize them before leaving themselves. There is no third option.

Two of the weightiest medical norms are here in collision: the prohibition against abandoning patients and the prohibition against killing them. Where it is impossible to evacuate patients and dangerous and medically futile to remain with them, one of these two norms *must* give way.

In the professions of medicine and nursing, there is a broad consensus on the twin issues of nonabandonment and euthanasia. While euthanasia has been heavily contested in the professional literatures, that is less so of nonabandonment. Loyalty and fidelity to patients and clients are commonly invoked as core professional values. Patients and clinicians stand in a fiduciary relationship. At the center is trust on the part of the patient and *a reciprocal commitment to be worthy of that trust* on the part of the clinician. Accordingly, it is a serious matter for a doctor to "fire" a patient: for nonpayment of bills or for imposing unnecessary risks on staff and other patients. Physicians are well advised to give notice in writing, and with ample time for the patient to obtain the services of another caregiver. Likewise, nurses know that they may not leave their units if there are not enough staff to care for the patients. While leaving a gravely ill patient alone, to die unattended and unmedicated, would be a paradigmatic violation of professional ethics—an egregious betrayal of loyalty—the pertinent principles were not conceived in the light of medical catastrophe.

Along with abandonment, euthanasia is also commonly prohibited by authoritative professional standards.

Facing the Dilemma

To fix ideas, let us restrict our focus to cases that arise only under the following three conditions.

1. The care setting has become hazardous to the point where clinicians are no longer under a duty to remain.
2. The patients who are being attended in the care setting are not expected to survive with the treatments that are available there. Nor is it expected that supplemental clinical resources will become available in time to improve their prognoses.
3. It is not possible to evacuate these patients.

There are at least three considerations that support excusing euthanasia under these specific circumstances.

1. Clinicians who abandon the care setting early, leaving others to take up the common burden, are able to sidestep the problem. Only the clinicians who stay on to the last will have to choose which of the two medical norms they will betray. To charge these men and women with criminal or professional misconduct would be to discourage or punish the very heroism they earlier displayed by remaining at their posts despite the hazards and to encourage early desertion as a way of avoiding censure. Taken together, these pragmatic considerations amount to a powerful justification for withholding condemnation.
2. Earlier, in Section II, I reviewed certain "yellow light" objections based on prematurity. I noted that steadfast clinicians might

refrain from ending the lives of intractably suffering patients out of a worry that such an irrevocable step would be premature—other strategies might still be tried. But forced abandonment puts a full stop to such reflection. Once the patient is unattended, no further care can be on offer. When the only other option is to abandon the patient (no care at all), it may be that *the best treatment* would be one that beneficently and painlessly ends life. The euthanizing of black-tagged patients under conditions 1 through 3 above may represent "appropriate care under the circumstances": the least-worst option. On this argument, forced abandonment would *justify* euthanasia rather than merely excuse it. Not only would it be a reasonable choice: it would be the right choice.

3. But even if it could not be shown that euthanasia is the preferred option, faced with the forced choice, it remains that neither option is plainly the wrong one. The ethics literature does not authoritatively prioritize the prohibitions on abandonment and euthanasia when circumstances dictate that one of the two must give way. The two norms seem always to be considered independently, perhaps because it is not imagined that they can conflict. Clinicians who are forced to choose between the two are therefore not in violation of professional ethics, considered as a whole. If it cannot be maintained that a clinician made the wrong choice under the circumstances, there is no basis for condemnation. Notwithstanding the violation of a weighty norm, the offense, if there is one, should be excused. The circumstances forced a choice between two weighty norms, one of which had to be violated. In the absence of an accepted priority rule, neither choice should be condemned, and either choice should be excused.

Were one to apply this standard to the events at MMC, here are the questions that would have to be addressed. First, did the conditions that followed Katrina require the evacuation of the hospital? A positive answer to this question might establish that the clinical staff was no longer required to remain in the hospital.

Second, were the remaining patients likely to die despite the best effort that might be made with the staffing and resources then available in the hospital? Was it reasonable to believe that supplemental clinical resources would not arrive in time to improve their prognoses? A positive answer to these questions would establish that the patients were not expected to survive.

Third, was it reasonable to believe that rescue efforts to evacuate the remaining patients would not arrive in time to improve their prognoses? A positive answer to this question would establish that the remaining patients were not expected to be evacuated.

Where all three conditions are satisfied, clinicians must choose between abandoning their patients or euthanizing them before leaving themselves. Paradoxically, *it is precisely because each of the two options stands as an egregious violation of an important health care norm, and because there is no third option, that neither violation can be rightly condemned.* We can only have compassion for those who had to face the forced choice.[6]

If my analysis of the issue is correct and if, in the end, it turns out to be applicable to the events at Memorial Medical Center, then, narrowly, as a matter of professional ethics and law, what clinicians did or did not do during the darkest hours of the New Orleans catastrophe might not be consequential. To be sure, patients suffered and certainly some died. And we can imagine a small number of clinicians, tired, overworked, despondent about the lack of support, having to make one of the most painful and vexing moral decisions human life can force upon anyone. We can imagine clinicians reasonably concluding that their hospital has become hazardous, that their patients cannot be evacuated nor are they expected to survive, and that no one is coming to help. We can imagine clinicians telling any patients who were still alert enough to understand:

> Because of the disaster, we can neither keep you alive for very long nor can we move you to a safer location. This hospital has become dangerous and help is not on the way. The staff must evacuate. We can leave you as you are, hoping for the best but realistically expecting something quite bad. Or we can provide you with drugs that will put

you into a deep sleep from which you will never awaken. You can make the choice to die soon, with us still here with you rather than after we have gone. We have no other option to offer. Please help us to make this decision.

While the argument from forced abandonment may have a broadly understood application on the battlefield, its requisite conditions are exceedingly rare in civilian settings. If the conditions were satisfied at MMC, that event might be one of only a handful where a civilian health care institution collapsed catastrophically. It should not be a worry that the decision to excuse euthanasia in these extremely rare circumstances will lead inexorably to the Nazi gas chambers.

The problem of euthanasia arises *in extremis*. In one case, the life of a suffering person approaches a ruinous and horrific end. In a second, rarer and less studied case, a collapsing health care system is unable to minister to the most grievously afflicted. It can be distressing to ponder what it might be like when such important matters go so dreadfully awry, and difficult to discern professional responsibilities when they do. But these tragedies do befall us, challenging our capacities to craft decent and just social practices, and to act rightly out of charity, compassion and respect.

NOTES

* I am grateful to Leanne Logan, Rosamond Rhodes, Michael Gross, Edmund G. Howe, and Thomas P. Gonsoulin for suggestions that have improved this essay. Most of all, I am indebted to Peggy Battin for her generous comradeship and counsel as this project unfolded. Some of these materials were drawn from an earlier article on euthanasia that I prepared for *The Encyclopedia of Social Problems* (Sage Publications, forthcoming).

1. The seventh floor of MMC had been leased by LifeCare Hospital. A separate hospital within a hospital, LifeCare patients were among the most gravely ill in the building (Deichmann, 2006: 64-65).

2. My sketch of these well-reported events is drawn from hundreds of sources, the most important of which were reports in the *New Orleans Times-Picayune* and the *New York Times*. Jeffrey Meitrodt's five-part series in the *Times-Picayune* ("For Dear Life: How Hope Turned to Despair at Memorial Medical Center") offers an excellent overview (Meitrodt, 2006). MMC's chief of medicine has written a first-person narrative of his experience during the episode (Deichmann, 2006).

3. If it is permissible, under the circumstances, to do some one thing oneself (leaping to one's death from a World Trade Center window), one must ask why it would not, by implication, be equally permissible to lend assistance to another who reliably and reasonably desires to do that same thing, but is physically unable to do so? While I believe this issue is worth pursuing, I will pass over it here.

4. Among the many proponents of this highly influential idea are John Stuart Mill (1985), John Rawls (1999), and Joel Feinberg (1987).

5. The issues here are well explored in John Rawls' *Political Liberalism* (Rawls, 1993: 35-40, 133-72).

6. It would be still be appropriate to condemn others who, in various ways, allowed or caused conditions to deteriorate to a point where only those two unwelcome options remained.

REFERENCES

Brock, Dan W. "Voluntary Active Euthanasia." *Hastings Center Report* 22:2 (March/April, 1993): 10-22.

Deichmann, Richard. E. *Code Blue: A Katrina Physician's Memoir*. Bloomington: AuthorHouse, 2006.

Dworkin, Ronald. *Life's Dominion: An Argument about Abortion, Euthanasia, and Individual Freedom*. New York: Vintage, 1994.

Feinberg, Joel. *The Moral Limits of the Criminal Law*. Vol. 1: *Harm to Others*. New York: Oxford University Press, 1987.

Kipnis, Kenneth. "Overwhelming Casualties: Medical Ethics in a Time of Terror." *In the Wake of Terror: Medicine and Morality in a Time of Crisis*. Ed. J. Moreno. Cambridge: MIT Press, 2003.

Masters, John. *The Road Past Mandalay*. New York: Bantam Books, 1979.

Meitrodt, Jeffrey. "For Dear Life: How Hope Turned to Despair at Memorial Medical Center." *New Orleans Times-Picayune,* August 20-24, 2006 <http://www.vendomeplace.org/press082006memorialhospital.html>.

Mill, John Stuart. *On Liberty.* New York: Penguin, 1985.

Rawls, John. *Political Liberalism.* New York: Columbia University Press, 1993.

———. *A Theory of Justice.* Rev. ed. Cambridge: Harvard University Press, 1999.

Sulmasy, D. P. "Death and Human Dignity." *Linacre Quarterly* 61:4 (1994): 27-36.

Swann, S. W. "Euthanasia on the Battlefield." *Military Medicine* 152 (1987): 545-549.

Jeff McMahan
Justice and Liability in Organ Allocation

THE DISTRIBUTION OF ORGANS FOR TRANSPLANTATION

SUPPOSE THAT THERE ARE TWO PEOPLE, BOTH OF WHOM WILL DIE VERY soon without an organ transplant. One organ becomes available. It is a perfect match for both people, one of whom can therefore be saved. It is virtually certain that no other organ will become available in time to save both. How ought the choice between the two people to be made? There are indefinitely many distributive principles that might be followed. The organ could, for example, be sold to the highest bidder. Or it could be given to the person whose need was manifest first: first come, first served. Many people believe that both possible recipients should have an equal chance of being selected. They may think that the decision should therefore be made randomly—for example, by flipping a coin. Both of these last two proposals seek to avoid being discriminatory. They appeal to considerations that are essentially arbitrary and irrelevant. By refusing to distinguish between the two potential recipients on substantive grounds, they seek to treat both people as equals— though it is worth noting that because these criteria do not require any exercise of judgment, they also enable those in charge of the distribution of organs to avoid any sense of responsibility for the outcomes of the selection procedure.

One common view, which in fact guides our practice in certain cases, is that priority should be given to the patient whose medical need is greater. Medical need might then be measured in terms of a patient's probable survival time in the absence of a transplant. Part of the rationale for allocating organs to those who will otherwise die sooner is that other organs may later become available for those who can survive longer. Giving priority to those whose medical need is greater is thus a means of maximizing the number of people who can be saved.

Some people think that just as it is important to save the greatest number of lives, so it is also important to achieve the greatest possible benefit per person by giving a certain priority to those individuals who will otherwise suffer a greater loss in dying. Those who hold this view think that decisions about allocation should be sensitive to the number of years a transplant recipient could reasonably be expected to live following the transplant. Suppose there are two patients who will both die tomorrow without a transplant and one organ becomes available. If one of them would die within a month even with the transplant while a transplant would enable the other to survive another 50 years, surely the organ ought to go to the latter.

Yet many people think that to allocate organs on the basis of a comparison of the benefits that the possible recipients are likely to receive is discriminatory and thus incompatible with treating patients as equals. Others, however, claim that what attention to equality really requires is not a random distribution that gives each patient an equal chance. Instead, what is needed is a distribution that would achieve the greatest equality among the potential beneficiaries in terms of some important respect in which people ought to be equal. One plausible respect in which people ought ideally to be equal is the number of years of life they get to experience. It seems unfair if, through no fault or choice of their own, one person gets to live 90 years while another gets to live only 20. So if, for example, an organ could be used either to enable a 20-year-old to live another 20 years or to enable a 40-year-old to live another 30 years, this ideal of equality would favor allocating the organ to the 20-year-old, even though he or she would derive a lesser benefit, measured in terms of the value we would seek to equalize.

Still others go further in claiming that length of life is a crude measure of both benefit and equality. We should, they argue, be concerned not just with quantity of life but also with quality of life.

On their view, if an organ could be used either to enable a 50-year-old to live another 20 years, though with a greatly reduced quality of life, or to enable a 45-year-old to live another 15 years with a high quality of life, there would be a strong case for giving it to the latter, if other considerations were equal. Giving the organ to the 45-year-old would arguably provide the greater benefit and reduce rather than increase the inequality between the two lives. Most people, however, find this sort of calculation disturbingly presumptuous and utilitarian.

Thus far I have merely offered some samples of the distributive principles to which we might appeal in allocating organs in cases in which the number of people who need an organ to survive exceeds the number of organs available for transplantation. The options are many and the debate about them is lively. In this essay I will not attempt to defend a complete account of the morality of organ allocation in conditions of scarcity. But I will defend one criterion, or the relevance of one consideration, that I have so far not mentioned. If I am right that this consideration is significant and ought to have a role in decisions about allocation, then at least some of the views mentioned above are unacceptable. At least in those cases in which the consideration I will discuss arises, we ought not to distribute organs by the use of a randomizing selection procedure, and many of the other criteria, such as medical need, likely degree of benefit, and so on, ought to be subordinated to the criterion I will defend.

KILLING IN SELF-DEFENSE

The best way to introduce this criterion is, surprisingly, to consider the ethics of killing in self-defense. Suppose that someone is rushing at you with a meat cleaver, determined to chop off your head. You have done nothing to provoke this attack; you are entirely innocent in all relevant senses of that word. The attack is unjustified and the attacker culpable. It is uncontroversial that if killing this culpable attacker is necessary to prevent him from killing you, then you are morally permitted to kill him. Yet while the permissibility of self-defense is uncontroversial in this situation, the explanation of why self-defense is permissible is not.

One view is, in effect, that self-defense needs no justification; it is always self-justifying. This is the view that informs the currently dominant theory of the just war. According to this theory, the reason combatants on both sides in a war are permitted to attack and kill combatants on the opposing side is simply that their adversaries pose a threat to them. This is the criterion of liability to attack in war: posing a threat to others. This is why all combatants are legitimate targets while noncombatants are not. It makes no difference, on this view, whether a combatant is fighting for a just cause or for an unjust cause. If he poses a threat to others, he is morally liable to attack.

This understanding of the justification for self-defense has no plausibility outside the context of war (nor even, in my view, within that context). According to this understanding of liability to defensive violence, if you engage in morally justified self-defense against the culpable assailant with the meat cleaver, you will then pose a threat to him and he will be justified in killing you. But that is clearly false; he cannot become justified in killing you by provoking you to engage in justified self-defense. We should conclude, as virtually everyone does outside the context of war, that there is no right of self-defense against a morally justified attacker.

Many people have thought that what is missing in the account of self-defense associated with the just war theory is an insistence that the attacker must be culpable—that is, that his action must be wrong and that he must be blamable for it—in order to be liable. That would exclude the possibility that people could become liable to attack merely by acting in justified self-defense. But to insist on culpability is to require too much. Suppose that the person rushing at you with a meat cleaver has been credibly threatened with being slowly tortured to death unless he kills you now. The level of duress may have overwhelmed his will and we may regard him as entirely blameless, or fully exculpated. But most people still believe that you would be fully justified in killing him in self-defense on the ground that he had made himself liable to defensive attack.

Some philosophers have argued that what makes a person liable to defensive attack is simply his posing an objectively wrongful or unjust threat, a threat to which the victim has done nothing to make herself morally liable. What matters is not whether the threatening person is blamable; it is whether he poses a threat *permissibly*. If he does, he does not thereby make himself morally liable to defensive attack. This view therefore explains why you do not make yourself liable to defensive attack when you engage in justified self-defense against the assailant with the meat cleaver. But if a person poses a threat that lacks a moral justification, and in particular if his act threatens to violate the victim's *rights*, then he will be liable to defensive action if the other conditions of justified defense (necessity, proportionality, etc.) are also met. This is true even if he acts under conditions that fully excuse his action, so that he is in no way blamable or culpable.

While the culpability criterion is too restrictive, the idea that posing an unjust threat is sufficient for liability is too permissive. It is right to insist that the threat must be objectively wrongful, and right to insist that the threatening person need not be culpable to be liable. But this view fails to insist on a condition that I believe is necessary for liability: namely, moral responsibility for the threat. Suppose that the story behind the person brandishing the meat cleaver is this. An hour earlier, he drank a glass of orange juice not knowing that a villain had put a powerful mind-control drug in it. The effect of this drug is to make the person who takes it incapable of resisting commands given by the first person he sees. The villain made sure that he was the first person his victim saw; he then commanded him to kill you.

In this version of the example, your assailant lacks all responsibility for the threat he poses to you. We might, to make it as clear a case as possible of lack of responsibility, imagine that the assailant is a helpless observer of the movement of his own body. His conscious mind is locked inside his head, watching in dismay as his body pursues you, wholly unable to exert his will to stop it. He is, in effect, an innocent bystander in relation to the movements of his own body. If this is the situation, there is no basis for the attribution of liability to this person. He does not threaten to violate your rights. For rights are moral constraints; they constrain the action of moral agents. But in posing a threat to you, this person is, temporarily, not a moral agent. Moral constraints do not apply to him in his present state; he therefore cannot violate them. If there is a justification for your killing him, it will apply equally to your killing an innocent bystander as a means of self-preservation—something that most of us believe is impermissible.

In short, moral responsibility for an unjust threat is a necessary condition for liability to defensive violence. It is also (together with the satisfaction of the ancillary conditions of necessity, proportionality, and so on) sufficient. It is moral responsibility for an unjust threat, and not merely posing the threat, that is the basis of liability to both self-defensive and self-preservative violence. Of course, the two usually go together: those who pose an unjust threat are normally responsible for it and vice versa. But in this last version of our example, the two have come apart: the assailant poses the threat but is not morally responsible for it, while the villain is responsible for it but does not pose it. Suppose that the villain cannot now stop the assailant from trying to kill you but that you can somehow avert the threat from the assailant by killing the villain, and that this will also have the effect of releasing the assailant from the effects of the drug. (I have tried to invent details for the story to make these stipulations plausible, but everything I have thought of sounds silly. So please just grant this general description.) In these conditions, the assailant would not be liable to attack but the villain would be. It would be permissible for you to kill the villain as a means of saving yourself from the assailant. In killing the villain, you would neither wrong him nor violate his rights; he would have no justified complaint against you. For he is himself responsible, through his own wrongful action, for the situation in which you must choose between his life and your own. It is not unfair to make him pay the cost of his own voluntary action.

This explains not only why it is permissible for you to kill the villain in this version of the example, but also why it is permissible for you to kill the assailant in the first version, in which the assailant is himself culpable for attacking you. In both cases, it is a person's moral responsibility for an unjust threat that makes him liable to necessary and proportionate defensive violence by the potential victim, or by third parties.

Notice, finally, that responsibility for an unjust threat is a matter of degree. And if responsibility is the basis of liability, then liability should be a matter of degree as well. This is recognized in the law. In general, for example, a person will be liable to criminal sanctions to a lower degree if he causes harm recklessly than if he causes the same harm willfully or intentionally, and lower still if he causes it negligently rather than recklessly.

THE RELEVANCE OF RESPONSIBILITY

How could any of this possibly be relevant to the allocation of organs for transplantation in conditions of scarcity? I will try to work toward a demonstration of the relevance of these considerations by degrees. I will do so by presenting a series of examples.

> *Reckless Driver (ex ante version)*
> A person is driving recklessly, aware of but indifferent to the fact that he is creating unreasonable risks to others. He is about to hit and kill a pedestrian. (It would be helpful to imagine that the impact would destroy her liver, causing her to die a few days later, though of course it is unrealistic to suppose that anyone could know this in advance.) Someone—either the pedestrian herself or a third party—could save the pedestrian by blowing up the car and with it the driver. (We might imagine that this occurs in a country, such as Israel, in which armed military personnel frequently have occasion to walk on public sidewalks.)

This is just one more case, albeit and unusual one, of defense against a person who culpably poses a threat to another. It is uncontroversial, in law and morality, that it is permissible to kill the driver if that is necessary to save the pedestrian. And we know why: the driver is morally responsible, to a high degree, for an unjust threat to the life of the pedestrian.

Villainous Patient (ex ante version)
A person needs a liver transplant to survive. He is at the top
of the waiting list for a transplant but his tissue type is very
rare and it has become evident that the probability is negli-
gible that an organ will become available in the standard
manner before he dies. Somehow he learns, however, that
your liver is the only known liver that is exactly the same
tissue type as his. He therefore attacks you with the intention of killing you in order to make your liver available for
transplantation.

Again it is uncontroversial that it would be permissible for you
or a third party to kill him if that were necessary to prevent him from
killing you. This is even clearer than in the case of the ex ante version
of the Reckless Driver case, since the villainous patient is culpable to a
higher degree than the driver is.

Villainous Patient (ex post version)
A person needs a liver transplant to survive. Learning that
your liver is of a matching tissue type, he arranges to have
you abducted and then has your liver extracted and transplanted into his body. You are nonetheless able to survive
for a few days through the use of a new device that can
temporarily perform most of the functions of the liver. It is
therefore possible for you and your assistants to track him
down, remove your liver from his body, and transplant it
back into your own. Although he may survive a few days
with the same device you have used, your removal of the
liver from his body will cause his death.

Assume that by the time the cumbersome mechanisms of the
legal system could be mobilized on your behalf, it would be too late
to save you, so that the only effective option for recovering your liver
is self-help. In these circumstances, I am not sure what the law would

say about your forcibly taking it back. But this much is true: it would not be an act of self-defense. The opportunity for defense passed when the thief successfully removed your liver and had it transplanted into his body. To remove your liver from his body now would be an act of killing in self-preservation, not self-defense. The thief is no longer a threat; he is now a bystander to your impending death, albeit a *guilty* bystander. Whatever the law might say, common sense morality says that you would be justified in taking back your liver, even if that would count as killing him. (I think it would not be a case of killing but a case of actively allowing him to die, but we need not pursue this here.) And again we have an explanation of why it would be permissible to do what would result in his death: he is morally responsible—indeed culpable—for the unjust threat to your life. He, not you, should pay the cost of his own wrongful action.

It might be argued that the difference between killing in self-defense and killing in self-preservation is relevant even in this case. In this ex post version of the case of the Villainous Patient, killing the villain to preserve your life involves *using* him in a harmful way, whereas in the ex ante version, killing him in self-defense does not. In Warren Quinn's useful terminology, killing the villain in self-defense is merely "eliminative" agency, whereas killing him in self-preservation is "opportunistic": it involves using him as a resource. But while the distinction between eliminative and opportunistic agency seems to have moral significance in many cases, it does not seem to matter in these cases. I think this is because in both the ex ante and ex post versions of the case of the Villainous Patient, the villain is fully liable to be killed because of his responsibility for the unjust threat to your life.

Next consider a variant of the case of the Reckless Driver.

Reckless Driver (first ex post version)
A person needs a liver transplant to survive. He is at the top of the waiting list for a donor organ. But he is driving recklessly and hits a pedestrian, destroying her liver. Now both he and the pedestrian will die soon without a trans-

plant. Remarkably, they are of the same tissue type. One organ becomes available that is thus a perfect match for both of them, but is unsuitable for anyone else on the waiting list. It can therefore be given either to the driver, who is at the head of the queue, or to the pedestrian, who has just joined the queue and thus would have a lower priority than the driver, according to rules of distribution that take into account the length of time that a person has been on the list, even though the pedestrian's medical need is the same as his.

It would, I believe, be unjust to give the organ to the driver. It must instead be given to the pedestrian. The driver has forfeited whatever claim he had to the organ in favor of the pedestrian, whose life he has culpably endangered. If the organ were unsuitable for the pedestrian, then of course the driver would retain his claim to it. It is not that he deserves to be passed over, or deserves to die. It is rather that by having culpably caused the pedestrian to need a transplant in order to survive, he is required to save her if he can, even at a cost to himself that is equivalent to, or even greater than, that which his action would otherwise impose on her. Having culpably created a forced choice between his life and hers, he must pay the cost of his own voluntary action.

Recall that it is uncontroversial that *if* the pedestrian or a third party could have prevented the reckless driver from hitting her and destroying her liver, it would have been permissible to kill him preemptively in order to do so. But the opportunity for defensive action has now passed. The only option is corrective or restorative action. I believe that if she or a third party could permissibly have *killed* him to prevent his action from killing her, it must now also be permissible to *allow* him to die (by denying him the organ he would otherwise have received) in order to prevent his action from killing her, even though his action now lies in the past. Indeed, I think two even stronger claims are true. I believe that if a third party could, at no cost to himself, have killed the driver to save the pedestrian, he would have been morally *required* to do so. Similarly, once the driver has hit the pedestrian and destroyed her liver, there is a moral requirement to give the available donor organ to the pedestrian rather than to the driver.

There is one more case in the sequence of reckless driver cases that is essential to my argument in this essay. But before turning to that example, I will introduce one further case that, though inessential for my purposes here (but not irrelevant, as we will see), nevertheless presents formidable challenges to common sense moral views.

Reckless Driver (second ex post version)
A perfectly healthy person is driving recklessly, aware of but indifferent to the fact that he is creating unreasonable risks to others. He hits a pedestrian, destroying her liver. She will now die soon unless she has a liver transplant, but there is no prospect of a suitable organ becoming available in time in the ordinary way. It is known, however, that the reckless driver's liver would provide an exact match. If his liver were extracted and transplanted into her body, she would survive, though he of course would die.

In this case there is no doubt what the law would say. It would be murder to take the driver's liver to save the pedestrian. I am not confident of my ability to speak for common sense morality here, but I suspect that most people would also think it morally wrong to kill the driver as a means of saving the pedestrian and that this moral belief is at least part of the explanation of why the law is as it is. Yet the challenge is to explain why it would be impermissible to kill the reckless driver in this case when it is uncontroversial that it would have been permissible, and perhaps even required of a third party, to kill him ex ante had that been possible and necessary in order to prevent the pedestrian from being hit by him in the first place. Why should he gain protection from the mere fact that his wrongful action lies in the past?

It is true that many people think that *defense* is nearly always justified, that it is privileged among possible justifications for the infliction of harm. And it is also true, as I have noted, that if the action that inflicts a harm has already occurred, defense is no longer possible. But I think it is an illusion that defense has a privileged place among justifications for the infliction of harm. It can be a matter of justice not just to prevent wrongful harms but also to rectify them once they have occurred. There is, indeed, an entire area of the law devoted to the rectification of previously inflicted losses: the law of torts. In tort law, if one person is objectively at fault in injuring another who was not herself negligent, the injurer owes the victim compensation as a matter of justice to restore her to the level of well-being she would have enjoyed in the absence of the injury. Of course, the compensation that is owed takes the form of a payment. And in the ex post versions of the case of the Reckless Driver, compensation cannot take the form of a monetary payment. Compensation in tort law is generally measured by an indifference criterion. A payment is deemed to compensate a victim for a loss if she would be indifferent between 1) not suffering the loss, and 2) suffering the loss and then receiving the payment. But for most people there is no amount of money that could compensate them, by this criterion, for the loss of their life. In the second of our ex post versions of the case of the Reckless Driver, the only way that the driver can come close to compensating the pedestrian is give her his liver—and even this would not fully compensate her. If we accept that it is just to force injurers to compensate their victims through monetary payments when compensation can take this form, why should we draw back when the only form of compensation is a vital organ?

One thought people tend to have at this point is that to cut a person open and remove his liver would be an extreme violation of his bodily integrity, and we tend to think of people's rights to bodily integrity as nearly absolute. In law, for example, a parent may not be coerced to donate bone marrow for her child, even if her child would be enabled to survive by a bone marrow transplant but will die without it. For even though it involves virtually no risk and is largely painless, the extraction of bone marrow from the parent's body does require the insertion of a needle into her pelvic bone, and thus, if done without her consent, counts as an invasion of her bodily integrity.

The suggestion that the issue here is one of bodily integrity finds support if we consider a further variant of the example. Suppose that instead of having destroyed the pedestrian's liver, the reckless driver has destroyed both her kidneys and that she needs a single kidney transplant in order to survive. The driver has two healthy kidneys and could easily survive with only one. Yet the law forbids the forcible extraction of one of his kidneys to save the pedestrian's life and I suspect that most people would agree that this would be forbidden by morality as well. If we may not take his kidney even when this would not threaten his life, this suggests that the main objection to taking the reckless driver's liver in the original case is not that this would kill the driver but that it would violate his bodily integrity.

Yet the problem with this appeal to the right of bodily integrity is that if it makes it impermissible to take the driver's liver after he has hit the pedestrian, it should also make it impermissible to kill him ex ante to prevent him from hitting the pedestrian. For we are imagining that in order to prevent him from hitting the pedestrian, one would have to blow him up along with the car he is driving. And it could hardly be true that while inserting a needle into a person's bone is a violation of her bodily integrity, blowing a person's body to bits is not.

I have discussed this example because it raises disturbing questions but, as I observed earlier, it has no essential role in the main argument of this essay. There is, however, one further ex post version of the case of the Reckless Driver that does.

Reckless Driver (third ex post version)
A person needs a liver transplant to survive. Her need for a transplant is the result of years of infection with the Hepatitis C virus, which she acquired from a blood transfusion administered with her parents' consent when she was a small child. (We might, just to bias the example a bit more in the direction I favor, imagine that she needed the trans-

fusion because of the loss of blood occasioned by being hit by a reckless driver as she was walking along the sidewalk.) She and another patient join the waiting list for a donor organ at the same time. This other person, whose medical need is the same as hers, needs a transplant because of an injury suffered in a single-car accident caused entirely by his own reckless driving. As one would expect at this point, he and the hepatitis patient share the same tissue type. A single donor organ becomes available that is an ideal match for both of them but is unsuitable for anyone else on the waiting list.

Had we not already discussed the other cases involving reckless drivers and villainous patients, it might not occur to us to suppose that the driver in this case might have a lesser claim to the organ than the hepatitis patient. But a consideration of the previous cases does pressure us to accepted that he has a diminished claim relative to hers. He is morally responsible for his own need for an organ; she is not. This makes him morally liable to the assignment of a lower priority.

This is not, like the second ex post version of the Reckless Driver case, an instance in which, in order to save the pedestrian, one must kill the driver as a means. In this case, the reckless driver would not be killed but merely allowed to die; and he would not be used as a means. This is a simple case of choosing whom to save when not all can be saved.

One obvious difference between this case and the previous two ex post cases involving reckless drivers is of course that in the other cases the driver is responsible for the *pedestrian's* need for a transplant. In this case he is not. He is responsible only for his own need. This case is therefore fundamentally different in what seems to be a morally significant way.

In one sense it is of course true that the driver in this case is not responsible for the threat to the pedestrian. He is in no way responsible for her need for a transplant. Yet in another sense he *is* responsible for a threat to her life. If he had not driven recklessly and injured himself, the organ that has become available would have gone to her. She could have been saved from the effects of the disease over which she has never had any control. But now, through his own reckless action, he has put himself in competition with her for the organ. He has, in other words, created a forced choice between his life and hers. And he has done so through action that recklessly endangered himself and others, action that now endangers the hepatitis patient, although in a rather indirect way.

It is true, of course, that the hepatitis patient threatens the driver in the same way that the driver threatens her. If she were not on the waiting list, the organ that has become available would go to him. So each poses a threat to the other. But the difference is that he is responsible for his need for the organ while she is not responsible for her need. He is therefore responsible for the threat he poses to her whereas she is not responsible for the threat she poses to him.

One might argue that the degree of his responsibility is too slight to make him liable to cede his claim to the organ to the hepatitis patient. All he is guilty of, after all, is reckless driving, and the only person he hurt is himself. I concede that this is relevant. I noted earlier that responsibility is a matter of degree and that liability should vary with responsibility, if other things are equal. To see how this is relevant in the present case, suppose that both the driver and the hepatitis patient could survive with only a partial liver transplant, though their quality of life and long-term survival prospects would be diminished relative to what they could expect from a full transplant. If the donor organ could be divided so that each could be given a partial transplant, that would probably be the best solution. If the division could be asymmetrical, it would probably be ideally fair to give the hepatitis patient the larger part, thereby enabling both of them to survive but offering her a somewhat better quality of life as well as better survival prospects. But she would not be entitled to demand the entire organ at the cost of allowing the driver to die.

I believe that the situation would be different, however, in a further variant of the first ex post version of the Reckless Driver case.

The driver is again a patient at the head of the waiting list for a liver transplant. But in this variant, he does not drive recklessly but instead intentionally and maliciously hits the pedestrian with his car and in doing so destroys her liver. Again a single organ that is a match for both of them becomes available, but in this variant it can be divided, so that each could have a partial transplant. Here it seems to me that the driver's claim to any part of the organ is very weak relative to the claim of the pedestrian. It would not be unjust, in my view, to give the entire organ to the pedestrian in an effort to compensate her as fully as possible for what the driver has done to her, while allowing the driver to die.

In the third ex post version of the Reckless Driver case—the version in which the reckless driver injures himself and thus puts himself in competition for survival with the hepatitis patient—it is not possible to divide the donor organ between the two. In this case, one of them can be saved and the other must die. In this situation, even though the degree of the driver's responsibility for his need for a trans-plant is modest, it is sufficient to give the hepatitis patient priority, since she is in no way responsible for her need for a transplant. In these circumstances, and in the absence of other considerations that might favor the driver, this asymmetry in responsibility decisively favors the hepatitis patient.

It is worth noting, before going on, that what I have said would not justify killing the reckless driver preemptively, to prevent him from injuring his own liver. Nor would there be a justification to kill him afterward, to eliminate the threat that his appearance on the wait-ing list poses to the hepatitis patient. For there is no necessity of defen-sive harming in this case. The threat to the hepatitis patient can be eliminated simply by allocating the organ to her. But suppose that, as is presently true, the allocation system does not take considerations of responsibility into account? Suppose that the officials who make deci-sions about the allocation of organs see that both the driver and the hepatitis patient appeared on the waiting list and the same time and have equivalent medical needs; and suppose that to decide between them the officials then flip a coin, with the result that the organ is scheduled to go to the driver. If the hepatitis patient, or a third party, could kill the driver in a way that would make it appear that he had died a natural death, would it be permissible to kill him to prevent his reckless action from depriving the hepatitis patient of the organ that she needs to survive and that would otherwise have been hers?

I do not have an answer to this question, which is similar to the question raised by the second ex post version of the Reckless Driver case, in which the driver recklessly damages the pedestrian's liver and has a liver that could be used to save her. In the present case, in which the driver is responsible only for his own need for a transplant, both the law and common sense morality clearly prohibit the killing of the driver. And no doubt there are many reasons why it would be morally objectionable to kill him to remove him from the waiting list. But this leaves open the question whether killing him would *wrong* him, or violate his *rights*, when he will otherwise survive by taking for himself an organ that, on the view for which I have argued here, ought as a matter of justice to be used to save someone else.

ALLOCATION OF LIVERS TO ALCOHOLICS

Many readers will have anticipated where this discussion is leading. Cases in which one potential transplant recipient is responsible for causing another person to need the same sort of transplant rarely, if ever, occur. But cases in which people are responsible for causing themselves to need a transplant, and thus for placing themselves in competition with others for an organ when there are not enough organs for all who need them, are common. The most notorious cases involve alcoholics who cause themselves to suffer from cirrhosis of the liver and continue to drink until they reach end-stage liver disease, when a liver transplant offers their only chance of survival. (Some people who are not alcoholics but who nevertheless drink heavily on a regular basis for many years can also cause themselves to suffer from the same liver problems that afflict some alcoholics. But these people account for only a small percentage of the number of cases of alcohol-induced liver failure. Thus, for simplicity I will refer only to alcoholics.) This is not a marginal phenomenon. In the United States, excessive consumption of alcohol is the leading cause of liver disease, so the problem is quite serious. And the cases, considerations, and arguments I have been discussing have implications for how this problem ought to be addressed.

The view I have sought to defend is that when a person is responsible to a significant degree for his own need for an organ transplant, and when there are not enough organs for all who need them, so that this person is responsible for placing himself in competition for an organ with others who are not responsible for their need for a transplant, priority ought to be given to those who lack responsibility for their condition, other things being equal. This view is, I believe, implied by the same principles that govern the ethics of killing in self-defense. These principles assert a strong connection between moral responsibility for conditions in which someone must die and moral liability to be the one who is killed or allowed to die. Because of this, a person's responsibility for his own need for a transplant is not a trivial factor; it is, rather, a factor that is not easily outweighed by other considerations.

Most alcoholics are aware that drinking threatens their health, and in particular their liver. Most are aware, particularly as a result of the publicity given to liver transplants undergone by numerous alcoholic celebrities (such as Mickey Mantle), that alcoholics have a high risk of eventually needing a liver transplant in order to survive. Many are aware, or ought to be aware, that organs donated for transplantation are scarce and that many people die because of the chronic shortage of donor organs. That these facts are common knowledge is important, since awareness of the risks they run seems to be a condition of significant responsibility for their own predicament when alcoholics reach the point at which they need a transplant to survive. Responsibility requires foreseeability. If we were to discover tomorrow that broccoli causes liver disease, we would not conclude that those who now require a transplant because of their high consumption of broccoli in the past are responsible for their need for a transplant. But because the facts about the connection between alcoholism and liver disease are well known, it is reasonable to regard most alcoholics who need a liver transplant to survive as responsible to a significant degree for their own condition.

If this is the case, the view for which I have argued implies that they should have lower priority in the distribution of livers for transplantation than those who have not contributed to their need for a transplant. When an alcoholic who needs a liver transplant has been aware, even if only vaguely (since even a vague awareness establishes a ground for negligence), that his continued drinking placed him at risk of liver failure, he is responsible to a significant degree for his own condition and therefore for the fact that others must now choose between saving him and saving the life of someone else who has not had the choice, as he had, of avoiding the need for a transplant. If he is allowed to compete with others for an organ, he then becomes responsible for a threat to them, though they are not similarly responsible for the threat they pose to him. Justice dictates in these cases that the organ be given to a person who lacks responsibility for her condition, if other things are equal (and they would have to be very unequal to outweigh considerations of responsibility).

OBJECTIONS
Equality
The suggestion that alcoholics should have lower priority in the allocation of organs for transplantation strikes many people as an affront to the equal worth of persons. It is worse than invidious; it is overtly discriminatory.

Yet to make responsibility for one's condition relevant to one's entitlement to treatment in conditions of scarcity is importantly different from other proposed departures from a system of distribution, such as an unweighted lottery, that would give all potential recipients and equal chance of receiving an organ. Most other proposed criteria for ranking potential recipients focus on factors that are beyond people's control: age, ability to benefit from treatment, social worth, and so on. To allow such factors a role in the allocation of organs may indeed seem incompatible with respect for the equal worth of persons. But responsibility for one's own condition is different. To hold alcoholics responsible for their action is to recognize their capacity for responsible agency and to hold them liable for their exercise of it. This is no less compatible with equal respect than recognizing the permissibility of self-defense or the legitimacy of punishment.

Punishing Vice

It is frequently argued that the idea of assigning lower priority to alcoholics derives from a Prohibition-era mentality, from religiously motivated moralizing about demon alcohol and the wickedness of those who imbibe it. To integrate this idea into policies for the allocation of organs would simply be a way of rewarding supposed moral virtue and punishing vice.

It should be obvious that there is nothing punitive, nothing retributive, in the argument I have given. I conceded earlier that even someone who bears the highest degree of responsibility, through morally culpable action, for his need for a transplant, may be perfectly entitled to a donor organ if there is no one else who needs it to survive but is not responsible for her condition. We may, however, go further than this. Nothing I have written implies that a person's general moral virtuousness or wickedness is relevant to his entitlement to an organ transplant. Suppose that there are two people of the same tissue type whose medical need for a transplant is the same. One is a convicted murderer serving a life sentence in prison who as a child was infected with Hepatitis C through a blood transfusion, while the other is a thoroughly nice person who destroyed his own liver in an accident caused by his own uncharacteristic reckless driving. Suppose that an organ becomes available that is an ideal match for both and is unsuitable for everyone else on the waiting list. Nothing I have written implies that it ought to be given to the nice person; rather, my argument favors giving it to the murderer. Whether there are further considerations that outweigh the nice person's responsibility for his own condition is a matter I will leave open—though for the record I will note my intuition that the organ ought, all things considered, to be given to him rather than to the murderer. The point here is that the argument I have advanced for assigning lower priority to alcoholics does not depend on any assessment of the moral virtues or vices of alcoholics.

Notice that a similar objection is still sometimes made to the imposition of a "vice tax" on cigarettes. But most people now understand that the purpose of the high tax on tobacco products is not to punish vice but to make smokers bear the costs of their own action. Because smokers make disproportionate demands on the health care system, thereby burdening others with increased taxes (under a national health system) or increased insurance premiums, the tax is meant to redistribute the costs of their action back to them, rather than allowing them to impose the costs of their own voluntary action on others.

Addiction and Responsibility

Another objection that is frequently stated is that even if a person's responsibility for her need for a transplant is a relevant factor in the allocation of organs, this has no bearing on the priority that ought to be given to alcoholics, since they are not in fact responsible for their liver disease. Alcoholism is itself a disease. Among the defining characteristics of the disease are *addiction* and *denial*. Addiction is a form of compulsion while denial involves an inability to recognize and thus to try to combat the compulsion. Together they absolve the alcoholic of all responsibility for behavior—such as continuing to drink even when it is known to be damaging to the alcoholic's health—that is entirely attributable to the disease. Thus, according to the deputy director of the National Institute on Alcohol Abuse and Addiction, which is a division of the National Institutes of Health, "although taking the first drink is a willful behavior, once the person is addicted, it's beyond their control" (quoted in Munson, 2002: 62).

There is much that could be said in response to this objection. I will make only a few brief points. The most obvious and important point is that many alcoholics do stop drinking and continue to abstain from drinking for the rest of their lives. I know many alcoholics who have done this. Most adults probably also know at least several alcoholics who have stopped, some even without professional assistance. So it just cannot be true that once a person is an alcoholic, it ceases to be within his control whether or not he continues to drink.

Many alcoholics are not unaware of their condition. They recognize that they are alcoholics and make efforts to control their drinking but fail. Still, the opportunity to exercise control remains with them, however many times they fail. Many of them make the decision to drink every day. In many cases, the reasons they perceive for stopping are insufficient to counter the temptation they experience to drink. If the incentives for stopping were stronger, many would stop. If, for example, it were true of some particular alcoholic that if he were ever to have just one more drink, he would immediately die an agonizing death, and if he knew this was true, it is highly probable that he would never have another drink. Most alcoholics could stop drinking in these conditions. So one way to help alcoholics in general would be to increase the costs to them of continued drinking in order to provide greater incentives for stopping. And of course one obvious possibility would be to assign them lower priority in the allocation of livers for transplantation. Many alcoholics know that under the current rules, if they destroy their liver by drinking, they will compete with others on equal terms for a transplant and thus will have a reasonable chance of surviving. If it were instead true, and they knew it to be so, that they would have almost no chance of receiving a donor organ if they were to destroy their liver by continued drinking, that would give them a significant incentive to stop drinking before it is too late.

We should, of course, recognize that alcoholics have diminished responsibility for their continued drinking. It seems undeniable that alcoholic addiction makes it extremely difficult not to drink, and that alcoholism does impair a person's ability to appreciate the nature of his problem. But diminished responsibility is not absence of responsibility, and even a small degree of responsibility can be morally significant. Negligence, for example, is treated as a basis of liability even when it is slight, and even though there are puzzles about how it can be a basis of liability. (How can we hold that a person ought to know what he does not know? Suppose he does not know that there is something that he ought to know. Is he then negligent for not knowing that there is something that he ought to know? And so on.) If, however, we were to rewrite the first ex post version of the Reckless Driver example so that the driver was guilty of negligence rather than recklessness, I would still think that he would forfeit his position on the waiting list in favor of the pedestrian he had injured.

Policy

Perhaps the most powerful objection to giving alcoholics lower priority in the distribution of organs for transplantation on the ground that they are responsible for their condition is that there are notorious problems in implementing the responsibility criterion as a matter of policy. Alcoholics with end-stage liver disease are a fairly clear example of people who have caused their own need for treatment. But people contribute to the causation of their illnesses in a great many ways and to varying degrees. Smoking and obesity are, for example, widely known to be causal factors in the etiology of many diseases, and they are matters over which people can exercise varying degrees of control. Yet it is difficult to determine in many cases whether and to what extent either factor has in fact contributed to a patient's condition. And it is even harder to determine the contribution that a patient's failure to get exercise or adequate nutrition might have made to his or her condition. There are, moreover, both chronic and acute conditions that result from people's choices to engage in ordinary activities such as sport, or from hazards to which they are exposed through their occupations, and so on.

It would be impossible to gather relevant information on all the ways in which most people have foreseeably contributed to their own illnesses. And even if we had perfect information on people's behavior, we still would be unable to determine in most cases the extent to which their informed choices had actually made a causal contribution to their disease. And even if we could somehow overcome both these epistemic obstacles, the task of weighing and comparing different people's responsibility for their illnesses (where responsibility is a matter not just of causation but also of foresight, control, and so on) would elude our best efforts. Finally, any genuine attempt to overcome these obstacles would inevitably be a costly bureaucratic quagmire.

So the responsibility criterion cannot be a factor in general decision making about the distribution of scarce medical resources. There remains the question whether we should employ it in limited areas in which its application is arguably not ruled out by epistemic limitations—for example, in choices between giving a liver for transplantation to an alcoholic and giving it to someone else who clearly has had no role in causing her need for a transplant. If we were to do this, the targeted group—alcoholics—would have a justified complaint about the comparative unfairness of our policies. They could complain that it would be unfair to assign them lower priority among potential recipients of liver transplants while not assigning lower priority to overweight or obese patients among potential recipients of heart transplants. I will not attempt to resolve this further problem of comparative justice. My aim in this essay has been limited: to show that responsibility for one's own illness is a morally relevant criterion in the allocation of organs and other scarce medical resources.

REFERENCES

Munson, Ronald. *Raising the Dead: Organ Transplants, Ethics, and Society.* New York: Oxford University Press, 2002.

Dan W. Brock
Health Care Resource Prioritization and Rationing: Why Is It So Difficult?

THE PRIORITIZATION OF HEALTH CARE RESOURCES AND RATIONING IS A paradigm example of difficult choices, and yet one might well wonder why. Individuals are continually forced every day to prioritize their own resources, deciding what to use them for and what to forego. The process could not be more familiar. Since our wants typically outrun our resources, and although we may regret what must be foregone, we learn to make the choices and move on to the next ones. So why is the very idea of prioritizing and rationing health care resources so troubling and controversial?

Americans are deeply ambivalent and inconsistent about health care rationing. On the one hand many like to pretend that it does not take place, but they fear being denied beneficial care, in particular payment by their health insurance plans for care they need. If rationing does not take place, of course, there is little to fear. On the one hand, many say that we are a rich country and have no need to ration health care, but they resist the rising costs of health care, particularly when they result in greater out-of-pocket costs to them. On the one hand, many say that life is precious and money should not enter into decisions about medical treatment, but on the other hand they resist the ever increasing proportion of both our national wealth and their own wealth that goes to health care. And on the one hand many recognize the need to limit the use of some health care, but resist those limits when they are applied to them or others about whom they care.

Now these inconsistencies might simply reflect a perfectly common and understandable desire to have more of a valued good like health care, but not to pay more for it. For goods that we must purchase in a marketplace, we soon learn that this is not a desire that can be satisfied—if we want more, we must be prepared to pay more, and so we must decide how much that more is worth to us in comparison with other uses for our resources. Most Americans, however, do not pay out of pocket the full costs of the health care they receive, but instead have most or all of the costs of their health care paid through health insurance. So unlike goods fully purchased and paid for in the marketplace, we do not bear the full, often most, or sometimes even any, of the real costs of the health care we consume. In the extreme, if we can get it for free, it is hardly surprising that we do not support rationing which will have the effect of denying some health care to us.

Rationing is the allocation of a good under conditions of scarcity, which necessarily implies that some who want and could be benefited by that good will not receive it. This allocation or rationing can take place by many means. The use of a market to distribute a good is one common way to ration it, since attaching a price to a good or service is one way of allocating it in conditions of scarcity and results in some who would want it and could be benefited by it not getting it. One reflection of our ambivalence toward health care rationing is seen in our resistance to having it distributed in a market like most other goods: most Americans reject ability to pay as the basis for distributing health care. They do not view health care as just another commodity to be distributed by markets. Despite this widespread perception, we are the only developed country without some form of universal health insurance, and so for the 46 million Americans without health insurance their access to health care often does depend on their ability to pay for it.

Rationing largely remains a topic that the public, its elected leaders, and many health care professionals prefer to avoid. The avoidance takes many forms. As already noted, a prominent one is to deny that significant rationing takes place. Perhaps we must ration health care resources that are physically scarce such as organs for transplantation, but rationing because of costs is less visible to the insured. Another strategy of avoidance is to employ a restrictive understanding of rationing that characterizes practices that are plausibly understood as rationing as not in fact rationing. When this denial becomes increasingly difficult to maintain in the face of the realities of the health care system, a typical alternative strategy then is to condemn rationing as unjust or unethical and to deny that it should take place. This fits the strongly negative connotation that rationing has with the public and with many health care professionals. If people widely believe that health care rationing does not take place, and that if it did it would be wrong, it is hardly surprising that we have not had a responsible public debate about when and how it should be done. But both of these beliefs—that health care rationing does not take place, and that if it did it would be wrong—are mistaken.

WHAT IS RATIONING?

One source of confusion about rationing is widespread misunderstanding about what it is, or at least widespread differences in people's understanding of what it is. As already noted, I understand health care rationing to be: the allocation of health care resources in the face of limited availability, which necessarily means that beneficial interventions are withheld from some individuals. Rationing can be understood narrowly or broadly, and this account is deliberately broad in order to capture the full range of cases where scarcity of resources, either economic (for example, money) or physical (organs, professionals' time, for example), results in patients not receiving some beneficial care. If we understand rationing too narrowly we will miss some cases that raise people's concern about rationing, which is that they will be denied some beneficial care.

Several comments will help to clarify this conception of rationing. First, at the patient care level, rationing of limited health care resources more commonly takes the form of failure to offer some care of expected net benefit to the patient rather than the denial of care that the patient or surrogate has explicitly requested. Health care professionals regularly act on judgments about whether a particular diagnostic test or treatment warrants its costs—not every patient complaining of headaches gets an MRI to rule out the rare brain tumor, not every infection requires the latest generation antibiotic when a less expensive one might do the job. But these judgments are typically made by the health professional before making a recommendation to a patient. As a result, much rationing goes unnoticed by patients or their families, which no doubt contributes to the common perception of many that rationing is relatively uncommon. Parenthetically, it also raises the ethical question of whether and when physicians may have a responsibility to inform patients or their surrogates about care of significant benefit that is not being offered to them.

Second, much rationing goes unnoticed by physicians as well because they merely understand it as good clinical care. It is not necessary to do an MRI on every patient presenting with a headache because in the absence of other presenting symptoms, the probability of picking up an otherwise undiagnosed brain tumor is so exceedingly small. But exceedingly small is not zero, which means that the MRI would have had some very small benefit in ruling out the tumor. Here and elsewhere physicians have developed formal or informal protocols and guidelines for the treatment of patients with various presenting symptoms, and those protocols and guidelines sometimes explicitly, but more often implicitly, reflect judgments that some diagnostic or treatment interventions promise too little benefit to warrant their costs. Many common diagnostic interventions such as MRIs, intravenous pyelograms (IVPs), and cardiac angiography use contrast agents that carry very small risks of allergic reactions. Low-osmolality contrast agents reduce those risks, yet are not used for most patients because such reactions are relatively rare and can generally be medically managed, and because they are many times more expensive than high-osmolality agents (Steinberg et al., 1992). Radiologists or cardiologists carrying out one of these procedures are aware that the safer agent is not being used, but do not typically think of this as rationing because they are just following professional practice and guidelines for the procedure. Physicians referring patients for the procedure will rarely even think about what contrast agent will be used, leaving that to the professional judgment of the radiologist or cardiologist. And the patient may be told that there is a very small risk of an allergic reaction, but will be assured that it can nearly always be medically managed and will not typically be offered the safer but more expensive contrast agent. So guidelines for sound clinical practice will reflect a rationing decision about what contrast agent to use, but once the guidelines are in place almost no one will think they are rationing care when they practice in accord with these guidelines.

Rationing can also take place at different levels in the health care system, and be more or less direct. When a hospital CEO allocates funds between an intensive care unit (ICU) and a primary care clinic, she makes a rationing decision that affects the level of resources and care available for patients in the ICU and in the primary care clinic. For example, the ICU budget will inevitably limit the number of beds in the ICU, which will in turn require the ICU manager to refuse admission when all beds are already occupied to some patients who would have benefited from ICU care. The ICU manager directly rations the ICU beds between competing patients, while the CEO makes a higher level resource allocation decision that indirectly results in the direct rationing of the ICU bed. Some may insist that the CEO's decision is an allocation, not a rationing, decision, but for our purposes that is a distinction without a difference since both decisions share the feature of allocating a limited resource that results in denying potentially beneficial interventions to a patient. When the CEO allocates money to the different units within the hospital, the patients that will be affected are not identified, whereas the ICU manager may have to deny admission to an identified patient. However, it would be a mistake to think that rationing only occurs with decisions that at the time they are made affect identified patients. To do so would exclude a great many decisions from rationing, such as what services an insurance plan will cover or what is on a hospital's drug formulary, even though they directly result in some patients not receiving beneficial care.

While this understanding of rationing includes more limits on care than are often recognized as rationing, it does not include all denials or failures to offer care. Rationing is the allocation of health care resources "in the face of"—that is, as required by—their limited availability. This excludes some cases of limiting patients' access to health care resources when the reason for the limitation is not their limited availability. For example, when care is not provided to a patient because it is believed it would be futile in treating the patient's condition, the reason is not its limited availability—it would be provided to the patient if it was believed to have any potential for benefit—but rather its lack of any expected benefit for the patient. This is not to deny that claims of futility (which the public will understand as treatment that "wouldn't work"—would not provide any benefit in the particular circumstances) are sometimes hidden rationing decisions to the effect that the very small or very unlikely benefit the treatment might provide the patient is not worth its cost. This latter judgment is a rationing decision and should not be confused or conflated with true futility judgments. More problematic as to whether it is rationing is when patients are not provided a treatment such as antibiotics because of concerns about their overuse leading in turn to their decreased effectiveness; this is usually seen as a public health concern, not a resource scarcity concern. However, it could be considered rationing because it shares the feature that potentially beneficial care is withheld from some patients for the sake of others, in this case others who will need effective antibiotics in the future .

Rationing also assumes that the limited resources allocated between competing patients or needs are, or would be, wanted by those patients; if not, then it is not rationing because the patients are not competing for limited resources. Treatments are often not provided to patients who for a variety of reasons have refused those treatments; this is not properly understood to be rationing, even if the care would have been beneficial to the patient. A possible exception to this is if patients refuse the treatment or services because they cannot, or decide not to use their limited resources to pay for it. Economists typically characterize markets for health care or other goods and services as rationing by price; the goods or services will be allocated by the market only to those able and willing to pay for them. And, of course, since 46 million Americans now lack health care insurance and many millions more are underinsured, patients in fact often do not receive needed and beneficial services because they are unable or unwilling to pay for them. As insured patients are forced to bear increasing out-of-pocket costs for care, they often do not receive needed and wanted care for lack of ability or willingness to pay for it.

Rationing does not occur only in order to limit health care costs. A prominent instance of health care rationing is the allocation of scarce organs for transplantation (Veatch, 2000). The limited availability of organs is not a result of concerns about limiting health care expenditures, but rather results from the limited number of donor organs available for transplantation; the scarcity is physical, not economic, required by the inadequate supply of organs for those who could benefit from them. Another important example of noneconomic rationing is the rationing that all health care professionals must continually do of their time. Spending a bit more, or in some cases even a lot more time with many patients would have some, even if often only small, additional benefit for those patients. When time is limited for patient visits because the waiting room is full, however, all health professionals must allocate the relatively fixed resource of their time between competing needs and patients.

THE NECESSITY, RATIONALITY, AND DESIRABILITY OF RATIONING

As noted earlier, when the fact that rationing regularly takes place is not denied, many people then respond that it is nevertheless wrong that it takes place. Perhaps rationing is inevitable in the face of limited physical availability of resources like organs for transplantation, although controversial proposals for markets in organs might reduce or eliminate that scarcity. Perhaps it is inevitable that rationing must occur if others limit resources available to physicians to care for their patients, but many deny that resources should be limited in this way. This is a mistake, however, and it is important to understand why. How could we avoid the need for rationing? So long as there is some limit to the resources available for health care, health care will have to be allocated to those who need or want it with not everyone getting all they need or want; that is a necessary implication of limited resource availability. Even if physicians were to try to limit having to decide who gets what (by, for example, giving all patients who ask for care anything that may benefit them until resources run out), this still involves making choices that inevitably determine who receives what care. So allocation in the face of scarcity is inevitable.

But is scarcity of health care resources itself inevitable? The only way to avoid scarcity in the health sector is to provide all services to all patients that have any positive expected benefit, no matter how small and uncertain the benefits, and no matter how high the costs. This is clearly impossible. Everyone might benefit from the health services available to the president, for example having a private physician accompany us when we travel, or from unlimited resources for research for diseases that we have or have some chance of getting. More mundanely, everyone would benefit from avoiding the small risk of allergic reactions to high-osmolality contrast agents if the much more expensive but safer low-osmolality agents were always used in diagnostic testing, or from having an MRI on the very tiny chance that a brain tumor may be causing the headache they are experiencing. Yet none of this would be possible without enormous increases in health care costs.

More important, even if possible, none of it would be rational or desirable. To avoid scarcity by providing everyone with all care of any positive expected benefit, no matter how small the benefit and how high the costs, would have enormous opportunity costs (Brock, 1993). We would have to devote enormous additional resources to health care that produced very minimal or marginal benefits when we could have used them in ways that would have produced vastly greater benefits elsewhere, such as in education, rebuilding the country's infrastructure, or taking more Caribbean vacations. Even within the health sector, providing all beneficial care for some patients regardless of costs would inevitably prevent us from treating other patients who would benefit more, unless resources to the health sector were literally unlimited. So the only way to avoid the need to ration health care would be irrational and undesirable (Ubel, 2000). It would also be arguably unethical. We would have to use resources in a very inefficient manner producing far less by way of overall benefits for the population served than if we did ration care. And since society has other ethical responsibilities to its citizens in areas such as personal and national security, education, and so forth, failing to ration health care would inevitably result in failing to meet these other ethical and political responsibilities and obligations.

THE PROBLEM OF INSURANCE

As pointed out earlier, most goods and services are allocated and rationed in the marketplace, and so access depends on the ability to pay. That form of rationing is generally uncontroversial. Even goods and services that meet other basic needs, such as for food and shelter, are largely distributed in the marketplace, supplemented by programs such as food stamps and housing subsidies for the poor, who otherwise would not be able to purchase them. Most Americans budget their incomes so that they can pay for food and housing. But health care is different from these other goods serving basic needs in ways that make it impossible for the vast majority of people similarly to budget for it. People's needs for food and housing vary, depending on factors such as metabolism and family size, but the variation is within a fairly limited range and it changes little or only slowly over time.

Needs for health care are very different. At any point in time individuals' needs for health care can and do vary greatly—most people will be generally healthy and have few if any serious health care needs, while a few will have very great and very expensive needs. Over time as well, even over a lifetime, individuals vary greatly in their health care needs and their health care use. A large proportion of health care spending in any year is accounted for by a relatively small number of very high spending individuals. Not only does individual health care needs vary greatly at any point in time and over time, but that variation is to a large extent unpredictable, and so it is not possible to budget for those needs the way we can for food and housing (Arrow, 1963). The standard market response to needs with these features of health care is to create insurance, which allows individuals to spread the effects of this variability and unpredictability in their needs across a large group. But the existence of health insurance contributes fundamentally to why allocation and rationing of health care are so difficult.

Suppose for illustration you have an insurance policy with 10 percent copays on your health expenditures. Then, faced with any health care spending decision, you need only ask if the contemplated health care is worth to you 10 percent of its real costs. Even that decision is complicated by lack of data and uncertainty about the benefits of many health care interventions; many common interventions probably lack expected benefits for significant numbers of patients who receive them, although there is often controversy about which interventions for which patients. Nevertheless, most patients will assume that their physicians will only recommend interventions that they expect to be of benefit to them and, in the face of uncertainty about benefits, will likely accept the recommendations when the cost to them of doing so is only a small proportion of the intervention's real costs. Insurance that reduces patients' out-of-pocket costs to only a small portion of their health care's real costs leave them with no economic incentive to try to determine whether that care is indeed worth to them its real costs.

A physician caring for this hypothetical insured patient who gets paid in the traditional fee-for-service system will have an economic incentive to do more rather than less for that patient because she will be reimbursed for each additional service rendered. Moreover, physicians have been traditionally taught as part of their training that their responsibility is first and foremost to their individual patient. On this patient-centered ethic, the physician's responsibility is to do whatever will be of benefit to her patient, to be a single-minded advocate for her patient. She is not to be an agent of society weighing the costs of the care she recommends, but only an agent for her patient's medical interests (Levinsky, 1984). So she will and should recommend any care with positive expected benefits without regard to its costs. This of course will lead to the resource use that we earlier saw is irrational and undesirable.

Now much has changed in recent years for this hypothetical patient and her physician. Patients now are being asked to bear increasingly more of their health care costs out of pocket as the employers and governments paying for their insurance seek to rein in the rising costs of health care. The insulation against the real costs of their care that insurance provides to patients is being significantly eroded. Most physicians also now practice in a very different environment than supposed in our hypothetical example. Few are reimbursed on a simple fee-for-service basis, but instead practice under a variety of economic incentives to do less for, to use fewer resources in caring for, their patients. Moreover, physicians are increasingly taught in their training to be cost conscious in their use of health care resources: gone is the old version of the patient centered ethic according to which physicians should do whatever would be of benefit to their patient without regard to costs. But it has not been replaced by a clear standard that tells physicians when and how to weigh the costs and expected benefits of care when making treatment recommendations to their patients. The standard of care has been changing from one that largely ignored costs to a more cost conscious standard, but the new standard remains both unclear and controversial. Rationing is now part of the physician's job, even if still often not called by its name, but how much and by what standard is not clear. In this period of a changing and not well-defined standard of care, it is hardly surprising that there is uncertainty and controversy about when and what rationing is justified.

This evolving standard of care affects insurers as well. They no longer reimburse without question any service that a physician or health care institution may render to its insurees, and they are increasingly tough negotiators about how much they will pay for covered services. But they too have no clear or uncontroversial standard for making these coverage decisions or carrying out these negotiations.

These changes toward a cost conscious standard of care and away from the physician's role as advocate only for his or her patients' medical interests without regard to the costs of the care they provide—together with the new incentives that physicians now typically encounter to take costs into account in caring for patients—mean that some rationing now takes place "at the bedside" (Ubel and Arnold, 1995). Many physicians in the past have held on to the hope that if rationing must take place, "society" or others allocating resources to the health sector will set those limits, and they can then continue to do whatever will benefit their patients within these new resource constraints. Their hope was that society, not physicians, will do the necessary rationing. But even if possible, this would not be desirable. Even if we possessed comprehensive and new cost conscious practice guidelines, which of course we do not, physicians would still need to retain significant discretion to depart from those guidelines when the specific circumstances of a particular patient are different enough from what the guidelines assume. As patients, we want them to have that discretion, which means they will have to exercise judgment about whether the circumstance of a particular patient warrant either using fewer or more resources than the guidelines recommend.

CONTROVERSIES ABOUT STANDARDS FOR PRIORITIZATION AND RATIONING

The issue, then, is not whether to ration care, or how to avoid doing so if we could, but how to do so ethically. There are two broad ethical considerations that should guide health care rationing, or the allocation of health care resources in the face of limited availability. First, the resources should be allocated efficiently so as to maximize the health benefits they produce. This is an ethical consideration, not merely an economic concern, because promoting people's health and well-being through efficient allocation is an ethical goal and allocating inefficiently results in the avoidable sacrifice of some patients' well-being. Second, the health benefits derived from limited health care resources should be distributed fairly or equitably; we are not and should not be indifferent to how resources are distributed to distinct individuals or groups. To achieve the first aim of efficiency, different health interventions are typically compared using cost-effectiveness analysis, which tells us how much health benefits will be achieved by those different interventions for the resources they use (Gold et al., 1996; Tan Torres et al., 2003). But while there is at least general agreement among health economists and policymakers about how to evaluate the efficiency of different interventions in producing health benefits, there is no analogous agreement about what is a fair or equitable distribution of those benefits. Controversies about what count as equitable distributions in the health sector are a fundamental source of the difficulty of prioritization and rationing choices (Brock, 2004).

Let me illustrate briefly some of the controversies about equity in the prioritization of health care resources. One concerns how much priority to give to life-prolonging care as opposed to care that improves or preserves quality but not length of life. Economic measures of health benefits, such as Quality Adjusted Life Years (QALYs), rely on individuals' preferences for tradeoffs in their own lives between length and quality of life to assign relative values to each. (A QALY is a measure of health benefits that represents one year of life extension in full health; see Nord, 1999). To take an example from a common measure, the Health Utilities Index, on a scale in which 0 is death and 1 is full health, finds that being "able to hear what is said in a conversation with one other person in a quiet room without a hearing aid, but [requiring] a hearing aid to hear what is said in a group conversation with at least three other people" is valued at .95, which is a 0.05 reduction in health on the 0 to 1 scale (see Health Utilities Index at <http://www.fhs.mcmaster.ca/hug/>). It would follow that if we want to maximize health in a population, we should be indifferent between saving one person's life who will live for one year in full health and preventing 20 people from suffering the hearing loss described above for one year. But many people would not be indifferent between these alternatives—they would prefer to save the one person's life for a year who would live in full health. While we consciously and unconsciously often trade off accepting risks of death for gains in quality of life within our own lives, when we are trading benefits and risks that will come to different people, many will give increased priority to life saving.

The psychological disposition not to let an identified person in imminent peril die or suffer very serious harm when we have the ability to save them or to prevent that harm has been dubbed the rule of rescue—we see it at work in many contexts, such as rescue attempts with no expense spared to save trapped miners or boaters lost at sea (Jonsen, 1986).

This issue arose 15 years ago in the most systematic attempt in the United States to prioritize different health services and interventions in the state of Oregon's Medicaid program, which serves many of its poor citizens (Hadorn, 1991). Oregon developed a list of treatment/condition pairs for the various services its Medicaid program provided—that is, treatments given to patients in a particular condition—which it then ranked from the most cost-effective to the least cost-effective. Its intent was to expand eligibility for the program to more poor Oregonians and then to use the program's limited resources to provide the most cost-effective interventions to the program's members. This had the intuitive plausibility of using the program's limited resources to maximize the health benefits for the population served. One among several similar results of Oregon's initial priority list was that capping teeth was ranked above appendectomies for appendicitis, despite the fact that the latter is typically a lifesaving intervention. While there were problems in some of the data that led to such results, this is nevertheless an expectable result from a cost-effectiveness prioritization. It arose because appendectomies are much more expensive than capping teeth—Oregon estimated that it could cap a tooth for over 100 patients for the cost of one appendectomy.

This has been called the aggregation problem: when should small benefits to many persons have priority over large benefits to a small number of persons because the former are larger in the aggregate? It is a problem that is especially pressing when the large benefits that a few would receive are lifesaving, as they were in this case. This and similar results were sufficient for Oregon to reject its initial cost-effectiveness standard for prioritization and to largely disregard differences in cost that led to this and similar results. It reflects that ordinary people's priorities are based on one-to-one comparisons—one tooth capping and one appendectomy—and then it is obvious that the appendectomy should take priority. Is it simply a mistake to ignore large differences in costs, as the one-to-one comparison does? It need not be. Some people express the view that it would be unfair for individuals' health care needs to be given lower priority simply because it is more expensive to meet them. Others express the view that priority should be determined by the urgency of individuals' health care needs—how seriously they will be harmed if their needs are not met—not cost-effectiveness.

This common psychological tendency to prioritize life-prolonging over quality of life improving care, without much regard for great cost differences between the two, contributes importantly to the difficulty of rationing. Here is a recent example of where giving that priority to life extending care can lead (Brock, 2006). Genentech recently developed a new drug called Avastin for the treatment of colon cancer. It extends the lives of colon cancer patients on average by a few months. Genetech plans to seek approval for the use of the drug in the treatment of breast and lung cancer where it appears to provide similar benefits. Oncologists consider it a good drug for the treatment of these conditions. However, the drug is extremely expensive. In use for colon cancer it costs over $50,000 per patient, and because it must be used at twice the dose for breast and lung cancer, it will cost over $100,000 per patient in those cases. So in the latter use, it will cost over $200,000 for each year of life extension it provides; its cost per QALY produced will be even higher since these patients' quality of life is significantly compromised by their disease and treatment. This is substantially more than typical limits used in evaluating lifesaving programs, but the new use is likely to be covered by Medicare because Medicare's criterion for coverage is whether the intervention is effective in the diagnosis or treatment of disease or injury, not whether it is cost effective in comparison with other interventions. (Avastin has recently been turned down for coverage by the National Health Service in Great Britain.) The prohibition in Medicare's new prescription drug benefit, Part D, on Medicare's negotiating drug prices with pharmaceutical companies further cripples Medicare's ability to make reasonable rationing decisions.

Another example of the psychological force of the rule of rescue also comes from Great Britain. In the 1980s, Henry Aaron and William Schwartz studied the different usages of a number of common health care interventions in Great Britain and the United States (Aaron and Schwartz, 1984). Then, as now, the British spent about half as much per capita on health care as we do. At that time they found a practice of not dialyzing patients with end-stage renal disease who were over about 55 to 60 years old, though there was no formal regulation in the National Health Service stating this age limit. What Aaron and Schwartz found is that primary care doctors generally told patients who were too old to receive dialysis something to the effect that "there was nothing more that could be done for them." Of course, patients would tend to understand this to mean that there was no further treatment for their condition, whereas in fact it meant that a social decision had been made not to fund treatment that would extend their lives. When some patients were able to get past the primary care gatekeeper to the renal specialist, they often received dialysis. At each point, physicians found it difficult to say to a patient face-to-face for whom there was a life-prolonging treatment that a social decision had been made not to provide that treatment. When life extension or lifesaving is at stake, people find it extremely difficult to deny the care to an identified patient who will die without it.

A second rationing controversy concerns what role, if any, age should play in prioritization and rationing. Some years ago Daniel Callahan proposed an age cutoff of 80 for life-extending care, arguing that after that age we should only provide care that improves quality of life and relieves suffering (Callahan, 1987). His proposal was extremely controversial and did not win many adherents, but proponents of rationing continue to cite the large amount we spend on care in the last year of life and more generally on the elderly. In part of course, this simply reflects the greater health care needs of the elderly, and if we should allocate resources to meet the most urgent needs then this high spending on the elderly may be appropriate. But a somewhat artificial example shows a reason for supporting a preference for the young, at least in prioritizing life-extending care (Williams, 1997): each year thousands of patients die on waiting lists for an organ transplant.

Suppose a liver becomes available, but there are two patients each of whom urgently needs it or he or she will die. The first patient is 20 years old and because of an unrelated health problem would have a life expectancy of 10 years with the transplant, whereas the other patient is 50 years old and would have a life expectancy of 15 years with the transplant. By usual measures, the 50-year-old would receive the greater benefit, 15 years instead of 10, and so if we want to allocate the scarce resource to produce the greatest benefit we should give it to the 50-year-old patient. But would that be fair? Shouldn't the patient who has only lived 20 years get the organ rather than the 50-year-old who has already had many more years of life, indeed many more than the 20-year-old will have even if he is given priority for the organ? Shouldn't the 20-year-old patient have a fair chance to get closer to a normal lifespan than the 50-year-old has already reached? Would it be fair to give the organ to the 50-year-old patient, thereby increasing still further the undeserved inequality in the years that each will live?

Now this is a limited and artificial example, but it illustrates why the young may have a stronger claim grounded in fairness for life-extending interventions than do the old. It is not that we get a bigger benefit because the young will, other things equal, live longer with the intervention—while in most cases that may be true, it is not the case in our simple example—but rather that if they do not get it they will have had so much less life. So the very difficult challenge and controversy is how to fairly take account of this preference for the young when we prioritize resources. It would be too simple to condemn this as unfair or unjust age discrimination because the ground for preferring the young precisely is fairness. Just to illustrate the complexity of the problem, it is doubtful that any priority should be given to the young for other non-life-extending care, such as palliative care aimed at relieving pain or suffering.

In suggesting above why the young should receive some priority for life-extending care I noted that not doing so would increase still further the undeserved inequality in the years that each will live. But health inequalities are not always undeserved, and that points to another difficult controversy for prioritization. Many health problems are the result of behaviors that are well known to be unhealthy and that people have failed to take steps to change (Wikler, 2005). There are all too many examples: smoking, alcohol and drug abuse, unhealthy diets and obesity, failure to comply with medical treatment such as controlling blood sugar in diabetes, lack of exercise, failure to use seat belts, and on and on. Alcoholism is now widely viewed to be a disease, but individuals could still be held responsible for failing to seek treatment for it. Smoking is addictive, but again there are interventions that enable people to overcome the addiction. Eating an unhealthy diet looks more like simply an unwise and unhealthy choice. So perhaps if people are responsible for their heath care needs because they freely chose to engage in behaviors that they knew were unhealthy and that caused those needs, they should have a lower priority for receiving scarce resources.

Shouldn't a patient whose liver fails from a genetic disease have priority over a patient whose liver failed as a result of 20 years of alcohol abuse for which he failed to seek treatment? (Moss and Siegler, 1991) The state of West Virginia has recently introduced expanded benefits in its Medicaid plan for patients who follow certain health promotion regimens; they receive priority for additional health services for their healthy behavior, rather than penalizing those who engage in unhealthy behavior (Bishop and Brodkey, 2006). Yet we know that behaviors like smoking, alcohol abuse, and unhealthy diets are disproportionately concentrated in the poor and are associated with other disadvantages the poor face—alcohol abuse is associated with other stresses of poverty, healthy foods are often much harder to obtain in poor urban areas, and peer pressure to begin smoking is greater in lower classes and smoking typically begins before children are old enough to be held responsible for starting. So again there are very difficult and controversial issues about when, if ever, health care resource prioritization should depart from considerations of need and benefit to take account as well of whether people's unhealthy behaviors are the cause of their health care needs.

And finally as a last illustration of controversies about what equity requires in prioritization and rationing of resources is the question of whether we should give special priority to those who are worst off (Brock, 2002). A widely shared feature of most theories of justice and most religious traditions is a special concern and priority for the worst off. Common aphorisms such as that you can tell the justice of a society by how it treats its least well-off members also express this view. This idea can take at least two different forms in health care prioritization. It could mean that we should give special priority to the poor, and not only because they generally have worse health. Or it could mean that we should give special priority to the sickest patients, even if we could produce greater health benefits by treating less seriously ill patients.

These two senses of the worst off—the poorest and the sickest—are to a significant extent combined in some cases, for example the homeless, though in other cases they can come apart. Should we focus resources on the homeless, for example, even if we could achieve greater health benefits elsewhere? The homeless, many of whom are chronically mentally ill with various other health problems, may be very difficult to treat effectively because the nature of their lives leads to poor treatment compliance. Consider a second example where the concern for the worst off can conflict with maximizing health benefits. Hypertension is known to be much more prevalent in poor urban black males than among more affluent suburban white males. If we want to give priority to the sickest, or those with the most serious risk factors, we should give priority in developing hypertension screening and treatment programs to those poor urban black males. But we would probably get greater health improvements from programs serving the more affluent suburban white males. Their greater resources, better access to the health care system, more orderly lives, and fewer life stresses will likely make them more compliant with efforts to control their hypertension. But it would hardly seem just to direct priority away from the poor urban black males who have greater health care needs because other unjust disadvantages they suffer will result in fewer health benefits from treating them. This would be to let the unjust disadvantages they already suffer be the basis for disadvantaging them still further when we prioritize health care interventions. Even if we decide to sacrifice some aggregate health benefits to ensure that the worst off are treated, we are still left with the unresolved problem of how much aggregate health benefits we should be prepared to sacrifice to do so.

MAKING RATIONING AND PRIORITIZATION CHOICES IN HEALTH CARE INSTITUTIONS

The structure of the American health care system also makes rationing choices more difficult than they are in many other countries. Other developed countries have one or another form of national health insurance or national health care system that covers all their citizens. This gives them several advantages in confronting prioritization and rationing decisions. Consider Great Britain, which has had a National Health Service serving all its citizens for decades. As already noted, Great Britain spends about half as much per capita on health care as does the United States, which requires some prioritization and rationing decisions that our higher spending permits us to avoid. Despite much lower spending, however, the British have at least as good health outcomes as Americans, suggesting that controlling or even reducing our health spending need not result in worse health outcomes for Americans (Banks et al., 2006).

The NHS is funded by general tax revenues, which enables the British to employ what is called global budgeting for the public health care system. It can do for health care what we can do for spending in areas like national defense, but not for health care. For our defense spending, the president proposes a defense budget, Congress debates his proposal, amending it in various ways, and votes a defense appropriation, which the Defense Department must then live within. Congress makes a decision about how much it is willing to have defense spending grow in the coming year, in many cases specifying which specific programs are funded, and then can enforce that decision through the appropriation process, though of course in the present time of war this process tends to break down. The British government can do the same thing for health care when it decides on a budget for the National Health Service, or NHS, which it must then live within. Various units within the NHS will in turn receive budgets that they must live within, requiring them to make decisions about how to use their available funds to best serve their population of patients. Aiding this prioritization process, the British National Institute for Clinical Excellence (NICE) evaluates the cost effectiveness of new medical technologies, broadly construed to include new drugs and devices, for coverage by the NHS (Buxton, 2006). Although NICE denies having any strict cost-effectiveness cutoff, analysis of its decisions suggests a rough $50,000 per QALY limit for coverage of new technologies. When a new technology is not recommended for coverage by NICE, that decision can be justified on the grounds that the limited funds in the NHS will be used instead to meet other patients' more urgent health care needs or where greater health benefits will be produced.

There are several features of a national health system like the NHS that facilitate resource prioritization and rationing. The first is the ability to do prospective global budgeting; that is, to make a public, politically accountable and legitimate decision about how much of the country's resources will be devoted to health care over the coming year. This in effect prioritizes health care against other public programs and responsibilities. Second, when physicians in the NHS make individual treatment decisions within constrained budgets, they can justify denials of beneficial care to some patients on the grounds that those resources will be used instead for other patients with more urgent needs or who will benefit more. The NHS is a financially closed system in which what is not spent in one place can be reallocated elsewhere where it will do more good. Third, NICE does evaluations of new technologies to determine whether they are sufficiently cost-effective to warrant coverage by the NHS. Fourth, a much smaller parallel private health sector in Britain that individuals can access through privately purchased health insurance or with their own funds out of pocket acts as a safety valve for individuals who want and are financially able to circumvent the NHS limits.

How do these features contrast with the American health care system? First, we cannot do prospective global budgeting because there are many independent health plans within the American health sector—government plans such as Medicare, Medicaid, and the Veterans Administration, as well as a multitude of private health insurance plans and self-insured employer plans. These may and do grow at different rates and there is no institutional or political mechanism in most of them to set and stay within a budget. Instead of setting a health budget prospectively and having to live within its limits, we can only add up a year or two later how much we have spent on health care. Second, because many parts of the American health care system are not financially closed, so that what is not spent for particular health care needs can be rediected to greater needs, physicians cannot justify withholding beneficial care from some patients on the grounds that the resources will go to other patients who need them more. Instead, they have no assurance about where the savings will go; they can as easily be directed to higher executive salaries or to increased profits in a for profit health plan as to other more needy patients (Daniels, 1986). Third, we lack any means of new technology assessment comparable to NICE in the American system. Indeed, Medicare, which is the largest single entity in the American health care system, is as already noted specifically foreclosed by law from using cost-effectiveness evaluations in making coverage decisions. Medicare is required by statute to cover an intervention if it is effective in the diagnosis or treatment of injury or disease, and attempts to change the statute to permit it to also take cost and so cost effectiveness into account have failed in Congress. Since many other health plans tend to follow Medicare's coverage decisions, ignoring cost effectiveness then spreads through the system. The fourth comparison is largely moot, since there is no tightly rationed national health care system, and so no parallel private system to act as a safety valve for it.

CONCLUSION

Ever growing costs of health care will increasingly force the practice and issue of health care resource prioritization and rationing into the open for public, professional, and political attention. We have explored some of the features of those practices and issues that make them ethically and politically difficult. Those issues will not be easily resolved, but avoiding them will not allow us to evade the need or reality of rationing: it will only mean that it will go on covertly and unexamined. That will lead neither to better nor more legitimate prioritization and rationing decisions.

REFERENCES

Aaron, Henry, and William Schwartz. *Painful Prescription: Rationing Hospital Care*. Washington, D.C.: Brookings Institution Press, 1984.

Arrow, Kenneth J. "Uncertainty and the Welfare Economics of Health Care." *American Economic Review* 53 (1963): 941-973.

Banks, J., M. Marmot, Z. Oldfield, and J. P. Smith. "Disease and Disadvantage in the United States and in England." *Journal of the American Medical Association* 295:17 (May 3, 2006): 2037-45.

Bishop, G., and A. C. Brodkey. "Personal Responsibility and Physician Responsibility: West Virginia's Medicaid Plan." *New England Journal of Medicine* 355:8 (August 24, 2006): 756-8.

Brock, Dan W. "The Problem of High Cost/Low Benefit Health Care." *Life and Death: Philosophical Essays in Biomedical Ethics*. New York: Cambridge University Press, 1993.

———. "Priority to the Worst Off in Health Care Resource Prioritization." *Medicine and Social Justice*. Eds. M. Battin, R. Rhodes, and A. Silvers. New York: Oxford University Press, 2002.

———. "Ethical Issues in the Use of Cost-Effectiveness Analysis for the Prioritization of Health Care Resources." *Public Health, Ethics, and Equity*. Eds. Sudhir Anand, Fabienne Peter, and Amartya Sen. Oxford: Oxford University Press, 2004).

———. "How Much Is More Life Worth?" *Hastings Center Report* 36:3 (2006): 17-19.

Buxton, M. J. "Economic Evaluation and Decision Making in the UK." *Pharmacoeconomics* 24:11 (2006):1133-42.

Callahan, Daniel. *Setting Limits*. New York: Simon and Schuster, 1987.

Daniels, Norman. "Why Saying No to Patients in the United States Is So Hard: Cost Containment, Justice, and Provider Autonomy." *New England Journal of Medicine* 314 (1986) 1381-1383.

Gold, M. R., et al. *Cost-Effectiveness in Health and Medicine*. New York: Oxford University Press, 1996.

Hadorn, David. "Setting Health Care Priorities in Oregon: Cost Effectiveness Meets the Rule of Rescue." *Journal of the American Medical Association* 265:17 (1991): 2218-2225.

Jonsen, Albert. "Bentham in a Box: Technology Assessment and Health Care Allocation." *Law, Medicine and Health Care* 14 (1986): 172-174.

Levinsky, Norman G. "The Doctor's Master." *New England Journal of Medicine* 311:24 (Dec 13, 1984): 1573-5.

Moss, Alvin, and Mark Siegler. "Should Alcoholics Compete Equally for Liver Transplantation?" *Journal of the American Medical Association* 265:10 (March 13, 1991): 1295-1298.

Nord, E. *Cost-Value Analysis in Health Care: Making Sense of QALYs.* New York: Cambridge University Press, 1999.

Steinberg, P., R. D. Moore, N. R. Powe, R. Gopalan, A. J. Davidoff, M. Litt, S. Graziano, and J. A. Brinker. "Safety and Cost-Effectiveness of High-Osmolality as Compared with Low-Osmolality Contrast Material in Patients Undergoing Cardiac Angiography." *New England Journal of Medicine* 326 (1992):425-430.

Tan-Torres Edejer, Tessa, and R. Baltussen, T. Adam, R. Hutubessy, and A. Acharya, eds. *Making Choices in Health: WHO Guide to Cost-Effectiveness Analysis.* Geneva: World Health Organization, 2003.

Ubel, Peter. *Pricing Life: Why It's Time for Health Care Rationing.* Cambridge: MIT Press, 2000.

Ubel, Peter, and Robert Arnold. "The Unbearable Rightness of Bedside Rationing: Physicians' Duties in a Climate of Cost Containment." *Archives of Internal Medicine* 155:17 (September 1995): 1837-1842.

Veatch, Robert. *Transplantation Ethics.* Washington, D.C.: Georgetown University Press, 2000.

Wikler, Daniel. "Personal and Social Responsibility for Health." *Public Health, Ethics, and Equity.* Eds. Sudhir Anand, Fabienne Peter, and Amartya Sen. Oxford: Oxford University Press, 2005.

Williams, A. "Intergenerational Equity: An Exploration of the 'Fair Innings' Argument." *Health Economics* 6:2 (1997): 117-32.

Sanford Levinson
Slavery and the Phenomenology of Torture

THE YEAR 2007 WILL BE THE SESQUICENTENNIAL OF THE *DRED SCOTT* case, perhaps the most reviled case in American constitutional history because of its endorsement of slavery as constitutionally protected.[1] Slavery might have been evil, but this did not prevent its full integration into the warp and woof of American constitutional law, not least because the presumed overarching good of creating and then maintaining a union took precedence over alleviating the plight of slaves. Even if most people believed that a society without slavery would certainly be better than a society with it, they also believed that eliminating slavery was not worth the risk of dissolution of the union and the presumed costs attached to that dire possibility. In this context, one might recall that Lincoln, in his first inaugural address, went out of his way to reassure the slave states not only that he meant no harm to their entrenched practices, but also that that he would support a proposed constitutional amendment that would in effect guarantee the maintenance of slavery in perpetuity, at least in the absence of a voluntary decision by the affected states to cease the practice. And it is worth recalling as well that the Emancipation Proclamation was notorious for failing to free a single slave in the four "union states" where slavery remained fully legal—Missouri, Maryland, Kentucky, and Delaware—not least because of fear of switches in loyalty especially by unionist Missouri and Kentucky slaveholders.

For many, torture is at least as evil as slavery. Yet we have learned, over the past five years especially, that for many Americans the presumed overarching good of maintaining our national security takes precedence over the plight of those subjected to highly coercive, even tortuous, means of interrogation. As with slavery, exceedingly problematic modes of interrogation are being integrated into the warp and woof of our present legal order. And, as with slavery, the possibility of terminating the practice is viewed by many Americans, when all is said and done, as potentially more harmful than maintaining it, with all of its acknowledged costs.

I believe, though, that the most direct reason to look at torture through the prism provided by a 150-year-old case involving chattel slavery is that the most fundamental legal and moral issues raised by slavery and torture are astonishingly similar. Both ultimately raise issues of "sovereignty"—that is, the possession of absolute and unconstrained power—and, therefore, the challenge to "sovereignty" that is implicit in any liberal notion of *limited* government. Both *Dred Scott* and those who defend torture today ask us if we believe that there are indeed categories of persons who quite literally have "*no* rights" that the rest of us are "bound to respect."

This article is divided into three sections: The first discusses why, as both a political theorist of sorts and as a lawyer, I find the issue of torture both compelling and yet intellectually and morally perplexing. The second section is built around my belief that the word "torture" tends basically to be a placeholder, which means that it needs to be filled in with concrete definitions and exemplars that are often lacking. Any serious discussion of the subject—including, obviously, its ethical dimensions—therefore has to confront the reality that there is almost certainly far less agreement than we might hope as to what even counts as torture, let alone if there are any circumstances that might justify its infliction.

This means, among other things, that any real progress with regard to establishing acceptable social policies—as distinguished from engaging in polemical argument—requires that we engage in an altogether unpleasant and grim task of offering fairly precise notions of what counts as torture. This carries with it the ineluctable consequence that to define x, y, and z as "torture" may be to suggest that a through w, however open to criticism and perhaps description as quite awful—perhaps even "cruel, inhuman, and degrading"—is still different from "torture" and thus not subject to the almost unique condemnation connected to the term "torture" and "torturer." One might, of course, say somewhat similar things with regard to "slavery" and "not-slavery," also oft unanalyzed notions.

The last section will take a considerably different tack, and it may be in tension with the thrust of the second section and its emphasis on specificity and concrete acts. I want to raise the possibility that "torture," in a profound sense, is less about concrete acts than about the creation of a phenomenological reality of total control. Indeed, if this effort is successful, it may become quite unnecessary to engage in the acts themselves. As David Sussman has suggested, one might have to consider the possibility that something accurately described as torture "need not involve touching the victim's body, so long as his physical environment is appropriately controlled" (Sussman, 2005: 27). This is no small point, for it suggests that we might be mistaken in concentrating almost exclusively on the extent to which torture necessarily entails what Elaine Scarry so memorably labeled "the body in pain" (Scarry, 1987). The essence of a totalistic system of political control, after all, is that it might not be necessary to inflict pain all that often so long as what Justice Holmes might have called the "sovereign prerogative of the choice to inflict pain" is ever-present. Defending the creation of such phenomenological realities should raise especially profound difficulties for anyone committed to any version of political theory that emphasizes the status of persons as rights-bearing individuals. It is at this point that I will return to the *Dred Scott* case and focus more extensively on contemporary implications of Chief Justice Taney's horrific sentence describing blacks as "having no rights that whites were bound to respect."

I

I begin with a brief excursion into autobiography. I arrived in Cambridge in 1962 to pursue a doctorate in political science. Because I had written a senior thesis at Duke on national security policy, I came to Harvard with the intention of becoming a member of that new breed called "defense intellectuals," a group who spent most of their time engaged in close analysis of the circumstances under which one could credibly threaten to use horrendous weapons that would almost certainly kill millions of people.

I recall being perplexed at the time as to how we decided what kinds of state-imposed deaths are legitimately "thinkable" and which, on the contrary, are subject to categorical condemnation. Why was it, for example, that the use of poison gas was universally condemned, and not only on the consequentialist grounds that it could not be adequately controlled to affect only the enemy and not one's own troops as well? Even to counsel the possibility of using such a weapon was to expose oneself as a barbarian in a way that was not the case if one suggested the wisdom of obliterating cities, if "necessary," as part of the Clausewitzian extension of politics by other means.

As it happens, for reasons that need not be gone into, I "migrated" from Henry Kissinger, Harvard's leading "defense intellectual" and the author of *Nuclear Weapons and Foreign Policy,* a leading book of the era, to Robert McCloskey and the study of American constitutional history. Yet I find myself returning to some of those earlier interests, in part because of the implications for certain classic questions in constitutional law. I continue to be perplexed by how we divide the world into thinkable—and altogether acceptable—modes of violence and those that are beyond the pale.

It is well to be reminded that Elaine Scarry's indispensable *The Body in Pain: The Making and Unmaking of the World* (1987) contains a chapter on warfare that is every bit as remarkable—and unforgettable—as its probably more famous chapters on torture. Scarry, like Homer in the *Iliad*, teaches us that the essence of war is a "contest" in which the metric is the ability to injure, main, and kill the enemy more successfully than the enemy can do in return. She invites us to imagine alternative forms of contests, such as, my favorite, a singing contest in which conflict would be settled through deciding who can sing the most beautiful songs. But we know that is fantasy, for war is injuring, maiming, and killing.

Moreover, in modern times, the injuring, maiming, and killing is most certainly not restricted to the actual soldiers or other "combatants" in organized warfare. The phrase "collateral damage" has entered into our technocratic vocabulary to capture this reality.

Scarry carefully distinguishes "war" from "torture" and argues that the latter is worse, in a fundamental way, than the former. That is just to say, perhaps, that she is not a pacifist. As a matter of fact, Scarry analogizes nuclear warfare with torture, which obviously raises the possibility that anyone who accepts what might be termed the "absolutist" argument against torture, to which I shall turn presently, should, at the very least, recognize that it compels as well the repudiation of nuclear deterrence as a military strategy. A retaliatory strike by definition occurs only after an initial attack, by which time it is obviously too late to save New York, Chicago, Tel Aviv, or whatever the target might have been. At that point, the only function served by a second-strike, if it is other than "counterforce" (as against "counter city") is pure revenge. Millions of innocent persons are incinerated for no apparent point beyond any satisfaction attached to revenge.

Would a decent, ethical person ever order, or carry out orders for, a second-strike?[2] One might well doubt it, which is, of course, one reason why theorists like Herman Kahn in the 1960s posited "doomsday machines" that would take such decisions out of the human realm and instead guarantee that the missiles would fly once the machine sensed that a certain line had been breached (Kahn, 1960). Kahn was responding to a real problem, which is the ethical madness of "mutually assured destruction" as a strategy.

These issues were once discussed with some vigor, though they appear to have fundamentally disappeared from the public realm. Although there is an increasingly extensive examination of the "ethics of torture," there appears to be surprisingly little interest in offering similar examination of the ways we conduct wars more generally.

At least one thoughtful observer, Georgetown law professor Louis Michael Seidman, has expressed deep concerns about what he views as the near obsession with the issues of torture and the treatment of detainees, however important they are, to the exclusion of sufficient concern about other aspects of the contemporary realities of warfare, both actual and proposed (Seidman, 2005: 881).

It is necessary to recognize the extent to which the present discussion of torture arises within the context of developments in the ways that cross-border warfare is now conducted. Most military conflict, at least for the past several hundred years, has arisen on a state-to-state basis. (By using the term "cross-border," I mean to elide the particular kind of military conflict subsumed under notions of "civil war" or "domestic insurgencies.") Indeed, the logic of deterrence requires that potential enemies have specifiable geographical "addresses" to which retaliatory strikes can be sent. Moreover, the "reciprocity" rationales for obedience to certain norms of warfare depend, at bottom, on the same sort of state-centered warfare and the willingness even of barbarian countries, such as Nazi Germany, to adhere to certain norms regarding treatment of prisoners of war if they believed it would lead to similar treatment being accorded their own captured soldiers.

Though some contemporary cross-border conflict fits this state-centered model, a fundamental reality of our current situation is the importance of what has come to be called "asymmetric warfare," often conducted by what my colleague Philip Bobbitt has labeled "virtual states" (Bobbitt, 2006). These groups lack addresses even as they may have the capacity to inflict warlike modes of violence, the most notorious example of which, of course, is September 11. Because threats of retaliation are thought, probably correctly, to be unavailing against such inchoate organizations, emphasis shifts from "deterring" attacks to gaining information that can fend off the occurrence of any such attack in the first place. Ironically, a robust system of deterrence and retaliation allows for a considerable measure of risk-taking, since it assumed that a rational enemy will be aware of the costs of aggressive action and behave accordingly. That model does not hold in conflicts with basically unlocatable virtual states. Note that this requires no untenable assumptions that the leaders of such "states" are more "irrational" than leaders of territorial states, only that they are subject to a very different risk calculus. So this brings us specifically to the debate about torture, which arises almost entirely because of the role that these virtual states play in contemporary public affairs and the felt need for accurate information about their future plans.

Perhaps this is the appropriate point to indicate that I have extremely mixed feelings about one common move in this debate, which is to question whether torture is *ever* effective in procuring accurate information. Even if one concedes, as I believe to be the case, that it far less effective than is claimed by some of its enthusiastic partisans, almost none of whom are experienced interrogators, there seems little reason to doubt that it has on occasion been efficacious. The Supreme Court of Israel, even as it courageously invalidated many modes of interrogation used by the General Security Services of that state, stated that "[m]any attacks—including suicide bombings, attempts to detonate car bombs, kidnappings of citizens and soldiers, attempts to highjack buses, murders, the placing of explosives, etc.—were prevented due to the measures taken by the GSS" (Supreme Court of Israel, 2006: 165), which, incidentally, were described only as "inhumane" and not as "torture" by the court.

If we could be confident that torture *never* worked, then there would in fact be nothing to debate. Only a sadist would defend coercive interrogation under such circumstances. But consider only a recent case arising in Germany, involving a 2002 kidnapping of an 11-year-old boy (Jessberger, 2005: 1059). The kidnapper was arrested while picking up the million-euro ransom. During his interrogation he refused to indicate where the youngster was. In fact, he had already murdered him. Finally, on the second day of the interrogation, which by now was four days after the kidnapping, a Frankfurt police officer, Wolfgang Daschner, ordered that pain be used to procure the information. A subordinate police officer told the defendant that his continued failure to cooperate would result in the infliction of pain that "he would never forget." Because of this threat, which was never carried out, the defendant confessed and indicated where the body was located. (He was subsequently sentenced to life imprisonment.)

Not only the defendant faced legal problems. The police officer and his subordinate were both charted with violating an absolute prohibition on torture in contemporary German law. The threat to torture is an offense in itself, so it is legally irrelevant that it was not carried out. A German court found both of the police officers guilty. (It is worth mentioning that Germany, as a civil law country, does not rely on citizen juries. One can well ask if any jury in the United States would have, or even should have, convicted the officers under these circumstances.) One strand of argument held that less dire means of procuring the information were available. Another held that the ban on torture was absolute.

As every legal realist knows, though, it is not enough, when examining a legal system, to know only what sorts of acts trigger formal legal liability. It is also important to know what the actual cost of violating the law is. And here things get especially interesting. The German court found that there were "massive mitigating circumstances" that justified only limited punishment. Although the relevant law allowed, and perhaps even demanded, some time in prison, the court instead only fined the two officers: 10,800 euros for the superior officer and 3,600 euros for his subordinate who actually issued the threat, and issued reprimands rather than requiring jail time. This has aptly been described as "guilty, but not to be punished," which suggests that the court and anyone who sympathizes with its "solomonic" solution finds this particular deviation from the ban on torture to be at least quasi-acceptable.

There are two further things that need to be said about the Daschner case. First, it had absolutely nothing to do with national security. Second, the number of potential innocent lives thought to be savable through the threat of torture was one. I leave it to the reader to decide whether Daschner was justly treated by the German legal system and what implications his case might have when national security is involved and when the purported number of lives at stake is considerably higher than one.

In any event, I believe that arguing that torture is *always* inefficacious is often simply an attempt to evade making a full-scale moral defense of an anti-torture position by presenting oneself in the posture of a utilitarian cost-benefit analyst who comes to the happy conclusion that the costs of torture, which are many, *always* outweigh any potential benefits. I can readily understand the temptation to make such an argument. It is not easy in the culture that most of us inhabit to be an unabashed "moralist" of the Kantian variety. It is relatively easy to "take rights seriously," including the right not to be tortured, if one believes that the costs of honoring the right are relatively limited—what Frederick Schauer labels the generation merely of "suboptimal" outcomes rather than "catastrophes" (Schauer, 1991). After all, the very point of rights, as Ronald Dworkin insists, is to privilege them over undeniable "gains" to the overall society. As with any other important value, one must argue that potential social costs are in some profound sense irrelevant, at least if we wish to maintain a self-image of a society that does indeed take rights seriously. It is not clear that model of "taking rights seriously" accurately describes our own legal order, at least when potential social costs move away from the merely suboptimal toward the catastrophic. And, of course, we can readily debate whether that model of "taking rights seriously" *should* prevail as we move along the spectrum of potential consequences. "Let justice be done though the heavens fall," however inspiring in some contexts, is not, I dare say, accepted by most people, including, I must add, moral theorists. On this point, I can do not better than to quote my sometime colleague at Harvard Law School, Charles Fried, who writes of the prohibition against "killing an innocent person [in order to] save a whole nation." "It seems *fanatical*," writes Fried, "to maintain the absoluteness of the judgment, to do right even if the heavens will in fact fall" (quoted in Levinson, 2006: 31-32. Emphasis added).

But such absoluteness appears to be required by the remarkably unequivocal language of the ban on torture set out in the United Nations Convention against Torture (CAT), one of the few human rights treaties ratified by the United States. Article II of the CAT states that *"[n]o exceptional circumstances whatsoever*, whether a state of war or a threat of war, internal political instability or any other public emergency, may be invoked as a justification of torture" (emphasis added). I have often described this as the most "Kantian" passage that I am familiar with in any legal materials. With a remarkable degree of self-consciousness, it appears to rule out appeals to what has become a chestnut of contemporary constitutional analysis in the United States: this is the ability to override what otherwise appear to be clear constitutional prohibitions by positing a "compelling state interest" that will authorize the override. Perhaps the clearest example is the statement of the First Amendment that Congress shall pass *no law* abridging freedom of speech or the press. Every well-trained constitutional lawyer knows that "no law" does not in fact mean "no law under any circumstances," but, rather, "no law unless the state can demonstrate, in the instant case, a compelling public interest justifying the limitation."

With regard to torture, that move appears to be ruled out. If one takes the CAT seriously, it appears to require that one must indeed allow the heavens to fall rather than engage in the particular injustice called "torture." Such a view is in direct conflict with what I term "the logic of the compelling state interest."

As David Luban has noted, the Senate, although it ratified the convention and, therefore, Article II, did *not* include the quoted language when passing legislation implementing the Convention against Torture (Luban, 2005: 60). One might, of course, castigate Congress for being remiss in not including the specific language of Article II. But consider the possibility that no responsible legislator—or at least no legislator who had read and been persuaded by Michael Walzer's classic essay on "dirty hands" (1973)—would actually vote for legislation that on its face appears to preclude even the *possibility* of a defense with regard to someone charged with torture.

Consider in this context a recent comment by Democratic Senator Hillary Clinton: "In the event we were ever confronted with having to interrogate a detainee with knowledge of an imminent threat to millions of Americans, then the decision to depart from standard international practices must be made by the President, and the President must be held accountable. That very, very narrow exception within very, very limited circumstances is better than blasting a big hole in our entire law" ("McCain Team," 2006). Interestingly enough, the article in the *New York Daily News* discussing her speech was headlined "McCain Team Mocks Hil Torture Loophole" and it included a dismissive comment by Republican Seantor John McCain's chief political aide stating that he was "shocked Sen. Clinton would try to have it both ways," perhaps referring to the fact that she had voted against the

Military Commission Act supported by Senator McCain and almost all other Republicans. But an official connected with Human Rights Watch also indicated his disappointment: "Once you open the door to this sort of thing, you legitimize the practice" ("McCain Team, 2006). But this, of course, is just to reopen the question set out by Fried and Walzer, usually on the opposite side of the political spectrum: Do we *really* believe that *no circumstances whatsoever* could possibly legitimize even one instance of torture or, as in Germany, the threat of torture? Or, on the contrary, do we elect presidents at least in part to make agonizing choices in the truly "hard cases" that might present genuine dilemmas as to how to protect the nation against potentially catastrophic threats?

II

At the very least, it should be crystal clear that any regime that absolutizes the prohibition of torture will place immense pressures on those charged with defining the practice. After all, by definition, "torture" can never be contemplated; the negative implication, though, is that "less than torture," even if abhorrent in its own ways, could, under at least some restricted circumstances, be used. There is thus a certain incentive to cordon off definitions of "torture" from the practices that one can in fact envision engaging in.

In the course of compiling a useful booklet, *Defining Torture*, Gail H. Miller writes that "a definition of torture must be clear, uniform, adequately strict, and universally accepted" (Miller, 2005: 5). There are two basic problems with definitions that do not meet these daunting conditions, both of them identified in a 1973 report issued by Amnesty International. "Given that the word 'torture' conveys an idea repugnant to humanity, there is a strong tendency by torturers to call it by another name. ..." One is surely not surprised that Amnesty International cautions us not to accept euphemisms for what ought rightfully to be denominated "torture." But it *is* surprising to read another warning, that there is a "tendency of victims to use the word too broadly not least to take advantage of the opprobrium attached to anyone even charged with "torture" (see Miller, 2006, quoting Amnesty International, *Report on Torture* [1973]: 29-30). Moreover, there is the practical problem, at least with regard to structuring a legal system, that those officials charged with complying with the laws prohibiting torture, and threatened with significant criminal punishment should they not do so, are entitled to some reasonably clear idea of kind of conduct will put them in legal peril.

Consider the recent debate regarding the Military Commissions Act (2006) over the incorporation of the prohibition by Article 3 of the Geneva Conventions of "outrages upon human dignity." President George W. Bush has received scornful criticism for asking "What does that mean, 'outrages upon human dignity'?" He argued that "our professionals" must have "clarity in the law" if they are to do their job, which is to interrogate persons and gain information vital to national security (Rutenburg and Stolberg, 2006: A11).

One of the points made by the president is precisely that the crux of the debate about interrogation does *not* concern travesties like Abu Ghraib. Not only are these indefensible but also, in fact, they receive no defense from any reasonable person. Rather, the debate is about the freedom of action we as a society are willing to accord trained professionals whose particular vocation is interrogation. It will not do, incidentally, to scoff at the creation of such professionals unless we are willing to engage in similar disdain for the military as a profession. All are devoted to thinking through the most freighted questions surrounding the use of force to attain national goals, including the goal of self defense. And, of course, we are necessarily discussing yet another profession, that of the law, with regard to establishing adequate control over professional interrogators to reduce—or, ideally, to eliminate—going over the line of what we as a society are willing to tolerate.

One of the more ironic aspects of the recent debate is that many members of Congress, supported by many who identify with the international human rights community, successfully objected to the Bush administration's desire to specify a set of prohibited methods of interrogation because of altogether justified fears that anything not specified would therefore be treated as permissible. So instead of indicating certain acts, such as "waterboarding," by which persons are made to feel that they are drowning, as prohibited, the Military Commissions Act instead offers a more general definition of torture as any "act specifically intended to inflict *severe* physical or mental pain or suffering." What counts as "severe" pain is, of course, not self-evident; nor is the task made any easier by the fact that a section defining "cruel or inhuman treatment" refers to *both* "severe or serious physical or mental pain," which invites any well-trained lawyer (at least in the sense that law schools define as "well trained") to differentiate between "severe" and "serious" and require that anything meeting the standard of "torture," rather than "merely" cruel or inhuman treatment, meet the severity requirement.

In any event, the wish expressed by Miller that there be a "clear, uniform, adequately strict, and universally accepted" definition of torture approaches the utopian. There is not now, and is unlikely to be in the foreseeable future, any such definition that could meet all four criteria. Anything that could possibly be universally accepted, as an empirical matter, is likely to be what lawyers sometimes term "void for vagueness."

This being said, I do not see how we can give up the duty of addressing specific acts, whether waterboarding, hypothermia, or sleep-deprivation, to name only the three most common discussed techniques that have been used by the United States over the past five years, and deciding whether they, and many others that could be mentioned, meet our criteria for torture or instead should be described as a less-condemnable mode of interrogation. That may turn out to be no great compliment if, for example, we agree that something, though not torture, is, nonetheless, "cruel, inhuman, or degrading." But then we must move on to attempt to discover the difference between what is only "coercive," or even "highly coercive," but not of sufficient magnitude to enter the world of the "cruel, inhuman, and degrading," let alone "torture."

There is, to put it mildly, something awful about such a conversation. Michael Walzer famously wrote about the duty of political leaders to accept the possibility of "dirty hands" (including the possibility of torture). Few lawyers or ethicists will be in a Walzerian position to decide between the Weberian duty of responsibility as against a ethic of ultimate ends. Our hands may therefore remain clean. But even if we remain commentators from the sidelines, we have a duty to sully our minds by way of wrestling with what kind of modes of interrogation we will deem acceptable.

The only way to avoid such inquiries is to declare that people suspected of possessing important information about major potential future harms—and who are suspected as well as in some significant sense being the "cause" of those threats, as through active membership in a group committed to terrorist activity—should basically be allowed to avoid any significant interrogation at all. That is, they should be treated the way we treat (or would like to believe that we treat) "ordinary" criminal defendants who are immediately read their "Miranda rights" and accept the advice of their attorney to say nothing. Once we countenance a "gap" between such defendants, who are arrested because of what they are suspected to have done in the past, and people we are interested in interrogating because of what they might know about the future, then we have no alternative but to get our minds dirty by attempting to discern the line between the "coercive but acceptable" and the forbidden movement into the realm of the unacceptable. Are 24 hours of sleep deprivation all right, but 36 to be forbidden? (And what, therefore, about 28?) Is a 14-day period of solitary confinement in a windowless room, even without having to listen to loud and jarring rock music, tortuous in a way that a three-day period, perhaps with the accompaniment of Led Zeppelin, not?

Heather McDonald, trained at Stanford Law School, is highly censorious of those who condemn most methods used by American interrogators. She describes as "light years from real torture" (MacDonald, 2005: 84) the methods allegedly used by American interrogators, though she does confess to a bit of uncertainty about "waterboarding." Jean Bethke Elshtain has also been critical of human rights activists who are promiscuous in their use of loaded terms like torture (Elshtain, 2006). But, recall, even Amnesty International conceded that at least some who were undoubtedly subjected to state oppression may nonetheless have been too quick to claim the label of "torture victim" for themselves.

"Meaning is use," Wittgenstein famously declared, and I think this is as true of the term "torture" as of any other morally loaded term. We must discuss what it is about *this* encounter or *that* interrogation that leads us to say, with confidence, that it is an instance of "torture," "cruel, inhuman, or degrading" conduct, or simply "highly coercive" interrogation? As I have already suggested, I do not think anyone really wants to engage in such conversations. They might lead us, for example, to decide that relatively little that occurred at Abu Ghraib counted as "torture," even if almost all of it surely exemplified "cruel, inhuman, and degrading" conduct that, of course, had nothing whatsoever to do with interrogation. Because of that elemental fact, Abu Ghraib therefore has less to teach us than some might hope when it comes to, for example, the activities of highly trained professional interrogators working for the CIA. Indeed, it is *these* individuals, and not the almost incredibly untrained amateurs at Abu Ghraib, who triggered the so-called torture memo within the Office of Legal Counsel of the Justice Department and subsequent discussions about American policy.

III

In thinking about the interrogation relationship even, or perhaps especially, when engaged in by trained professionals, I want to return to Heather MacDonald, who writes that "[u]ncertainty is the interrogator's most powerful ally; explored wisely, it can lead the detainee to believe that the interrogator is in *total control* and holds the key to his future" (MacDonald, 2005: 86. Emphasis added). She is critical of procedures whereby American techniques of interrogation have been made public. Not only does this provide "al Qaeda analysts with an encyclopedia of U.S. methods and constraints." More to the point, in a way, is that any constraints on interrogation methods "make perfectly clear that the interrogator is not in control." Thus she quotes an unnamed "senior Pentagon intelligence official" who "laments" that "[i]n reassuring the world about our limits, we have destroyed our biggest assets: detainee doubt" (MacDonald, 2005: 94-95).

David Sussman's far more sophisticated analysis of torture—and his attempt to answer the question "What's Wrong with Torture"—equally emphasizes the crucial role of absolute vulnerability. "Victims of torture," he wrote, "must be, and must realize themselves to be, completely at the mercy of their tormentors" (Sussman, 2005: 6). "The asymmetry of power, knowledge, and prerogative is absolute: the victim is in a position of complete vulnerability and exposure, the torturer in one of perfect control and inscrutability" (Sussman, 2005: 7). "The torturer . . . makes himself into a kind of perverted God. . . ." Sussman quotes Jean Amery's reference to the "agonizing sovereiginty" exercised over him by the person who tortured him (Sussman, 2005: 26). Sussman thus answers his question by suggesting that "[w]hatever makes torture distinctively bad"—worse, say, than the infliction of "collateral" damage on innocent victims of a bombing raid—"must have something to do with the sort of interpersonal relationship it enacts, a relationship that realizes a profound violation of the victim's humanity and autonomy" (Sussman, 2005: 19).

As it happens, Sussman, like Elaine Scarry, links torture, understandably enough, to the infliction of pain. It would be perverse to deny the ubiquitous empirical connection between torture and "the body in pain." But, as Sussman and Scarry both note, we inflict pain all the time on innocents as part of the conduct of the "injury contest" we call war, even if we did not directly "intend" that innocents be harmed. And, frankly, I find the recourse to "double effect" arguments to distinguish between ethically admissible injuries, maiming, or killings of innocents and those that are instead condemnable often to be quite facile. Too often they serve as a way of avoiding responsibility, by reference to the purity of one's intentions, rather than acknowledging the awful costs that can be exacted by the pure in heart.

Nonetheless, I do agree that what distinguishes torture from these other sometimes abominable acts in the world is that only the former requires a phenomenology by which the victim is made to realize that he is a totally rightless individual, a pure object of the interrogator's will, with no way of affecting his own future other than by giving the interrogator whatever he or she wants. (Even suicide is in effect prohibited, as at Guantánamo, where hunger strikers are being force-fed lest they be allowed what the US military has described as a "victory" in the "asymmetric warfare" being conducted by the hapless detainees against the Americans.)

Thus we return to *Dred Scott* and the question of whether we wish as a country to adopt as a method of interrogation the creation of a belief that we indeed recognize no limits, that any forbearance is merely a sovereign "act of grace" that can be succeeded, in an instant, by wrathful infliction of pain. Ironically, one might argue that the successful inculcation of such complete dependence and vulnerability will *lessen* the need to inflict the pain itself, inasmuch as a "rational" detainee will have every incentive to submit early on in the process.

One might recall in this context the controversy provoked some 30 years ago by the publication of *Time and the Cross,* by Robert Fogel and Stanley Engerman, one of whose theses was that the frequency of violence against slaves was significantly less than that assumed by most abolitionists. The reason was simple: so long as slaves knew that violence was possible whenever a master so wished, then they would behave in ways that minimized the likelihood of bringing about that violence.

The slave was treated as having sufficient human agency to decide, in effect, whether or not it would be "necessary" for the master to punish him or her. The master would prefer to minimize the incidence of violence; after all, the slave was a productive asset who might indeed be harmed through the infliction of violent methods of discipline. Similarly, a professional interrogator would presumably prefer to minimize the incidence of violence as well. But one of the most insidious features of this phenomenology is that it is the person being interrogated, rather than the interrogator, who in some sense becomes "responsible" for the level of pain to be inflicted. Just as a parent sometimes tells a child, "I wish I didn't have to punish you this way, but you leave me no alternative," so does the torturer in effect blame the person being tortured for "forcing" the torturer to the next level of inflicting pain.

Can such a phenomenology successfully operate if the person being interrogated is actually made to feel that he or she has rights that the interrogator is bound to respect? No doubt, as many memoirs show, such assurance may lead people to cooperate, not least because this basic recognition of humanity may run counter to assumptions made about the nature of the enemy. But, obviously, one must also be aware that if it is known that there indeed are limits to the modes of potential interrogation, then it may well be the case that our enemies will train themselves to withstand whatever we are legally able to throw at them, just as American soldiers are trained to withstand harsh interrogation practices. Interrogators will feel it incumbent to use whatever legal methods of interrogation are allowed, including those that are "highly coercive" and even, perhaps, "cruel, inhuman, and degrading," in an effort to break the will of the person being interrogated. Yet the victims of such interrogations can reasonably hope for the immense satisfaction of outlasting whatever is done to them. Indeed, to break will be a sign of moral weakness. Thus the need to move toward total domination.

Even if there may be some truth in the assumptions made in the last paragraph, I am unwilling that the United States adopt, or be perceived as adopting, what I am labeling the "*Dred Scott* policy" of stripping individuals of any rights whatsoever. Indeed, as I prepared this paper, I realized that in a very real sense those who are tortured are *always* treated worse than many slaves were, as an empirical matter, treated. Thus Dred Scott himself was allowed to marry, and Dred and Harriet Scott apparently were able to preserve an intact family with their two daughters. Many slaves, of course, had it far worse, but one of the many anomalies of the *Dred Scott* case is that we realize that Dred Scott was in fact treated with a measure of humanity by his owner. That can never be said with regard to someone who is tortured. This obviously does not serve to justify slavery, and one can be sure that the Scott family had a ubiquitous awareness that they were indeed at the mercy of their "master's" power.

IV

Every time I return to systematically thinking about the issues raised by torture, I find myself moving closer and closer to the "absolutist" positions embraced by writers such as Ariel Dorfman, Elaine Scarry, David Luban, and Jeremy Waldron, not least because I become ever more distrustful of my own government and the good faith of those who profess these days to speak for the American people. If one adopts Judith Shklar's basic definition of liberalism as the avoidance of cruelty, then nothing is easier, in a way, than adopting an absolute ban against a practice whose every aspect instantiates cruelty.

But, at the end of the day, and of this essay, I realize that I remain in the Walzerian camp. What one most wants if political leadership with the kind of *character*, as well as disciplined mind, to be

able to wrestle with the sometimes demonic aspects of public responsibility and retain public trust. The most fundamental question facing
a modern democratic order is whether it is likely to produce leaders with adequate character to play the complex—some, of course,
would say incoherent—roles assigned them by Walzer, who requires
leaders to abandon, when necessary, the ethic of ultimate ends in
favor of the ethic of political responsibility, but to feel suitably guilty
about doing so. Whether we can hope for such character in leaders
produced by our modern political order is, thankfully, the subject for
another essay.

NOTES

1. An earlier version of this article was prepared for delivery at the
   Edmond J. Safra Foundation Center for Ethics, Harvard University,
   October 27, 2006.
2. I put to one side the question whether a decent and ethical person
   would engage in policies that he or she believed would increase
   substantially the risk of nuclear war in the first place, as, arguably,
   was the case with John F. Kennedy's decision to impose a blockade
   on Soviet ships traveling to Cuba during the Cuban Missile Crisis.
   See my review of Abram Chayes' 1974 book, *The Cuban Missile Crisis:
   International Crisis and the Role of Law* (Levinson, 1975: 1185). I argued
   that Chayes avoided any serious discussion of this issue.

REFERENCES

Bobbitt, Philip. *Terror and Consent.* New York: Knopf, 2006.
Elshtain, Jean Bethke. "Reflections on the Problem of 'Dirty Hands.'"
    Torture: A Collection. Ed. Sanford Levinson. New York: Oxford
    University Press, 2006.
Jessberger, Florian. "Bad Torture-Good Torture: What International
    Criminal Lawyers May Learn from the Recent Trial of Police Officers
    in Germany." *Journal of International Criminal Justice* 3:5 (2005).
Kahn, Herman. *On Thermonuclear War.* Princeton: Princeton University
    Press: 1960.

Levinson, Sanford. "Fidelity to Law and the Assessment of Political Activity (Or, Can a War Criminal Be a Great Man?)." *Stanford Law Review* 27:4 (April, 1975): 1185-1202.

Levinson, Sanford. "Contemplating Torture." *Torture: A Collection.* Ed. Sanford Levinson. New York: Oxford University Press, 2006.

Luban, David. "Liberalism, Torture, and the Ticking Bomb." *The Torture Debate in America.* Ed. Karen Geenberg. Cambridge: Cambridge University Press, 2006.

MacDonald, Heather. "How to Interrogate Terrorists." *The Torture Debate in America.* Ed. Karen Geenberg. Cambridge: Cambridge University Press, 2006.

"McCain Team Mocks Hil Torture Loophole." *New York Daily News,* October 16, 2006 <http://www.nydailynews.com/front/story/462237p-388764c.html>.

Miller, Gail H. *Defining Torture.* New York: Cardozo Law School, Florsheim Center for Constitutional Democracy, 2005.

Rutenberg, Jim, and Sheryl Gay Stolberg. "Bush Says G.O.P. Rebels Are Putting Nation at Risk." *New York Times,* September 16, 2006: A11.

Scarry, Elaine. *The Body in Pain: The Making and Unmaking of the World.* New York: Oxford University Press, 1987.

Schauer, Frederick. *Playing by the Rules: A Philosophical Examination of Rule-Based Decision-Making in Law and in Life.* Oxford: Oxford University Press, 1991.

Seidman, Michael Louis. "Torture's Truth" *University of Chicago Law Review* 72:3 (Summer 2005): 881-918.

Supreme Court of Israel. "Judgment Concerning the Illegality of the General Security Services Interrogation Methods." *Torture: A Collection.* Ed. Sanford Levinson. Oxford: Oxford University Press, 2006.

Sussman, David. "What's Wrong with Torture." *Philosophy and Public Affairs* 33:1 (December 2005): 1-33.

Walzer, Michael. "Political Action: The Problem of Dirty Hands." *Torture: A Collection.* Ed. Sanford Levinson. New York: Oxford University Press, 2006..

Jonathan Moore
Deciding Humanitarian Intervention

"HUMANITARIAN INTERVENTION" MEANS ACTION BY INTERNATIONAL actors across national boundaries including the use of military force, taken with the objective of relieving severe and widespread human suffering and violation of human rights within states where local authorities are unwilling or unable to do so. This essay will attempt better to understand decisions about humanitarian intervention from the narrow perspective of looking at the proximate considerations attendant to the intervention itself, particularly focusing on the priority of ground-level implementation and the recognition of the integral relationship between military action and reconstruction. Since what is confronted on the ground will be determinative, it is important to see if the decisions from above can be better connected to the realities below. The inherent complexity of the subject will be confirmed here using selected cases with which the author has experience in the field; concepts and constructs identified that have been developed in attempts to frame the problem; constraints faced by the policymakers indicated; and moral aspects of the enterprise considered.

It should be painfully obvious that the prospect of humanitarian intervention engages all sorts of competing factors, principles, interests, and motivations, and the trade-offs among them. Choices on intervention are made in a morass, essentially in chaotic circumstances, with infernal variables and unpredictables; they involve potentially irreconcilable confrontation between macro geopolitical forces and the more localized interests to be discussed later. There is a plethora of disparate actors jockeying to find common ground and motivated by more selfish goals, attended by hypocritical rhetoric, with the result determined by a winnowing down of power and pragmatism.

The purpose here is to identify some weaknesses, both in the range of factors applied in decisions on humanitarian intervention and in the criteria and models that are available for guidance, in order to suggest their possible strengthening. At the same time there will be an attempt to measure the adequacy of moral consciousness in the process and, finally, speculation as to whether, given the huge external, strategic forces at work, such refinement would make any difference.

A review of some specific humanitarian interventions that have taken place should begin with mention of two interventions from the past and one from the present that fit our description: Tanzania's invasion of Uganda, Vietnam's of Cambodia, and America's of Iraq. All three: were unilateral (the United States, leading the charge, managed to recruit some others in accompaniment); were aimed at regime or at least dictator change (Idi Amin, Pol Pot, and Saddam Hussein); and all claimed humanitarian purpose embedded in other, more national interests (of the three, Tanzania might be said to be the purest). Looking at what has happened since, both backward and forward, should give cause for caution; but then it is hard to know how much better or worse it would be without the interventions, and depending upon who is making the judgment.

The brief sketches, highly selective, of some recent interventions included here—Somalia (1992), Rwanda (1994), Haiti (1994), Kosovo (1999), and Afghanistan (2001)—illustrate why making decisions to initiate them were so knotty; they will also reacquaint us with the consequences and begin to lay a base for perceiving how such decisions might be better made in the future. Not much better, since the size and array of problems and the capacities and motivation to address them do not match, but perhaps some improvement.

Somalia

It's difficult to remember that the original intent of the US intervention in Somalia was successful in that approximately 100,000 Somali lives were saved and a swelling refugee population severely reduced—a huge humanitarian catastrophe was prevented. But the agenda shifted incrementally, 18 US soldiers were killed and savaged in a firefight, and amid characterizations of failure and humiliation, the United States pulled out with major consequences to follow, in Rwanda and Haiti, for instance, as well as in Somalia. The administration of President George H. W. Bush began the intervention late in 1992, driven by humanitarian urgency despite doubts about the absence of direct US interests, the wanting criteria of the Powell Doctrine, and getting sucked into ancient tribal battles. Change at the top of the US government did not help in shaping a coherent strategy, and the incoming administration of President Bill Clinton inherited a US presence without a clear mission.

Once committed, and along with the admirable progress in feeding and protecting suffering and vulnerable Somalis, the US military role evolved from protecting relief efforts and relief workers, to attempting to provide a broader security and stability, and then in October 1993 to targeting one of the warlords in response to his earlier massacre of Pakistani United Nations (UN) peacekeepers. The intervention lost the neutrality of humanitarian relief by taking sides in Somalia's internal conflict. As former UN Undersecretary General Brian Urquhart put it: "The moment a peacekeeping force starts killing people, it becomes part of the conflict it is supposed to be controlling, and is therefore a part of the problem" (Traub, 2006: 12). It was not so much that this "mission creep" had occurred—it would have been enormously difficult to avoid—as that its likelihood had not been anticipated. The UN Security Council had given its authority under Chapter VII of the UN Charter for military intervention to address massive human rights violations and because the civil war in Somalia represented a threat to international peace and security. But the joint UN-US effort never worked well, with rehabilitation efforts at odds with military operations, and the UN peacekeepers operating under restrictive rules of engagement and effectively separate from the American forces. In its exit in March 1994, fueled by US public opinion that had turned strongly against the involvement, the White House claimed that never again would it allow US soldiers to have to operate under UN command, although this in fact had not been the case. Even a US admiral and former member of the National Security Council staff serving as the special representative of the UN secretary general, with a Marine general as his deputy, could not manage the conflicting authorities and roles in this country with no national government of its own.

It is difficult to accept the certainty, let alone the arrogance, of hindsight. But there are several lessons that can be drawn from the Somalia experience that are echoed in other interventions and a greater appreciation of those lessons could be useful for future decision making about humanitarian intervention. One is, don't do it unless you are prepared to make it work and to stick it out when things get rough, which they will. Adequate understanding of the local environment, not just political-security, but cultural, is essential in any viable calculation to understand what is required and what might happen, instead of operating superficially under "best case" and "do it on the cheap" scenarios. The necessity of understanding the connectedness of the humanitarian, security, political, and rehabilitation requirements is crucial, along with recognition of the natural tendency of military activity to dominate and at times to overwhelm other efforts. Even under a multilateral mandate and UN umbrella, the drawbacks of US dominance of other actors must be expected. Sustaining popular support at home, and being prepared to buck it when it turns sour if that is necessary, are important elements. Related to this is the question of whether it is necessary to make a strong national interest argument along with the humanitarian imperative to make the policy stick, and whether this was done adequately in the case of Somalia.

Rwanda

Rwanda is generally, and properly, regarded as a morally deficient and tragic refusal by the international community to intervene to stop the genocide that took place between April and July 1994. The Security Council had previously acted and UN peacekeeping soldiers were on the ground in Rwanda at the time, having replaced French troops to protect and oversee the Arusha peace agreement designed to head off the civil war between the Hutu-dominated government in Kigali and the Tutsi rebel offensive mobilized from inside Uganda. This agreement was regarded as extremely fragile; if the UN presence in Rwanda could nudge it into sustainability girded by an unlikely convergence of benevolent behavior on the part of the various interests and forces involved, then so be it. But it was not robust enough in numbers, staffing, equipment, and mandate to handle a real war or a massive ethnic explosion. When the UN commander in Kigali was told about the onset of the massacre, he realized that he did not have the assets to withstand it, so he sounded the alarm to UN headquarters in New York. He was asking for a renewed, upgraded intervention, and desperately. The response he got fell somewhere between distractedness and evasion. Although many believe that fast and concerted UN action at that point could have significantly defused the onslaught, no one knows that for certain; it may have already become a case of missed opportunity. In any event, it was foolish to expect in the first place that the UN could have acted with robust dispatch. Rwanda was not a priority issue, Africa was not a priority region, Somalia had not worked. Action had already been taken, the resolution passed, the admonitions pronounced, the troops in place; been there, done that. The major powers that enable these things were otherwise occupied, and not in accord. The peacekeeping forces were notoriously hard to recruit and weak as serious fighters. The key intelligence from the field was unable to be distinguished from the wealth of discordant reports. The UN's opaque, contorted, and laggard bureaucracy was just that.

There is no intent here to make excuses for a truly awful lack of moral resolve and efficacy, and it is not certain that a better designed and implemented decision making could have made any difference, especially given the political and institutional environment that inevitably constrains and even distorts such processes. It is interesting if sad to speculate that perhaps Rwanda is a case where only a rapid unilateral invasion, unmandated by the Security Council, by a powerful and efficient force, could have done the job. In the instance, the United States not only refused to support further action by the Security Council, but also lobbied with others against it: a "dog in the manger." The United States refused to label the atrocities "genocide," at least partly because it did not want to act as obligated under the Genocide Convention, and at one point it used the spurious argument of wanting to protect the UN's credibility for the future by keeping it from failing in this case. By the time it and others reversed their position, in embarrassment and wan hope that it could still help to send more UN forces to Rwanda, it was pathetically too little, too late. The killing was stopped by the victorious Tutsi rebels when they won the civil war and the surviving genocidaires fled. Boutros Boutros-Ghali, the UN secretary general, in a situation report to the Security Council of May 31, 1994, fumed that the "delay in reaction by the international community to the geno-cide in Rwanda has demonstrated graphically its extreme inadequacy to respond urgently with prompt and decisive action to humanitarian crises entwined with armed conflict. . . . We all must recognize that we have failed in our response to the agony of Rwanda, and thus have acquiesced in the continued loss of human lives" (*Report of the Secretary General*, 1994, para 43). But neither he nor his lieutenants could ignore the confines of restrictive Security Council mandates, and in any case there is a difference between those who mandate something to be done and those who are obligated actually to try, somehow, to get it done. The principal factors on the US side dictating inaction were that Rwanda was not considered a threat to its national interest and the humanitar-ian urgency to the extent that it was recognized at all was not sufficient in itself. They were followed by the questionable operational feasibility of actually being able to prevent this disaster, given the huge obstacles present, which tend to be obscured by moral fervor.

Haiti

The US military "intervasion" of Haiti in September 1994, authorized by the UN, although not by the Organization of American States, turned out to be a peacekeeping rather than a war-fighting mission. The "de facto" military government, which had ousted Haiti's democratically elected president, relinquished power when the planes were in the air. Economic sanctions, which had been in place against the government in Port-au-Prince, with some cost to the humanitarian needs in the country, had not worked, but the threat of military action in the service of humanitarian purposes did. Relying on the continued presence of US military forces, United Nations agencies, bilateral programs, and NGOs working with the restored Haitian government led by President Jean-Bertrand Aristide fairly quickly began cooperative efforts to try to establish stability, alleviate human rights abuses, and build up the country. Eventually, UN peacekeeping forces supplanted US troops.

The decision to intervene was provoked and justified by multiple needs: to alleviate human rights violations and deprivation, to reverse a breakdown in civil order, to avert a large refugee flow, and to achieve regime change by ousting a junta that was systematically oppressing its citizens and ransacking the country. Each objective supported the others, making a justifiable case. The UN Security Council resolution cited "a threat to peace." But there was little public support in American public opinion or in the media. The White House deliberately led with the argument for humanitarian need, with "national security" coming a close second. The decision was aided by strong advocacy from the Congressional Black Caucus, the demographic reality of substantial Haitian populations living in the United States, and the confidence that even if the targeted Haitian leaders did not flee, the military challenge would not be great. The opposition could be intimidated and any resistance mopped up easily, with major support expected from the Haitian population eager to see the highly popular Aristide returned to power. Yet the decision took significant political will for the Clinton administration to buck the sentiment against it, particularly in the wake of the Somali debacle.

The intervention was generally regarded as a success from the point of view of its motivation, execution and immediate results. Yet the Haiti experience did not produce a consensus ethic for the US on humanitarian intervention, perhaps because it too neatly synchronized humanitarian need and national interest, was uniquely close to America's shores, and proved easy militarily with limited violence, casualties, and collateral damage to civilians.[1] And one swallow does not make a spring.

What happened afterward in Haiti, an eventual break between the international actors and the Haitian government and resumption of political instability and violence, does not shed much light on the decision to intervene. We are reminded that social and economic progress and nation-building in an impoverished country without strong institutions and an established culture of democracy and rule of law take a long time, and is both tightly connected to the phenomenon of intervention but can never be assured by it. In this instance, the assistance efforts by multilateral organizations and national governments and their investments in reconstruction and development, more sustained and better coordinated than usual, either could not be put to effective use or fell prey to weakness in indigenous capacity and leadership. There were real disappointments but no rude surprises here; no evidence in what has happened since to challenge the decision to intervene and barely enough for us to be able to argue that it made enough difference.

Kosovo

After the negotiations at Rambouillet in February 1999 failed to stop the violence in Kosovo, the United States and NATO started the bombing in March. This intervention was controversial then and remains so. Again, the mix of humanitarian and political interests was present. Some believed that the former was too much of a cover for the latter, that the principal motivation was to keep Serbian leader Slobodan Milosevic from expanding his power westward, plus NATO's desire to restore an image that had been blotted in Bosnia. David Rieff bitterly characterized Kosovo as calling forth "a brave new world of human rights—a world in which sovereignty is conditioned on the rulers treating the ruled decently, and in which, if they abuse that privilege, they are properly condemned as having forfeited their right to rule and are laid open to military intervention from the outside" (Rieff, 2002: 201).

Although the humanitarian crisis in Kosovo was real, no one should be startled when nations with the power to intervene with the use of force and can see their interests being served by doing so seize and exploit as much as a smidgeon of humanitarian need to help justify it. Also, the proportionality of motivations in intensely complex situations with vicious cost-benefit ratios and tradeoffs is extremely difficult to measure. Even further, a working definition of national interest should be deep enough to include acting for moral purpose anyway, rather than being so wimpish as to exclude and relegate it to a separate and optional category.

In Kosovo, there was concerted and efficient ethnic cleansing being conducted by Serbia: Albanians were being killed, and there appeared to be no way to stop it except by bombing—but only from 80,000 feet, which would not be surgical and with civilian casualties likely to be extensive. There were other trade-offs: employing massive violence on a problem versus needing to quell the inclination to resort to force by the populations affected. Demonstrating that national sovereignty cannot be protected unexceptionally and that human rights malefactors better watch out versus the desire for retaliation felt and paranoid nationalism engendered by being so violated. The sprawling, ubiquitous operation the UN and NATO would subsequently set up after the destruction of war to police Kosovo, run its government, help reconcile its hostile populations, and guide it to self-government versus the harm done to internal capacity-building transmitted by the conceit that deep-rooted problems could be solved by outsiders with their own interests playing a dominant role. The need not to be paralyzed by complexities, obstacles, and uncertain outcome versus the danger of resorting to radical extremes just to be sure to take some action. And there was the curious sidebar of moral asymmetry—was it wrong to keep the pilots and planes out of harm's way at such a great height while blowing up people and facilities on the ground, or was it right since that was the only way to get the job done?[2]

The Serb forces surrendered in June and with a cease-fire the stabilization and reconstruction forces from outside descended with a vengeance, with all of their bureaucratic weight, intramural infighting, and confident prescriptions intact. Although there had been no prior public commitment to assume the responsibilities consequent to the bombing, the international community was quick to respond by the time it was over. NATO took over the security and initial policing responsibilities and divided the province into different sectors headed by US and European military contingents. The UN directed the civilian side, working with the OECD and the European Union and allocating tasks under four umbrellas: humanitarian, administrative, human rights, and development. But the last was interpreted in practice to mean economic and financial institution building, which left reconstruction and development programs in a secondary role. Ambitions were heavy and expectations high, and given the investments planned and the time-frames projected, at the very least they were inflated. The military elements, in their size, strength, and discipline, and assigned the highest priority mission, dominated the factionalized civilian enterprise. Although there were mechanisms to coordinate the two, those who had hoped the partnership would work smoothly were frustrated, and earlier skepticism about how well such collaboration would function in an environment of continued political and ethnic hostility was confirmed.

This is not to argue that the Kosovo intervention was a mistake. Here is another example of big and militarily-capable powers taking it upon themselves in a coalition to intervene without UN Security Council blessing, which only came in the aftermath in endorsing clean-up and build-up efforts, then pursued with sincere and tenacious effort. Among questions with hesitant answers is whether the explicit political commitment to preserve a pluralistic society, certainly noble, was wise. The incendiary hostility thickly laden in the air at the bridge over the Iban River in Mitrovica between ethnic Albanian and Serb enclaves remains. The human rights dimension of the intervention is hard to judge, and Kosovo's political future is still in contention. Taken as a whole, the action and follow-up brought measures of progress, and much was learned about this fragile business, but whether these lessons can be put to use and—given the trials, disappointments, and various kinds of costs which were suffered—the influence they may carry in future intervention decisions is unclear.

Afghanistan

The military intervention in Afghanistan initiated by US-led coalition air strikes against Taliban targets on October 7, 2001, barely qualifies as a humanitarian one. The Security Council had immediately condemned the attacks on the World Trade Center the day following, and in late September paved the way for the US invasion of Afghanistan by okaying actions to combat international terrorism deemed to be a threat to international peace and security. The desired multilateral mandate was in place. But the decision to intervene in this manner was dictated by military and political stimuli, which did not so much include humanitarian intent as attached it piggyback as a compelling accessory. The decision to intervene was not cluttered by whether but driven by how. It is important to note that the United Nations, with the support of the United States and others, had for some time prior to the air strike been engaged in humanitarian assistance in Afghanistan and in working on a transitional government and postwar political structure with the widespread participation of Afghanis. The UN Special Mission to Afghanistan was in place, the UN's principal nation-building impresario, Lakhdar Brahimi, was on duty and reappointed as the secretary general's special representative, and the diplomatic-political process that would produce the Bonn agreement devising a plan for governing the country was close to signing. The UN did not follow the military action of others, it was already in Afghanistan in a humanitarian and political role, and the two operations were subsequently folded together

Critiquing how this merger worked reminds one of the story of the dog standing on its hind legs in a bar singing an aria—what was important was not the quality of the performance but that it had been attempted at all. The problem being attacked was of Himalayan magnitude and Byzantine complexity. The military element unsurprisingly dominated the dual enterprise from the start. Not only did security come first, and military action supersede the humanitarian and rehabilitation efforts of the UN and the NGOs, but the US war-fighting against Al Qaeda after the surrender of the Taliban restricted the efforts of other military forces to achieve badly needed general security and stability throughout the country. Although the Security Council on December 20 authorized a new, UK-led International Security Assistance Force (ISAF) to maintain security in Kabul and environs, it made it clear that the US Central Command would maintain authority over this new force "so that activities between the two factions do not conflict with each other, and to ensure that there is no interference to the successful completion of Operation Enduring Freedom."

For a considerable period of time the United States blocked efforts to expand the size and geographical mandate of the ISAF, which otherwise could have provided better security for populations in outlying provinces and permitted less inhibited civilian humanitarian and reconstruction efforts by the Afghan central government, UN agencies and NGOs. Policies on how to deal with the warlords and other local commanders were set more by the international interests in wiping out the terrorist enemy than by indigenous requirements for serving the basic needs of local communities and the linking of the central government to them. Of course subsequent events in Afghanistan have proved both that establishing adequate security is necessary for effective humanitarian and development tasks to be undertaken effectively and that the efforts to fulfill this basic requirement have so far failed. In many cases, military efforts to provide infrastructure repair and support for local needs were invaluable, but they were too few and sometimes paid serious costs. The experiment of creating provincial reconstruction teams has attempted to integrate security, humanitarian, and reconstruction programs in a mutually reinforcing manner but in most cases the symbiosis has fallen short.

Comparatively speaking, and based on a realistic appraisal of what was actually feasible given the time-frame, which was much too short, and the resources, which were too little, and the simultaneous needs, which were much too numerous and urgent, the various actors from the international community and the Afghan leaders performed impressively. There was too much corruption, lack of local capacity decimated during 18 years of war, competition among the outside agencies, political factionalism, weak and badly allocated aid flows, unending insecurity problems, and so forth. But these realities are all inherent, normal, and to be expected, and the continuing efforts at collaboration across actors, agencies, and tasks as nation-building was pursued perhaps can not as a practical matter be done much better. Progress was made; yet it could turn out that the job was just too big. The authorities who made the decision to intervene militarily may have felt they could leave the responsibility for fully assessing the local political and economic conditions and needs to the UN and the civilian operators. Could they have been expected to better anticipate the narcotics problem, the unneighborly troublemaking across the Afghan borders, the diversion of military and financial resources to Iraq? And if they had, would it have made any difference in their decision? No. But the resources committed were inadequate: time, money, talent, concentration, and troops. Above all, and yet again, the military force was not provided in enough strength up front, and everything else suffered accordingly.

THERE ARE VARIOUS THEORIES, MODELS, AND INVENTORIES AVAILABLE that can be used as guidance for those who exert influence in a decision to intervene with military force—interventions intended partly, at least, to relieve humanitarian suffering. A summary review of some of them reveals considerably useful framing of the question, variations in approach, and no template for general application. The decision making followed in individual cases differs widely; it is diffuse, inchoate, and essentially reactive in nature. The participants in such decision making at the national level are not always easy to identify, tend to be secretive, and produce public descriptions of deliberation and motivation not always consistent with the facts. At the multilateral level, there is more disorder, with a cacophony of vying national positions, becoming more focused incrementally through extensive diplomatic consultations and political bargaining. This is the dynamic context in which the substantive arguments, the matrix of factors at issue in the making of these difficult choices are considered. There are several relevant conceptual frameworks for identifying and organizing them.

"Just War" Considerations

The just war ethic starts with a presumption against the use of force, and then sets out moral criteria, which could together constitute or would be necessary to justify an exception. There are a number of them: legitimate authority, just cause, right intention, last resort, proportionality of objectives and means, noncombatant immunity, and reasonable expectations of success. The application of this doctrine in cases of humanitarian intervention involves interpretation of certain of these standards in an effort to fit the generic circumstance. This could include, for instance, expanding the standard of just cause in the direction of a duty to intervene, requiring multilateral authorization for the action, and a particularly tough means test. J. Bryan Hehir believes that: "The 'just causes' for intervention must go beyond genocide. The intellectual and political challenge is to identify a wider ranger of exceptions without eroding the presumption against intervention" (Hehir, 1995: 7).

This is useful guidance, and it also provides an example of the difficulty in applying good precepts to complex crises. How "humanitarian" must a crisis be and how much of an intrusion of other purposes should be allowed in the exception? Are the violence and threats to international security sufficient to justify the violation of national sovereignty? How much effort in what categories is needed to correctly define the use of force as a "last resort"? Is it possible to adequately assess investment and outcome in advance so as to establish reasonable hope? With no ideal model to determine what we should do, just war theory and the questions it confronts is a valuable framing of moral reference.

The Responsibility to Protect

The concept of the responsibility to protect, articulated by the International Commission on Intervention and State Sovereignty, draws upon just war doctrine in attempting to guide humanitarian intervention (Evans and Sahnoun, 2001). It is closely linked to "the right to intervene" and to the principle of sovereignty as responsibility. It has been criticized both for providing too much justification for intervention and for being too restrictive of it. It can be used as a resource to help think through the pertinent issues and provides some useful operational principles for "military intervention for human protection purposes."

The commission's recommendations cite "large-scale loss" of life or ethnic cleansing to define just cause; rely too much on UN Security Council performance and multilateral participation regarding right intention and authority; apply stringent standards for prevention and last resort, vaguer language addressing proportionality, and a "do no harm" approach to reasonable prospects. While its operational advice sounds the right warnings in stressing clarity, lack of ambiguity, and precision (for example, "unequivocal communications and chain of command," and "total adherence to international humanitarian law"), it also betrays a certain naiveite about what military operations actually involve and commanders confront. The report properly calls for maximum coordination with humanitarian agencies; it does not note the dangers of inhibition of indigenous capacity. On balance, it covers the key bases and constitutes an impetus for humanitarian intervention, but with serious restrictions attached.

The Powell Doctrine

This set of criteria, attributed to former Joint Chiefs Chairman and Secretary of State Colin Powell, concentrates quite straightforwardly on the interests and responsibilities of the military when undertaking virtually any major US military action, and thus includes those undertaken that support humanitarian causes. But it is not narrowly drawn. It has several components, or questions to be satisfied before action is taken, and prominent among them appear: vital national security interest, overwhelming force, clearly defined political-military objectives, doable mission with costs and consequences carefully analyzed, and widespread public and congressional support. This formulation is particularly interesting in two respects. First, it focuses on successful implementation. It enforces the point that it is not a good idea to apply military force, to make war, without a very good chance of success. Second, with its insistence on public and congressional support, it suggests not only that the military does not want to be abandoned politically in the middle of a fight, but that if a democratic system is not behaving democratically when it decides to make war, it will be in serious trouble. It is no secret that the Powell Doctrine was largely applied in the Persian Gulf War and largely ignored in the US invasion of Iraq.

Two additional principles of the Powell Doctrine have particular relevance to the utility of just war theory. One is the requirement for broad international support for the given military action. This is consistent with the emphasis on multilateral authorization and support, which is advanced as a needed adaptation of the theory in order to deal with humanitarian intervention. The other is the need for a credible exit strategy. This appears to be inconsistent with the theory's acceptance of the principle that the immediate military and humanitarian action cannot be separated from the obligation to follow-up with stabilization, rehabilitation, and nation-building efforts. It is interesting to note in this regard that the Pentagon has recently endorsed a new priority to train and prepare its soldiers for stabilization and reconstruction duties to accompany adequate capacity in combat missions and skills.

Presidential Decision Directive 25
Presidential Decision Directive 25 was issued in May 1994 and was characterized by the US State Department as the "Clinton Administration Policy on Reforming Multilateral Peace Operations" (State Department, 1996, executive summary). It was produced with the uncomfortable hindsight of the Somalia experience as an attempt to provide a "framework for the decision-making process guiding whether to engage in

humanitarian interventions." It was a comprehensive and sophisticated effort, which was not greatly commended by the foreign policy establishment—because it did not solve the problem by removing the associated dilemmas and dangers, and was criticized by the human rights community—on the grounds that the document was deliberately designed to make humanitarian interventions less likely to be undertaken.

The official summary of the document warns that "any recommendation to the President will be based on the cumulative weight" of its multiple factors "with no single factor necessarily being an absolute determinant." This admits the huge difficulty of both weighing the individual points and assessing their relationships in such a formidable listing. Nothing seems to be left out, which is a good start, but the result calls for a quantitative skill and qualitative judgment required to parse the whole problem, which is severely intimidating. Where will the right process, people, and time be found to reach a good decision out of such a multitude of often competing factors?

There is a reassuring redundancy in that similar criteria appearing in the directive are included in the other iterations examined. Without citing all of the items in this framework, there follow some that deserve particular mention. When deciding whether to vote for a proposed United Nations peace operation, the directive wants the United States to be sure there is international backing and participation, a proper understanding of "where the mission fits on the spectrum between traditional peacekeeping and peace enforcement," a mandate and available resources sufficient to fulfill the mission, and a finding that the consequences of inaction are unacceptable. It also asks in the case of Chapter VI peacekeeping activity that a cease-fire be in place, and for Chapter VII enforcement operations that a significant threat to international peace and security is established. In cases in which US military personnel are expected to actually be involved in combat, additional rigor is necessary, including the commitment of sufficient US funds and forces, tight command and control systems, and clear objectives, plans, and "endpoint."

United Nations Documents

Obviously, there is considerable experience at the United Nations that should throw light on multilateral efforts to reach decisions on humanitarian intervention. The UN Charter articulates the grand mandates of the organization, acknowledging that peace, security, or development cannot exist without the others. Secretary General Boutros Boutros-Ghali's 1992 "Agenda for Peace," commissioned by the Security Council, contains some early hints relevant to humanitarian intervention. Boutros-Ghali's charge was to make recommendations for strengthening the UN capacity for preventive diplomacy, peace-making, and peacekeeping, but he added postconflict peacebuild-ing as a category of his own, believing it to be integrally connected to the others. For this package "to be truly successful [it] must come to include comprehensive efforts to identify and support structures which will tend to consolidate peace and advance a sense of confidence and well-being among people" (*Report of the Secretary General*, 1992, para 21). The December 2004 report of the High-level Panel on Threats, Challenges, and Change, entitled "A More Secure World: Our Shared Responsibility," recommended that the Security Council "adopt and systematically address" a set of agreed guidelines for deciding whether or not to authorize the use of force and emphasized the need for "good conscience and good sense." It enumerated a quite familiar "five basic criteria of legitimacy": 1) seriousness of threat; 2) proper purpose; 3) last resort ; 4) proportional means; and 5) balance of consequences (*Note of the Secretary General*, 2004, paras 205, 207).

These references are general in character. One would expect that an especially fruitful source of documentation for understanding better how multilateral actors go about determining humanitarian intervention would be the reports that the Secretary General makes to the Security Council prior to the Council taking action, as well as the Council's authorizing resolutions themselves. And they should not be ignored. But it is difficult to extract useful insights let alone identify patterns suggesting the inventories and methodologies being employed. Part of this is because much of the serious examination and negotiation takes place in fragments and increments, behind closed doors and with watered-down results. Perhaps most important is the fact the Security Council doesn't want guidelines and has always resisted them. In any event, the process and the outcome is dictated not by any overarching frame of reference or cogent system but rather by the result of a cacophony of national interests scrambling to find the formula in a given instance which can attract the most support and gore the least oxen. And the process rewards the powerful because of the structural advantages they enjoy in the UN but more so because they have more resources and capacity to act.

DISTILLATION OF BOTH THE SPECIFIC EXPERIENCES OF HUMANITARIAN intervention and the theories and concepts available by which to better understand and guide them, taken together, produces a few propositions for consideration.

First, no viable template or doctrine exists for good decision making. Although a general profile comes vaguely into focus and some common characteristics are present, the processes, participants, and factors employed are variable and disorderly, helter-skelter. There is a certain logic to this, given the nature of the hydra-headed beast and the chaotic environment it lives in, and to attempt to impose a conventional, artificial, or rigid model on this challenge would be foolhardy, even if feasible. There are limits to how much can be done better, given the limitations and pathologies found in the very nature of the human species and the slow pace of our moral evolution, but we can presumably try harder, and identifying some weaknesses in approach and performance could help. Among the problems to keep in mind is the limited ability to analyze an extraordinary complexity of dissimilar phenomena, tangible and intangible, which are constantly changing and beyond the control of the decisionmakers. It is almost as difficult to look back to evaluate results that have already occurred as it is to project in advance what the consequences might be if a given course were adopted. Did we do less harm than good? Did the "collateral damage" (for example, destruction of civilian lives and infrastructure) suffered outweigh the stability established? Did the military force preempt the humanitarian success? Will our objectives have been achieved a year from now? It is difficult to know for sure.

Second, the policymakers who have the authority to make decisions are not the ones who have the power to follow through with the supporting actions, which are necessary to insure success over a period of time. There is a lack of continuity in this respect, a serious disconnect. The stamina of the political will and the delivery of the funding pledged is not guaranteed, and the accountability for such obligations undertaken at the time of the decision to intervene is subject to disappearance.

Third, although the trade-offs will remain ferocious—for example, sovereignty vs. invasion, lives saved vs., lives lost, acting with sufficient speed vs. delay in exhausting other options first, allowing wars to take their natural course vs. intervening with violence that could extend them—there are several specific issues that deserve attention. They relate both to preparation and implementation, and although they may not quickly respond to reason, they will attract serious trouble if poorly accommodated. The following list is intended to help strengthen the inventory of factors to be addressed by the intervention deciders.

1) The seductive impact of poor attention to implementation. The lack of priority given to the requirements of successful implementation in a decision to intervene results in two dangerous manifestations of over-optimism. It seems that frequently the United States misjudges what is actually likely to happen, underestimates the complexity of the situation, and is left unprepared for the full dimensions of the unfolding crisis. Closely related, the cost estimates—in troops, time, talent, and especially money—of humanitarian interventions, which include some manner of follow-on support for nation-building, are invariably low-balled. The result is too little restraint, a lack of reality discipline. The law of unintended consequences is ignored, as is a sophisticated appreciation

of how human beings can actually be expected to act. There are explanations for both of these psychologies. Officials are more comfortable with "best case" rather than "worst case" scenarios; the "can do" confidence of Americans does not tolerate skepticism even in decidedly non-American contexts; it is better to ask for money incrementally, rather than to scare funding sources, such as the taxpayers, with too big a tab too early. But to some extent inadequate and misleading projections are simply incompetent; they were not calculated seriously enough, over-ambitious policy and politics trumped responsible real cost analysis. This becomes even more problematic as the future unfolds and extended involvement requires more investment, which the policymakers of the moment will effectively have no influence over. Either the future leaders will themselves believe in the continuing investment, or they will be trapped into paying up, or they will give it up.

2) Ignorance by decisionmakers about the complexities in the field. Greater understanding of local history, culture, behavior, prejudices, conflicts, actors, and levels of development is necessary, both to assess the likelihood of success and to prepare competently to pursue it. The process of choice must give a high priority to mobilizing and providing access to this kind of knowledge about the environment where the intervention will be attempted. The high priests of strategy and power politics, the headquarters generalists, should not be left unenlightened in order that the interests of the interveners do not overwhelm the interests of the people intending to be helped.

3) The inherent linkage between the application of military force and subsequent efforts at repair and development. They are integrally connected. The forceful means employed is driven by a political goal, which inevitably becomes implicated with social and economic dynamics, which are by nature moral. Not only is it true that development cannot progress without security, but also the reverse: security cannot be sustained without development. This relationship is recognized theoretically and rhetorically, but

not necessarily in terms of clear-eyed foresight and preparation, commitment, and capability. Planning an intervention involving military force must include a strong assessment of what commitments flow directly from it and what is required to deal with them and the ability to act accordingly. Yet how far must the decision-makers project the obligations of their immediate policies into the future to make them responsible and legitimate? Nation-building, and the efforts of fragile states not to fail, takes generations, yet the intervening states do not have the priorities, attention span, patience, or resources to help forever.

4) "Exit strategy" for the troops versus sticking it out through nation-building. This trade-off is in the crux of the problem and it gets a lot of attention, but needs more, particularly within the deliberations about whether to intervene in the first place. Future events cannot be easily predicted, and adaptability must be maintained, but the initial decision must address as resourcefully and courageously as possible the operational implications existing in a political and moral context. How fast and well can indigenous security capacity be developed? What nonmilitary entities are available and competent to undertake which reconstruction tasks? Is the entrapment of sustained occupation adequately calculated? How deeply embedded are the ethnic hostility and the human rights problems in the insecurity of the country?

5) Nation-building and self-sufficiency. As establishing security and protecting human rights morphs into more advanced reconstruction and capacity building, the tension rises between helping a nation get on its feet and substituting for its own growing competence. Those who are planning intervention must begin to assess the levels of existing capacity and to provisionally allocate appropriate tasks, roles, and phases for the international and the domestic actors in advance. This exercise in itself will impose foresight on the basic decision and give priority to the afflicted society's early responsibility for solving its own problems. With what kind of partnership can the root causes be attacked? In what ways and how far

can impositions of pluralistic democracy can be pressed? In what ways should international assistance restrain itself to allow local assets to gain strength?

6) Multilateral and "unilateral" interventions. The broad consensus in the international community for intervention with proper multilateral authorization and implementation is naturally reluctant to validate the need for other kinds of action if the desired approval or capacity is not available. The point is that unilateral action outside international law is a bad idea but not that it can simply be prohibited, given how dire the circumstances might be, the paucity of antidote, and the motivation of the intervener. This is especially relevant given the possibility of action by coalitions of the willing, which may carry some international credibility even if not that of the UN Security Council, and the reality that the UN frequently mandates collaborative support after the fact. These kinds of interventions should not be exempt from attempts at stringent criteria and standard-setting by the international community. This is admittedly dangerous territory, but ignoring it will not make it disappear or discipline it.

THERE IS A PROBLEM WITH ATTEMPTING TO BOOST THE POLICYMAKER'S competence about humanitarian intervention by concentrating more rigorously on implementation and the realities in the field. Giving adequate attention to the pitfalls, requirements, and specific details of effectively carrying out an intervention—along with needing to deal with large strategic issues and domestic political pressures—tends to crowd out more intangible factors, the idealism needing to accompany the existential.

Of course, morality is central in the definition of the kind of intervention we are considering. When violence is applied across political and cultural boundaries in response to humanitarian need, the situation is charged with moral purpose. And if it is true that "to be moral is to be operational," that is, that moral precepts left in the abstract and not applied in practice will lack impact, then morality must be dynamic; it requires political action (Moore, 1998: 7). The moral and the political do not remain separate realms but interact. The political policymaker faces the dilemma of ensuring that the political serves the moral rather than dominating it. This is a sufficiently difficult task, one often to be avoided. It requires determining how to apply moral reasoning to actual policymaking; avoiding the arbitrary imposition of rigid doctrine sacred to one culture upon a different one; and adopting a willingness to choose when different moral imperatives come into competition with one another.

The political and bureaucratic environment in which the people who participate in intervention decisions find themselves is not conducive to moral reflection and reasoning. The interests and stresses are more Hobbes than Kant; metrics carry greater weight than imagination. Ideology aside, the decisionmakers are made suckers for realpolitik. Tony Lake and Roger Morris, writing about Vietnam and the Pentagon papers many years ago, referred to "the normal mechanical perversity" of a system characterized by "bureaucratic infighting, immersion in technical details, personal hesitations of men caught up" in their careers that "imposed a style of behavior on its members which precludes open and forceful concern with human issues" (Lake and Morris, 1971: 12).

The structure and methodology of policy analysis and policy formulation and decision, the incentive and reward system operating here, do not encourage the systematic injection of moral factors. Although there are differences in the two settings, this is true for both national governments and the UN. In the former case, the deliberations are more nationalistically self-absorbed, although a common body of values may carry implicit weight. In the latter case, there is more vying of national interests and ideological conflict, but the greater pluralism can provide a broader range and more openness in attempts to define the common good. Acknowledging the immediate, almost preemptive pressures the decisionmakers are under produces a premium on strengthening the inclusion of our spiritual values as integral to our policy choices.

In what manner might this goal be advanced? Perhaps a listing of key issues that display intangible aspects along with empirical interests in the mix of factors being deliberated could help.

1) Responsible assessment discouraging action. Perhaps the biggest moral conundrum lies in the danger that, by being as thorough as possible in setting criteria and as encompassing as possible in the calculation of the requirements and consequences of intervention, the more reason will argue against supporting it. Cost is an illustration of this: Can a rigorous projection of resource needs in advance of an intervention, for instance, be justified if such an estimate by itself preempts the intervention? Would it be better to take a less costly approach to intervention, approaching the problem less in its totality and guided more by the limited capacity of the interveners to act, and thus assuring a greater chance of approval? Should the major, long-run commitment to getting at the root causes from which these humanitarian crises spring be separated from shorter-term efforts at humanitarian relief, security, and stabilization?

2) Broader participation and greater transparency in decision making. It will not automatically follow, but a strong argument can be made that the larger engagement of diverse actors with different perspectives and the more open and transparent the process of deciding whether to intervene or not the more likely it will be to get a good decision. The underlying values of the society would be better able to enlighten its policies. Narrow membership and secretive roles are poor prescriptions for dealing with decisions of this complexity and magnitude. Democratic principles are served in both respects: the diversity of the participants better represents the varied interests in the polity, and the openness of the process encourages public education and debate not only suitable but required in a participatory, representative, and self-governing system. Closed, hidden examination also affords greater possibly of deceit as to the true motivation of the policy being contemplated—for instance,

puffing up the importance of the humanitarian practice as cover for less justifiable or popular reasons.

3) The seductiveness and illusory nature of war. Before deciding to employ military force in a humanitarian intervention, yet having determined that the humanitarian crisis will persevere without it, war's unusual proclivity to justify itself, to suck up most of the oxygen and to take on a life of its own, should be fully appreciated. Once military force is seriously contemplated it tends to be assumed that it will work better and do less harm than is likely to be the case. War understandably moves from last resort to domination very quickly. This point is related to the doubt about violence ending rather than begetting violence, and the notion that destroying the village is necessary in order to save it.

4) The corruption of humanitarian values and space by needed collaborators. As humanitarian crises become more complicated by multiplying problems and also by multiplying actors with the requisite expertise—military, diplomatic, and economic—to deal with them, the ability of humanitarian actors to do their job according to their philosophy, tradition, and best practices can become severely compromised. They can be preempted, their integrity is endangered.[3] Yet there must be enough security for emergency relief to be carried out, which, in turn, must be connected to rehabilitation, political development, and economic progress. Band-aids are not enough: there must be both saving of lives and building of livelihoods. But the partners available for connecting these links create invasive problems for the others. It is ugly and messy. Is it impossible to have effective collaboration among differing components that are essential to the overall mission? No one entity can do everything; everyone needs someone else whom they will not be able to obtain on their exclusive terms. How pure can each afford to be?

5) Being careful not to inhibit local capacity. In order to truly help the local actors and assets in a fragile state catch hold and develop into sustainability, the international community must invest serious levels of funds, time, and talent. But it must be careful to build local

capacity and not substitute for it or the efforts can be corrupting rather than empowering. Michael Walzer has a somewhat different way of making this point: "So it seems best that people who have lived together in the past and will have to do so in the future should be allowed to work out their difficulties without imperial assistance, among themselves" (Walzer, 1995: 55). Because there are many different and shifting variables in this outsider-insider relationship, the right balance is extremely difficult to achieve, requiring time, adaptability and discipline.

6) The artificial apartheid of national interest and international good. In the making of policy, we have a bad habit of regarding realism and realpolitik separately from idealism and an encompassing humanity. As a result, the concept of national interest can arbitrarily be narrowed into a gratuitous nationalism by excluding the critical value to it of the interests of others beyond our borders and culture. This Manichaeanism is both dangerous and unnecessary. The shared political and moral problem here is to figure out how to protect our own survival and prosperity while advancing safe and sustainable lives of others, on the grounds that the latter is central to the former. Living on an increasingly interdependent planet replete with huge dangers and opportunities, this intimacy may be more a matter of balance than of choice, but is not generally perceived as an urgent one. Michael Ignatieff has looked at the same point the other way around: "What needs to be understood more clearly—however pessimistic the implications—is that when conscience is the only linkage between rich and poor, North and South, zones of safety and zones of danger, it is a weak link indeed" (Ignatieff, 1995: 13). That is, unless the more self-interested motivations are present when also attempting to fashion a global human strategy, the energy and assets necessary for that attempt to succeed will be lacking. Should our decisionmakers be armed to include moral values in pursuing "vital" national interests, and discouraged from defining national security so prominently in terms of military power?

AT THIS POINT WE ARE NOT EASILY ABLE TO JUDGE WHETHER THOSE inter-ventions that have been undertaken represent good decisions or not. This is because it is inherently difficult even retrospectively to calculate the costs and benefits, the harm and the good. We do not know what would have happened if the given interventions had not taken place and if the commitment and resources were directed somewhere else. And, above all, in the true sense they are not yet over, the results and consequences are still playing out.

Also, although humanitarian interventions are deserving of individual scrutiny and deeper understanding, it can be misleading and distorting if they are not examined along with our many other crisis categories: for example, nuclear proliferation, AIDS, avian flu, terrorism, global warming, extreme and widespread poverty, and the gap between rich and poor. Unless we are able to view our vari-ous problems and our limited resources with an integrated perspec-tive, we will not be able to figure out which actions to take: where, when, how much, and with what relationship to each other. We tend to overspecialize and overcategorize, using separate policies to deal with interwoven problems. This tenacious disconnect is also mani-fest between theory and practice, headquarters and field, expatriate and indigenous, immediate and long-term, the disproportionality of need and response. We seem left with the need to fill the gap between principle and action, the moral and the operational, without knowing how.

The original challenge of the intense complexity and difficulty inherent in humanitarian intervention can be emphatically exposed by revisiting a point made earlier. This involves the principle that mili-tary action in support of humanitarian goals should not be approved unless there is a commitment to carry through and provide subsequent support for the reconstruction and nation-building that is integrally connected to the action. This means that without a reliable assurance of the needed wherewithal to make the fulfillment of such a long-term commitment feasible, the intervention should be rejected. But this leaves the humanitarian imperative inert. It seems to be a bad idea to set standards to ensure that something be done right that then turns out to preempt the something that needs to be done. In order to avoid this debilitating catch-22, some compromise of the established principle is needed. This could be to intervene less ambitiously—that is, to limit the commitment to follow-up the intervention throughout nation-building. Where might the "end" of intervention lurk along the continuum between emergency aid and long-term development? Is it possible—acknowledging the various risks involved—to define an operational juncture following the initial military-humanitarian action, at some stage of security and stabilization but before local capacity and sustainability can be assured, beyond which the interveners are not obligated to go in order to justify the initial action? This is the kind of dilemma that requires the application of collective intelligence with the courage to choose in the face of moral ambiguity. Of course, it must not be forgotten that humanitarian action does not simply disappear when military forces are not involved or fail in their job, and that it will proceed however inhibited and limited as best it can under the existing circumstances.

Looking at our experience with humanitarian interventions so far, at the available constructs for guidance, and at perceived shortcomings in the way decisions are undertaken, we can see that, although there may be some useful ideas for our continuing efforts to understand and execute better, the options are very limited. As we have seen, the multifariousness and disorder is pronounced: the process is ad hoc and erratic, the participants tend to be hidden and unaccountable, the criteria and motivation highly variable. Decisions are subject to accidents of personality and presumptions of ideology. Surely attempts should be made to offset such shortcomings, but they will remain formidable and stubborn. The two lists concocted above intending to identify issues to which the decisionmakers should be more attentive—one generally addressing implementation issues and the other generally considering moral questions—are overlapping and reinforcing, which is unsurprising given the implicit argument that they are mutually essential. These inventories probably should be advocated and incorporated into whatever decision making matrixes are in use. But this does not get very far; there is a feeling of futility here, we are still behind the curve. Trying to understand better the difficult choices that are directly relevant to humanitarian intervention, there comes the recognition that there are no reliably sound ways of making them.

There are two realities that are largely responsible for this and that have not yet been directly addressed. The first reality is composed of the the larger powerful and overwhelming external forces, ambitions, strategies and tsunamis beyond the ability of this particular arena of decision making to predict or influence, even to fully comprehend, which will tend to dominate and moot the choices made here. These are not made in a cocoon or masters of their own fate, but are largely derivative; which would be so even if they were able to be made more competently. Second, the international community has not yet decided to attack the plethora of enormous, interacting challenges it faces with sufficient will, resources, determination, and unity to have a decent chance of meeting them. Here is our most ruthless truth; it influences everything and its costs are inestimable. Humanitarian interventions are both a product and a victim of this incapacity. Launching them is like steering into a hurricane, and any devoted effort to understand and strengthen our ability to decide what to do with them must recognize this.

NOTES

1. Richard Haas, former director of the State Department Policy Planning Staff, wrote: "And there is no coherent 'Clinton Doctrine'— unless that means a willingness to intervene when the domestic political cost of standing aloof exceeds the cost of a carefully staged and limited operation" (Hass, 2000: 136).
2. An exchange between two housecleaners in the kitchen of a wealthy American suburb in February 1999 discussing possible forthcoming NATO bombing in Kosovo: Paul: "If you're going to do this, then you have to rebuild afterwards, and that'll take too long to do." Jimmy: "It's one thing if our army is fighting another army inside a coun-

try, but if our army is killing civilians that's something you can't ignore."

3. In the Iraq Steering Committee, made up of representatives from the UN Secretariat and its operational agencies and chaired by Deputy Secretary General Louise Frechette, there were intense discussions subsequent to the US-led invasion of Iraq about the proper UN role there. Strong opinions divided over whether the UN presence should be limited to a largely independent humanitarian role or should in addition take on political and reconstruction functions under the authority of the US-led coalition. Secretary General Kofi Annan decided in favor of the larger but subservient role.

REFERENCES

Evans, Gareth, and Mohamed Sahnoun. "The Responsibility to Protect." *Report of the International Commission on Intervention and State Sovereignty* (December, 2001).

Haas, Richard. "The Squandered Presidency: Demanding More from the Commander-in-Chief." *Foreign Affairs* 79:3 (2000).

Hehir, J. Bryan. "Intervention: From Theories to Cases." *Ethics and International Affairs* (1995).

Ignatieff, Michael. "Moral Disgust." *Social Research* 62:1 (Spring 1995): 96.

Lake, Anthony, and Roger Morris. "The Human Reality of Realpolitik." *Foreign Policy* (Autumn 1971).

Moore, Jonathan, ed. *Hard Choices: Moral Dilemmas in Humanitarian Intervention.* Boulder: Rowman and Littlefield, 1998.

Note by the Secretary General to the UN General Assembly: Follow-up to the Outcome of the Millennium Summit. 2 December 2004. A/59/565.

Report of the Secretary General: An Agenda for Peace: Preventive Diplomacy, Peacemaking and Peace-keeping. 17 June 1992. A/47/277-S/24111.

Report of the Secretary General on the Situation in Rwanda. 31 May 1994. S/1994/640.

Rieff, David. *A Bed for the Night: Humanitarianism in Crisis.* New York: Simon and Schuster, 2002.

Traub, James. *The Best Intentions: Kofi Annan and the UN in the Era of American World Power.* New York: Farrar, Straus and Giroux, 2006.

United States Department of State. "Clinton Administration Policy on Reforming Multilateral Peace Operations (Presidential Decision Directive 25)." 22 February 1996.

Walzer, Michael. "The Politics of Rescue." *Social Research* 62:1 (Spring 1995).

Mary B. Anderson
To Work, or Not to Work, in "Tainted" Circumstances: Difficult Choices for Humanitarians

IN 2004, AS THE FIRST ANNIVERSARY OF THE US ENTRY INTO IRAQ approached, I was asked by colleagues to go to Iraq to conduct some training workshops for the local staff of international nongovernmental organizations (NGOs). I am an American. The NGOs I would be working with receive US government funding for some programs. If I went, would I be reinforcing a military operation by advancing a "hearts and minds" campaign? Or would I be demonstrating concern and support for local people involved in efforts to alleviate suffering and contribute to redevelopment?

A few years ago, I was asked by a colleague if my organization would be willing to visit an international corporation—working in a country that is known to abuse its citizens—in order to review the effects of the corporate operations on the people in their area. The corporation is criticized by human rights groups for working in this country but, through their own investigations, felt they were benefiting people in the area. If we went, and found that the corporation's assessment was correct, would we be complicit in supporting oppression? Or would we be contributing to an approach toward helping people who live under difficult circumstances?

I begin this article with two of the many possible personal stories I could cite to raise one difficult choice that frequently confronts international humanitarian agencies: When is it right, and when is it wrong, to work in "tainted" circumstances?

For international humanitarians, the decision of whether to enter, or stay, in compromised and compromising political and military settings is one that must regularly be faced. It is in the nature of humanitarian work to go to unsettled areas where existing governance and social structures are inadequate for handling crises. International help is provided when situations are out of control and beyond "normal." Such situations are often "tainted."

What do we mean by tainted circumstances? We use the term "tainted" to refer to the broad range of situations where, for example, government officials are more concerned with personal wealth and power than with the well-being of the people, or where international aid is manipulated by warlords and fighters to serve the ends of war or where international diplomatic, or military actors expect humanitarian assistance to "pick up the pieces" of failed diplomatic initiatives. In these and other such circumstances, the question arises: By working in this system and with these people, although we are here to save lives, are we also complicit with and supporting inhumane or oppressive processes?

In his famous extended essay written in 1970, *Exit, Voice and Loyalty*, Albert Hirschman explores how individuals and groups can express their dissatisfaction with systems that go into decline. He provides what he himself calls "numerous baroque ornamentations" to his wise and careful examination of the options for individuals and groups to express themselves through "voice" (speaking out against problems) or "exit" (withdrawing support or leaving), mitigated by and processed through the filter of "loyalty." Hirschman begins his discussion with a focus on customers or staff of firms that go into decline, but he extends the application of his analyses to other types of organizations and even to nation-states in ways that are helpful for thinking about the difficult choice we examine here about when is it right and when is it wrong for people involved in humanitarian assistance to work in tainted circumstances.

Hirschman's core question could be translated for the humanitarian context as: "When political and military conditions are tainted and, thus, will likely taint actions undertaken under their aegis, should humanitarians stay involved and try to exert 'voice' in order to change or improve the situation from inside or, alternatively, should they 'exit' by refusing to work under such circumstances?" Both options would be directed toward exerting influence to improve the situation for those living under oppressive or inhumane arrangements. Either could arguably be undertaken in the spirit of humanitarianism as a part of the process intended to alleviate suffering and save lives.

A review of the experience of many international humanitarians as they have encountered this difficult choice in a variety of locations and circumstances suggests that the direct translation of Hirschman's framework into this context misses an important redefining dimension. Whereas Hirschman deals with the options that people face for dealing with an organization of which they are a part, humanitarians continually confront the challenge of decision in situations of which they are not, intrinsically, a part. Humanitarians cross borders and insert themselves into other people's countries and circumstances. As "outsiders," international humanitarians make choices directed not toward changing the behavior of the agency or organization of which they are a part, but instead they make choices directed toward changing the political realities under which other people live or die where they, as outsiders, have elected to become involved. Therefore, any choice humanitarians make about whether or not to be present, or whether or not to speak out, has implications both for them and the situation (as in Hirschman's cases), and also for people who are a part of the situation into which these outsiders elect to insert themselves.

Acting as outsiders, international humanitarian workers decide, first, whether or not to intervene. If they decide positively, they may subsequently face a decision as to whether to stay or to leave. In both of these decisions, they also have the added choice of whether or not to exercise voice and, if so, to whom.

In this paper, we shall explore the choices regarding avoidance or entry, staying or exit, and voice or silence that are faced by international humanitarians. We shall do so, as described below in part I, from an experiential basis, reviewing and analyzing the experiences of many international humanitarians as they have faced these decisions and made their choices. Part II will describe a range of the circumstances in which humanitarians face such choices in order to highlight the multiple and conflicting dimensions involved. Part III will outline the arguments made by humanitarians both pro and con for each alternative, and in Part IV we shall conclude by reviewing what the evidence shows about how to proceed. We shall argue that we cannot, and in fact need not, determine a single answer to this dilemma, but instead should continue to decide each case individually. We suggest that, rather than establishing a fixed rule of choice, we should pursue approaches that provide guidance as we grapple anew with the choice each time it presents itself.

PART I: THE SOURCE OF OUR EVIDENCE

I direct an organization that is involved with many agencies worldwide that provide humanitarian and development assistance and work on peace-building and conflict resolution. In addition, we join with international corporations that have operations in troubled societies. We work with these partners to gather their broad cumulative experience and compare and analyze it to learn how to be increasingly effective. We join with these partners to assemble and learn from their collective experience as one way of improving our positive impacts on people's lives (through humanitarian, life-saving aid; through social and political development; and through peace and conflict-resolution).

Every one of the individuals and agencies with which we collaborate crosses borders to work in other countries with the intent of being helpful to and supportive of the people who live in those areas. Very often, these individuals and agencies—and we with them—work in areas where leaders pursue self-interest at the expense of their populations. Further, increasingly in North American and Western Europe, the foreign policy establishments expect humanitarian agencies to fit within and further their international political agendas. Even when these agendas are benign and supportive of poverty alleviation, it is a challenge to the "purity" of humanitarianism to be aligned with the foreign policy of individual nation-states. When these agendas pursue war or other policies that themselves give rise to humanitarian crises, the choice of humanitarian agencies to respond to these needs is further complicated.

Over the years of working with our colleagues in these agencies, we have seen many instances when they have faced the choice, posed here, of whether to stay engaged or to withdraw, to speak out or remain silent, to go to a site to work or to refuse. We have listened to their explanations about how their desire not to justify some immoral or inhumane act has been faced and, in that setting, "resolved." This broad field-based experience provides the evidence, and grounds, for the discussion that follows.

PART II: EXAMPLES OF THE DIFFICULT CHOICE

A selection of field-based experiences illustrates the kinds of situations where humanitarians face the difficult choice we are considering. Some of these situations are extreme; others less so. Nonetheless, the examples provided below are not atypical or unusual. They arise regularly and repeatedly. They demonstrate the several layers of complexity that, when taken together (as they always must be), make easy analysis and facile choice impossible.

A. Whether to Enter, or Not

Humanitarian agencies, and individuals, regularly face the decision of whether to start up work in a new emergency location. For NGOs that are mandated, and ready, to respond to human need wherever it occurs, this should be an easy decision based solely on whether people in that setting need the kinds of help we can offer. However, given that there are never sufficient resources to respond equally to all needs, choices among competing needs are inevitable. What criteria can humanitarians use to make such choices? How much control do they exert over these choices and how much are these choices "tainted" by other factors?

The example with which we opened this paper illustrates how difficult this choice can be. Many humanitarian agencies struggled with the decision about whether or not to prepare to provide humanitarian aid to Iraq even as the threats of the US government to invade gained credibility. Some felt they had to be prepared lest they fail to respond to genuine human need. Others felt that to prepare for such an invasion was, in some sense, to sanction it or, only a little less onerously, to accept its inevitability.

After the invasion and the establishment of the "Provisional Authority," the decision was no easier. The US Agency for International Development set rules by which US NGOs would be subject to the oversight of the authority, which was a direct challenge to their independence. Some US agencies refused to work in Iraq while others negotiated some variations in the conditions under which they did so. NGOs from other countries also struggled to decide how, if at all, they could work effectively in a country under "military occupation" where even their access and processes would, necessarily, be affected by military movements and decisions. Good friends and colleagues involved in humanitarian work came down on opposite sides of this decision. As the situation has grown worse in Iraq, the tensions surrounding these choices made three and four years ago still affect the US NGO community.

The decisions of donor nations about which countries, and which groups within countries, will receive priority are always a reflection of international politics. As some crises receive more international attention (and money) than others, humanitarian NGOs constantly review and struggle with the ways in which these decisions affect their decisions about where and with whom to respond.

Further, in some locations, as humanitarians decide whether or not to respond to a crisis, they are aware, in advance, that local political realities will circumscribe their access and dictate the conditions under which they can deliver help to people in need. Local politicians will determine who they can serve and who they cannot serve. Local regulations will allow some forms of help and not others. Local powers see international resources as a means to exert their own agendas and control. These circumstances are constantly present in civil war situations such as those that existed in Bosnia-Herzigovina and in southern Sudan in recent years. Knowing that such constraints can, and often do, serve nefarious purposes, NGOs have to decide whether to enter this situation. Should they respond to the needs they can serve and live with the reality that others will not be served *and* that this, in itself, supports the political will of the faction that controls their access? Or should they shun involvement in order not to be complicit with and reinforce such intergroup domination?

Finally, where governments are new and unproved, often in post-conflict situations, international aid workers have to decide whether or not to work with them. When newly formed, postconflict governments include former warriors known to have been directly involved in atrocities during the conflict, do outsiders—who have a choice—work with this government (thereby helping strengthen it), or do they shun it until it proves itself as competent, not corrupt, and legitimate? International development and humanitarian NGOs have faced this choice many times in recent years in places such a Mozambique and Afghanistan, to name only two . When is a government "worthy" of support and when should one withhold involvement?

B. Whether to Stay or Leave

Once in a country, humanitarian agencies may become aware of or encounter new circumstances that are disquieting in their implications for how their aid is used. Realizing their possible complicity in these circumstances, humanitarians face the choice of whether to stay and continue their work or to leave. Having entered a community and become involved helping local people, the decision between staying and leaving is difficult.

A striking illustration of the stay or leave dilemma confronted humanitarians soon after the genocide in Rwanda. Thousands of Hutus fled to what was then Zaire as well as to Tanzania. As people crossed these borders, the international humanitarian community responded by setting up refugee camps and supplying lifesaving aid. Within a very short time, it became clear that some number of people in the camps, particularly at Goma, were *genocidaires*, who had committed and sometimes spearheaded violent crimes. There were reports that they were using the camps as a base for regrouping and recruitment. Further, even if these individuals had not been engaged in continuing as fighters, NGOs questioned whether they, as humanitarians, should be providing assistance to people who had just committed the crime of genocide. Did they "deserve" humanitarian assistance? Some agencies left; others stayed.

Just as difficult is the choice made today by NGOs working in countries such as Zimbabwe. There the government sets rules for humanitarian action that limit where and how assistance can be provided. Some communities, seen by current political powers to be the "opposition," are designated as "off-limits" to NGOs and can receive no aid. By denying support to these groups, these political forces hope either to force the opposition to leave or to force people to change their political allegiance. The question for humanitarians is: Should they remain in the country, under these circumstances, contributing to this internal assertion of power/exclusion/dominance? As inflation and exchange rate rules make each dollar that NGOs import serve fewer and fewer people, humanitarians are finding the choice ever more challenging.

The pressures of choice are intensified for humanitarian NGOs when international tensions heighten. When the election in the Palestinian Territories (PT) brought Hamas—a political force deemed by some to be a "terrorist organization"—to power, some donor governments withdrew all but the most basic support from humanitarian efforts. International NGOs have had both funding and political pressures put on them to withdraw assistance.

Here the difficult choice is less whether they should stay and serve the Palestinian communities where they have been working. Most humanitarian NGOs seeing continuing and serious need would choose to stay. The difficult choice is faced by NGO administrators and decisionmakers. If they continue to provide aid in an area that has been deemed by their own government to be "terrorist," to what extent will this affect their ability to tap this government's funds for work elsewhere and in the future? Is staying in the current situation of sufficient importance that it can justify a failure to be able to respond to future situations because of lack of funding?

The conundrum posed by Hamas's ascension to power is all the more ironic because, in recent years, European donor governments have been reexamining the effect of their development aid to the territories. Because the assistance they provide to the PT is subject to some Israeli regulations, they have become concerned that their assistance is helping that government maintain its control over an occupied/controlled area. Further, they are struggling with the possibility that they help maintain the occupation/control by lessening the impacts of some Israeli policies. For example, as Israel built the wall/barrier to separate Israel from the Palestinian Territories, international donor support very often helped people adjust to the new village configurations that resulted. When a village was divided by the barrier, donors sometimes helped people move to new homes in order to reunite the village or, if access to health care had been cut off, they built a new clinic inside the wall. As they considered these issues, donors weighed the inadvertent support for policies with which they did not agree against the likelihood that, if they ceased funding, the living conditions for Palestinians would become significantly worse.

C. Whether to be Quiet, or Speak out

When deciding whether or not to enter a situation, or, once there, whether or not to stay, there is always an additional decision encountered by humanitarians. This is the choice about whether or not to "go public" with their concerns. If an agency on which people depend for life-saving assistance speaks out about crimes or oppression they witness, will they be denied entry (through restriction of visas or import licenses) or risk summary deportation? If an agency is known to advocate for human rights elsewhere, will its staff then be excluded from other troubled areas where their assistance could have helped? Humanitarians regularly wrestle with the choice, and the implications of the choice, of silence versus speaking out as it affects the likelihood of survival or of suffering among the groups they seek to help.

For example, agencies that have established humanitarian and development support programs in Burma/Myanmar experience strong pressure not to criticize the actions of that government publicly because they believe (with experience to back this belief) that such outspoken criticism would result in expulsion. Is it "better" to remain quiet and provide help to people who live under a restrictive regime or to speak out and not be able to maintain a presence inside a country?

In all three of these decisions—whether to enter, whether to stay and whether to speak out—international politics and money, and local politics and money, can taint the choices and the impacts of the choices that humanitarians make. The examples we cite here are only a small sampling of multiple encounters where taintedness arises in the course of providing humanitarian assistance. Nonetheless, they show that the decision of presence is an ongoing one, shaped and challenged by political and funding realities, that rise and ebb but that are seldom entirely absent.

PART III: ARGUMENTS FOR AND AGAINST ENTERING, STAYING AND BEING SILENT

The outlines of the arguments for and against presence and silence have been illustrated by the examples in part II. Here we draw out each—those for and those against—more fully.

Whether to Enter: The Pro Argument

Those who argue that one should always go where there is human need, regardless of the political context, do so from a strong commitment to the "humanitarian imperative"—namely, that those in need of assistance have the *right* to receive it and those who can provide assistance have the *right* (and obligation) to provide it. Human suffering, they feel, must always be responded to wherever and whenever it arises. If the world puts barriers in the way of delivering such aid, this does not release humanitarians from the obligation to try. Under any circumstances, it is better to try to reach those in need and to do what can be done than not to try and to reach no one.

Using Hirschman's framework, the decision to go to a tainted situation is linked to "loyalty" to the humanitarian imperative. Rather than a loyalty to an organization or a state, international humanitarians are loyal to a principle that they apply not only in their own circumstances but which justifies their crossing borders to work in areas not their own.

Those who argue in favor of presence cite two fundamental humanitarian principles: neutrality and impartiality. They argue that humanitarians have no business engaging in, or taking sides in relation to, politics. Political activism is, they say, the job of local people, not international "outsiders." They eschew "political interference" as inappropriate for non-nationals. They accept the complications of the circumstances where they work, but feel that someone must take on the specific role of humanitarianism, separate from and independent of political and monetary forces.

Believing that all human life is of equal value and focusing solely on responding to human suffering wherever it exists, they live by and reassert this universal value.

Whether to Enter: The Con Argument

Those who argue against becoming entangled in tainted circumstances also argue from a principled and moral basis. When deciding not to go to tainted circumstances, these humanitarians argue that refusal to participate in such situations demonstrates a strength of opposition that can exert power to bring change. They cite the many historical examples where people simply let bad things happen and, by failing to take action against these, in effect condoned and buttressed oppression or violence. Knowing the power of humanitarianism as an expression of an international conscience of concern for people's suffering, they use this as leverage to highlight political situations that harm their citizens. Knowing that oppressive governments survive more on the silence and inactivity of the majority than on its strong approval, they take the actions available to them to shun such circumstances—usually also with "voice." That is, they make clear in public ways the conditions that cause them to shun the tainted context, and by this, advocate for or "add their weight to" an effort to change it.

In our discussion, we have chosen to use the word "tainted" to describe the circumstances that force the difficult choices we are considering. This word has two dimensions. It highlights that, not only are some situations very bad, but that such tainted situations can also "taint" those who become involved in them. The word connotes the process by which disease or decay or putrefaction spreads, contaminating what it touches. "Tainted" implies the tendency of a morally corrupt situation to corrupt the morals of those who are in it. Taintedness may spread and spoil those who come within its reach.

Those who argue against going into such circumstances stress this relationship. They believe that some circumstances are so complexly negative that it is impossible to do the good we mean to do without becoming tainted by the circumstances in which we work. They feel that the purity of the humanitarian imperative, and the purity of the principles of neutrality and impartiality, are so compromised by such situations as to become meaningless.

Whether to Stay: The Pro Argument

The argument for staying in a situation that is tainted or seen to have deteriorated to such an extent that a choice must be (re)made follows the same lines as the decision to go to such situations. The choice is driven by the commitment to help people under whatever circumstances to the extent possible.

However, an additional dimension is added once work has been undertaken. Those who argue that, once there, humanitarians should stay point to experience that shows that the very act of withdrawing assistance has negative effects. They argue that when international humanitarians leave a bad situation, it exacerbates or prompts further violence and conflict. In conflict areas, they observe that when international agencies withdraw, this signals local fighters that conditions are getting worse. In some instances this causes the fighters to take preemptive action to ensure they are not caught off guard by the "other side." Further, proponents of staying say withdrawal of international actors in response to deteriorating circumstances sends a message that committing violent or inhumane acts can actually drive out the international community. This has implications for the security both of other international humanitarians as well as for local people. Further, they note the positive impacts of an international presence in preventing or mitigating human rights abuse. If internationals leave, this removes one form of protection they feel that humanitarians can offer to people in need.

Because of these added negatives of leaving, those who argue in favor of staying differentiate the choice to stay from the choice to enter a location. They feel that although it may in some circumstances be right not to enter a tainted situation, once there, the obligation to remain becomes preeminent because of these added negative impacts.

Some people add a future-directed argument to support the decision to stay even under nefarious circumstances. As noted earlier, they fear that to become engaged in the political situation that affects aid delivery in any location is to risk, in subsequent disasters, exclusion from responding to need because local authorities might refuse entry to an agency that has highlighted political problems in other areas.

Whether to Stay: The Con Argument

Humanitarians who argue that it can be right to leave a situation that has deteriorated (or been discovered to be severely tainted) note the power of the threat, and the impacts, of withdrawal. Some agencies set standard criteria for decisions about whether to stay in a troubled setting or to leave. For example, some have established the rule that, if any of their staff are threatened or killed, they will immediately withdraw. Making this condition clear from the beginning of an intervention can, they argue, greatly improve the security of humanitarian agency staff. They note, however, that the threat is only believed if, in fact, the agency is prepared to carry through on its threat.

Even with such rules in place, however, specific circumstances can shape the timing or framework for such decisions. Is withdrawal threatened or carried out? Is it partial or total? Does one take time to arrange the departure so that hardship is lessened or leave immediately to make a point? Does one leave permanently or conditionally, stipulating some desired change that will justify reentry? Proponents of withdrawal feel that these subchoices all can be used to improve the leverage they hope to exert by leaving.This leverage, they feel, has two dimensions.

The pragmatic dimension derives from its impact as a threat or actual departure to support a change processes. The argument here emphasizes the leverage that international humanitarians have to highlight wrongdoing and to call the world's attention to inhumane and abusive actions. The threat of withdrawal or actual leaving is accompanied by public speaking out about conditions. The purpose is to influence the situation for the better.

The moral dimension of withdrawal arises from the message it sends about the inhumanity of the situation. Further, those who advocate this are concerned about the possibility they see of becoming tainted by inhumane restrictions on their work. People who take this position feel that they cannot continue to operate within a harmful setting because this could, and could be seen to, support or condone it. They feel the moral imperative of taking the action that is within their power and, as outsiders, they feel their only real option is to withdraw physically. This group also observes that, precisely because they once showed their commitment to the people in this situation, the very difficulty of the decision to leave carries a special moral force. Taking this action is, they feel, an essentially humanitarian thing to do in support (rather than abandonment) of the people they came to serve. Withdrawal in this sense is always combined with voice: public speaking out, explaining why the withdrawal is necessary and the circumstances that drove them to this decision.

Whether to Voice Objections: The Pro Arguments
Those who choose to speak out also do so from their moral or ethical commitment to humanitarianism. Their arguments mirror the discussions offered by Hirschman about how people effectively use "voice" to change failing situations. It is both right and, they hope, effective.

They note that silence in effect supports an existing system and this inevitably ends by corrupting even the good that one would have wanted to do. To be silent in the face of inhumanity is to deny the basis of humanitarianism and, through silence, to allow and condone inhumanity.

They also note that voice very often is effective. "Name and shame" campaigns, such as those conducted by Amnesty International, have had important influence. Abuses have been stopped by international pressure brought to bear on offenders. If one truly responds to suffering, they argue, one mechanism for doing so is through voice.

The Con Arguments

Those who decide not to speak out weigh the good they know they can do for those they serve against the possible (but uncertain) good they might do by speaking out. They recognize the likelihood that, if they voice public concern, they will be expelled from the situation, leaving behind and unattended the needs that humanitarians are committed to serve. They point to occasions where "name and shame" has not worked but, instead, caused abusers to become ever more isolated, defensive and harsh in their actions.

Engagement: A Variation on the Choice Based on Presence and Quiet

Above, we suggested that the conditions of being an outsider, with loyalty to a universal principle of humanitarianism, who can choose whether or not to enter a humanitarian crisis and respond to need in other people's circumstances, changes the framework for the choices of exit and voice for international humanitarians. One manifestation of the difference is an argument for "engagement."

In some sense, engagement is a hybrid of nonexit and nonvoice. It is an approach that combines presence with quiet, but not silence.

Proponents of engagement describe it as involving an active presence that asserts both a commitment to the humanitarian mandate and a commitment to the correction of the injurious situation. Its proponents argue that it is possible both to provide humanitarian assistance to people in troubled situations and to recognize and directly interact with the causes of the deleterious circumstances under which suffering occurs.

Engagement also involves voice. However, the voice is not broadly public, but is focused instead in an "off-the-record way" toward specific actors who are guilty of creating and maintaining the harmful circumstances or capable and well positioned to directly change it. Humanitarians who take an engagement approach do not condone silence, but when they use voice, they do so quietly.

Those who argue for engagement recognize that their approach involves direct interaction with people whose values and actions are at sharp odds with their own and with circumstances that are abhorrent to them. However, proponents of engagement hold that there is no way for a humanitarian to be "pure." They contend that shunning a situation or leaving it has effects on people's lives and suffering and the political situation in which they live. Not to go into a situation is, also, to allow some things to occur that, had one been there, it may have been possible to stop. Because both nonaction and action have impacts on reality, they believe that avoidance of warlords or abusers is an impure choice.

Perhaps the best known exemplars of what we mean by engagement are the representatives of the International Committee of the Red Cross (ICRC). This agency has taken on a role of working in situations and with perpetrators of war, imprisonment, and other forms of violence. They act as monitors of human conditions under these injurious circumstances and often, through off-the-record appeal to those responsible, have been successful in bettering conditions of imprisonment, treatment, etc. By being "quiet" with what they find, the ICRC representatives have been able to go behind lines, visit people imprisoned, and enable some changes to occur that, had they refused to work there or insisted upon public denunciations of the wrongdoing they find, would not have been possible. Many prisoners of war have testified to the importance of this kind of engagement.

One ICRC protection officer is quoted this way: "In my experience, engaging even the worst abusers in this manner may yield unexpected results: you give a fellow the choice between solving the issue quietly, among ourselves . . . or putting him on the line by raising the case with his superiors. Not only may you solve the issue, but you may create a bond of confidence . . . an ally who does not perceive you as an enemy, and who may be useful to solve future cases" (Mahoney, 2006: 50).

The argument for engagement over silence or absence does not depend only on established procedures and the kind of reputation that ICRC has. Individual humanitarians also take this approach.

One NGO worker reported his experience with engagement in Liberia a number of years ago. He was assigned to head his agency's program in an area of a war-torn country that was under the control of a particularly unsavory warlord. He thought of strategies for avoiding this person's control or of asserting his own power to withdraw as leverage for ensuring that he had freedom to serve people who needed his agency's help. But, he reports, he decided to try "a different approach." He asked the warlord for an appointment. When they met, he asked permission to provide food and medical assistance to people in the area. The warlord granted this permission. He then asked if he could meet, weekly, with the warlord to report on how the work was going. Again, with some surprise, the warlord agreed. The NGO worker tells how, after some weeks of sitting together on Friday afternoons during which he would tell of the conditions and changes in villages in the area, the warlord finally asked, "How do you know these things about children's malnutrition? How do you know about their health status?" The NGO worker responded, "We go to the villages and talk with people." And he described the methods for assessing health status that his staff used. The warlord then said, "May I go to the villages with you sometime?"

As the NGO worker recounted this story to a group of colleagues, he was careful to say that he did not think he had changed the warlord's "soul" or turned his behavior from inhumane to humane. However, he did note that this individual had no previous experience with governance or attention to civilian well-being. Rather, all of his energy and attention had been focused on controlling populations and managing fighters. International NGOs that had provided humanitarian assistance in that area before had, in effect, taken care of civilian needs for the warlord. The change that the engagement approach had achieved, our colleague thought, was to open up another possibility for this man who, perhaps, could begin to imagine other ways of operating with the people in his region.

It is important to make a distinction between voice and transparency. Proponents of engagement argue that they use a quiet voice directed toward affecting positive change in a deleterious situation, rather than public denouncements. But, simultaneously, they say they are completely transparent about the fact that they are engaging with people whose values or actions they find wrong. The fact of their engagement is not secret. Because the ICRC is transparent about its *way* of working, it can also maintain its quiet about what it finds where it works so long as people perceive this as being an effective way of helping improve conditions. As one staff person of Amnesty International said about the ICRC, "It is what it does behind the scenes, what we do not hear about, that is so important, the confidential meetings, the protests, the reports" (*Financial Times*, 2005: W2). The NGO worker also was transparent with all the people in the region where he worked about the fact that he was regularly meeting with the warlord and about the content of their meetings. Had he not been so, he could have seriously jeopardized the trust of the communities with whom he worked.

Arguments against Engagement

People who argue against engagement say that it is optimistic (some would add naively optimistic) for those who pursue engagement to believe that working with people who commit war crimes or other forms of abuse has any chance of changing them. Critics of engagement feel it is presumptuous and possibly self-delusional to think that one can exert any real influence in nefarious processes.

Hirschman raises this point in his analysis of government officials who are part of a foreign policy office that goes to war. He describes officials who, even though they strongly oppose the war, justify staying in their positions by claiming that worse things would happen if they were not present, doing what small things they can to mitigate bad decisions. Hirschman notes that such people sometimes assume the mantle of "martyrdom," claiming to suffer as they stand alone amid hostile forces holding out for good. He also notes that these individuals usually continue to enjoy comfortable salaries as well as other perks of the position they hold. Hirschman accuses such people of operating from a "delicious mixture of motives" (Hirschman, 1970: 116) that includes at least as much self-interest as moral grounding.

A similar criticism is applied in the humanitarian world. Although humanitarian workers may not enjoy comfortable salaries or perks, humanitarian agency administrators are mindful of the need for institutional survival. When they object to policies and, at the same time, work within their confines and with the administrators who enacted them, they can be challenged as to whether they are pursuing an engagement approach to improve the situation or whether they are pursuing the funds that are available for the work in that area.

Humanitarian critics of engagement further point out the insidious tainting of tainted processes. Even if one begins engagement, they argue, with full commitment to "witnessing" for a moral position, the constraints imposed on one's work can circumscribe and distort that witness. They feel that those who pursue engagement may be rationalizing their presence and thinking that they have more moral power than they do.

Additional Factors that Affect the Choices

It would seem that there is no clear, unambiguously pure choice to be made about when and when not to respond to humanitarian needs. Arguments both for and against each choice all include strong moral positions as well as conscious political analyses.

Even these arguments do not capture all the dimensions of the choices that are experienced, however. Before concluding with our comments about how humanitarians might build on existing experience as they encounter these decisions in the future, we will turn briefly to a description of additional factors that also influence choices.

What other factors play into and complicate humanitarian choices regarding entry, voice and engagement? We observe five additional elements that often arise when humanitarians face these decisions.

First, there is a broad historical influence in some choices. For example, with regard to the decisions to provide assistance to the Palestinians, the European history of the treatment of the Jews, and the establishment of a separate Jewish state shape the extent to which donors are willing to be critical of Israeli policies.

Second, organizational histories also influence such choices. The example of the ICRC's continuing pursuit of engagement is a case in point. Likewise, the fact the Medicins sans Frontieres (MSF) on occasion chooses to withdraw from problematic situations arises from its own history. MSF was founded by Bernard Kouchner who, having worked for the ICRC, found he disagreed with the institutional limitations on "voice." He therefore established MSF as a humanitarian agency that is committed to speaking out when the staff feels it is justified by circumstances.

Third, organizational or personal identities influence choice. Again, the decision to work in Palestine provides an example for Christian agencies that are drawn to this area because it is the "Holy Land."

Fourth, one's relationship to the cause of suffering can shape choice. For example, some US-based agencies (and individuals) felt a particular urgency to work in Iraq after the US invasion in order to counter some of what they saw as the damage done by their country.

Fifth, some agencies undertake a calculus of good/harm through which they try to assess, on balance, whether the positive impacts of their work outweigh the negative ones, or vice versa. Which factors one puts on each side of the balance sheet can also be shaped by the above considerations. The example cited above of whether or not to stay in Zimbabwe reflects such a calculus.

The point here is that choices of entry, presence, and voice are layered with overtones and undercurrents of past histories and identities that go beyond an assessment of current politics or other "evidence."

PART IV: WAYS FORWARD FOR HUMANITARIANS

This paper has cited examples and ideas from day-to-day, on-the-ground operations and discussions of international actors trying to do what is right in a complicated and, often compromised, setting. From this basis, what can we say about how to go forward? Which options and alternatives have been seen to work best, to stand the test of time, and how might these be referenced for making these difficult choices in future settings? It seems clear that there is not a single "right" choice available to humanitarians with regard to either presence or voice. However, I do believe that the experiences of many making such choices, and the continuing discussions that surround these decisions, provide some pointers for the future. My own conclusions of what these might be follow.

The first obvious point to make, from the experience gathered, is that there is no choice that is completely "pure." Because of the layered and complex circumstances in which humanitarians work, each choice has both positive and negative potential impacts on the lives of the people to whose needs humanitarians want to respond. Experience would also seem to show that there is no straightforward moral calculus by which to assess the weighting of good versus harm of any choice. How, for example, can we weigh one life that we know we can save today against a number of lives that may be lost or oppressed in the future, or vice versa? Attempts to claim purity, or clarity of relative good and harm, should be suspect.

As a result, I would conclude that variety is reassuring and accomplishes more good than a single choice might. Rather than seeking a uniform and consistent answer across all humanitarian efforts, therefore, I welcome the fact that humanitarians make differing choices. Even though I decide to shun a location, someone else will decide to go there to respond to local suffering. When one agency withdraws where they find their work too compromised, another agency will conclude that the ends it feels are most important will be served by staying. Perhaps this multiplicity of responses can add up to cover the range of humanitarian goals, both alleviating immediate suffering *and* changing the conditions under which it continues.

In this way, I welcome and appreciate the range of responses that humanitarians of good conscience pursue and would not try to convince all others that they follow whatever light I hold. That said, I find that consultation with trusted colleagues is an essential factor in deciding whether and when to respond, shun, stay, withdraw, speak out, or engage quietly. It is far too easy to think that I have weighed all factors in my own mind when, we know, the reason these choices are difficult is precisely because of their complex and multi-layered nature. To think that I can consider all factors alone is arrogant and unwise. When faced with such a choice, I would always seek out (and recommend that others do so too) the counsel and wisdom of many friends and colleagues. I would try to listen to both those whose proclivities match my own and to those who hold starkly different opinions. Without these arguments in my mind, I mistrust any decision I might make.

An additional factor that I would always consider, alongside the possible impacts my choice may have, would be what in my organization we call the "implicit messages" of any choice. Sometimes the messages we send are as important as the direct impacts we have. With whom are we showing solidarity? What principles are we promoting? What are the likely misinterpretations of any choice we make? Who will these serve and who will these harm?

Finally, it is important to acknowledge that any choice is a combination of personal/moral and political/practical considerations. The specifics of each circumstance require their own analysis. A choice made only on political considerations will likely be too colored by temporary and partial understandings of complicated power relations. A choice made only on moral considerations will likely be too naïve in relation to interpretations and impacts. A difficult choice is just that—difficult. But, for humanitarians, such choices are also inevitable. Understanding and deciphering the factors that make such choices difficult, and the range of options that exist, based on past experience, can bring us to the point of each successive decision better prepared to make a good choice in that moment.

REFERENCES

Financial Times, June 18-19, 2005.

Hirschman, Albert O. *Exit, Voice, and Loyalty: Responses to Decline in Firms, Organizations, and States.* Cambridge: Harvard University Press, 1970.

Mahoney, Liam, *Proactive Presence: Field Strategies for Civilian Protection.* Geneva: Centre for Humanitarian Dialogue, 2006.

C. Fred Alford
Whistle-Blower Narratives: The Experience of Choiceless Choice

ONE MIGHT ARGUE THAT THE VERY CONCEPT OF A CHOICELESS CHOICE disqualifies the action undertaken as ethical.* Ethical choices are by their very nature the result of willful choice, even if they are not always the result of rational reflection—as when, for example, someone runs into a burning building to save a child's life. By the end of this essay, I hope you will be convinced that dividing the world in this way is not useful. Not only because the way one lives so as to find oneself in a position of choiceless choice is itself an ethical act, but also because the person one is so as to be placed in a position of choiceless choice is already an ethical fact. More important than judging these ethical actors, however, is understanding the people they became. Listening to their stories is the best way to do this.

I have sought to understand the whistle-blower, one who speaks out against illegal or unethical practices in the organization where he or she works. Most whistle-blowers are fired (though it is admittedly difficult to measure these things).[1] Theirs is an act of considerable consequence, especially when one considers that among fired whistle-blowers, most will lose their homes and ultimately, their marriages. A majority will turn to alcohol or drugs for some period during their long journey (Miethe, 1999: 58, 78-79; Rothschild and Miethe, 1996: 15-16; Glazer and Glazer, 1989: 206-207; Alford, 2001: 19-21).[2]

While I devoted considerable time to interviewing whistle-blowers, a majority was spent attending a whistle-blowers support group, listening to whistle-blowers tell their tales. In addition, I stayed several days and nights at a retreat on a farm for stressed-out whistle-blowers. The farm had been purchased by a retired psychologist with a large clientele of whistle-blowers (not the best way to get rich in the mental health field) who had graciously opened his farmhouse door to almost any whistle-blower who needed a place to get away for a few days (or even longer in several cases). Stories heard there for the third or fourth time at three in the morning took on a whole new dimension as some of the defensive walls came tumbling down—not just for the teller of the tale, but for the listener as well. There is something terrifying about the experience of whistle-blowing; Daniel Ellsberg, the Vietnam-era whistle-blower, compares the emotional experience to that of a space-walking astronaut who has cut his lifeline to the mother ship (Alford, 2001: 5).

Because I spent most of my time listening to whistle-blowers talk with each other, mine is a narrative analysis: an account of the structure of whistle-blowers' stories. To be sure, some of these stories they told to me, but most I first heard whistle-blowers tell to each other. The structure of the whistle-blower support group, or perhaps I should say its ethos, was for the members to go around the table telling their stories. Since I attended the support group for over six months, and since many of the attendees were regulars, this meant I heard many of the same stories again and again. That turned out to be a boon, as it was only after the third or fourth hearing that I began to get the point.

There is another reason I employ narrative analysis. Much of my previous research has involved bringing psychoanalysis to bear on social theory. I originally thought I would do this with the whistle-blowers, uncovering the depth psychological sources of their acts. Soon, however, I came to recognize that asking these men and women about their childhoods, or interpreting their stories about being crushed by organized power in psychoanalytic terms, would be embarrassing to me, and an insult to them. Instead, I turned to narratology, which allowed me to stay strictly on the surface, at least in one respect.

To be sure, there remained a conflict. The whistle-blower wants his or her story told in his or her terms: the content is everything. I, on the other hand, became more interested in the form of the story, the subject of narratology. Especially after I realized what I was doing, I always felt a little bit of a traitor to the whistle-blowers, who so wanted their stories to be told verbatim. In my defense I can tell you that I shared the proofs of my book manuscript with half a dozen members of the whistle-blower support group, and the book with a half-dozen more (Alford, 2001). Only one said she felt used, and I still receive letters, phone calls, and e-mails from whistle-blowers telling me that my book has been helpful to them in understanding their experiences.

WHISTLE-BLOWER NARRATIVES

Three prominent themes of whistle-blower narratives became apparent. The three themes are choiceless choice, stuck in static time, and "living in the position of the dead." The third theme represents, I believe, a resource for richer narrative forms, as well as richer lives. Choiceless choice contains a subcategory, paranoid narrative. One might be inclined to call it a counternarrative; better to call it the most narrative of narratives.

My inspiration is Lawrence Langer's *Holocaust Testimonies: The Ruins of Memory* (1991). Langer discovers an almost overwhelming impulse to transform the narratives of survivors into inspirational tales. Most listeners cannot or will not hear the shattered meaning that can never be made good, or even meaningful—if, that is, we equate meaningful with whole, coherent, and inspiring, not cold and broken. Whistle-blowers have gone through far, far less than survivors. Just having finished rereading Primo Levi's *The Drowned and the Saved* (1988), I can appreciate the reader who finds any comparison between the whistle-blower and the Holocaust survivor offensive; Levi might have found the comparison offensive. Let me be clear. I am not comparing the suffering of whistle-blowers and survivors. I am arguing that an analysis of the broken narratives of survivors can help us understand the broken narratives of whistle-blowers. More precisely, analyses of those who listen and fail to hear the broken narratives of survivors can help us better understand the broken narratives of whistle-blowers.

CHOICELESS CHOICE

"I did it because I had to . . . because I had no other choice . . . because I couldn't live with myself if I hadn't done anything . . . because it was speak up or stroke out. . . . What else could I do? I have to look at myself in the mirror every morning?" This is what most whistle-blowers say (the comments of several strung together to form a single quote), and the question is how to regard this almost universal explanation, one that is generally offered gratis—that is, not in response to a question about "Why'd you do it?" There is something formulaic about the explanation, but that does not mean empty. The trick will be to find out what the explanation is a formula for. The answer is that choiceless choice is a formula for relief from the almost unbearable regret of having let oneself be sent on a suicide mission.

Consider the parts of the self as actors in a narrative.[3] "Actants," they are called. The mark of the actant is that one person may play several roles; one person may play more than one actant. Actants are a class of actors with an identical relationship to the goal of action. Provide the actants with a plot, and we have a story. Let us call it the plot of plots—the structure of all narrative according to Greimas (1983):

> A given order is *disturbed*.

> The *sender* establishes a *contract* with the *subject* to bring about a new order of things, or reinstate the old. The sender is an imparter of values, sending the subject on a quest.

> The subject becomes *competent* by virtue of values and attributes imparted by the sender: these may include the desire to restore order, the obligation to restore order, and the ability to restore order.

> The subject goes on a *quest* whose goal is to obtain the object for the benefit of the *receiver*.

> As the result of three basic tests, the subject fulfills his part of the contract and is rewarded, or fails to fulfill his contract and is punished.[4]

The stereotypical love story exemplifies the plot of plots. He is both the subject and the receiver. She is both the object and the sender. Four actors (subject, receiver, object, sender) are incorporated into two actants. The merging of the sender with the object and the receiver with the subject occurs frequently, as in the love story: the subject's desire for the object is what sends him on his quest. It is for this reason that the sender is often called the power. But when the character of the subject is the main issue, the sender (power) merges with the subject. This is the case with every whistle-blower narrative.

The sender is the whistle-blower's character and values; the subject is the whistle-blower in his role as organization man or woman. Choiceless choice is what happens when the sender speaks to the subject in a voice the subject cannot resist. In fact, it is useful to think about the sender as the power of the beloved. We understand what it is to be bewitched by love. How much more compelling it is to be bewitched by one's own values and beliefs; how much more difficult it is to escape that Siren's call.

Deliver me from this kind of love, the Greek prayed, and for good reason. More than one whistle-blower wishes he had the foresight to tie himself to the mast, though a middle-aged whistleblower I will call Jim Bower did not put it quite that way. "If I knew then what I know now, I'd have told my wife to shoot me before letting me call [my congressman's] office."

Not many of us know what it is like to be overwhelmed by our own beliefs. Not, perhaps, because we have not been, but because this type of freedom comes frighteningly close to compulsion, so we blink and call it choice. Some whistle-blowers experience the sender as a virtual dictator, destroying their lives and then walking away, leaving the subject to pick up the pieces. If it is the contract between sender and subject that explains choiceless choice, it is a contract between unequals. But then love was always like that, says Plato, desire a virtual slave to its object (*Symposium*, 203b-e). "I loved my job," said one whistle-blower, "but it was nothing compared to how much I loved the job I gave myself, protector of the public. Now I don't have either. It reminds me of when my parents died one right after the other."

In "What is Freedom?" Hannah Arendt (1956: 151) argues that freedom is acting from a principle. "Action, to be free, must be free from motive on the one side, from its intended goal as a predictable effect on the other." Our motives are more likely to control us than vice versa. And the results of our acts depend upon events far from our control. Only when we give ourselves over to our principles are we free. With the term "principles" Arendt means an idea or value that inspires us from "without," from the outside in. We do not make our principles. Our principles make us. This sense of the term *principle* is identical to what I am calling the sender.

Jim Bower continued. "Once I blew the whistle, I was free. I could breathe for the first time in years." Better than Arendt, the whistle-blower knows that this freedom does not last. Or if it does, it is because he or she has had to rethink the meaning of freedom. "I was free to say what I thought was right, and now I am not free to work in my career. When was I more free, then or now?" Bower does not know.

Most of us think that freedom is about having and making choices. Arendt comes closer to the truth, writing about freedom as though it were surrender to principle. But even this is an idealization as far as the whistle-blower is concerned. The whistle-blower understands that the freedom he has experienced comes closer to compulsion, one that can seize a person and not let go until it has destroyed just about everything else the whistle-blower cared about: career, home, family.

Bower concluded by saying, "I'm glad I didn't have a choice. I don't think I could live with myself if I thought I chose all this. . . ." One might argue that this statement "proves" Bower had a choice, that his experience of compulsion is a way of avoiding responsibility for the consequences of his acts. It could be; these things are impossible to know for sure. One might, however, as easily conclude that the reader who cannot believe Bower was compelled may be defending against the possibility of such a threatening experience—that one could lose everything one cares about after being seized by an overpowering principle, almost as though it were a god.

Was Jim Bower too loyal to a principle, a principle that was insufficiently loyal to him—that is, insufficiently complex to take all of his interests as a person into account? I do not know. I do know that senders are often like that. How to live with someone who is so terribly loyal to his principles that they can make mincemeat of everything else he or she cares about? How to live, in other words, with the kind of person who is the sender to oneself—that is, the subtext of most whistle-blower narratives.

If the sender is supposed to make the subject competent, then it is a strange competence indeed, one that renders the whistle-blower unable to perform that most basic American act: making a living from one's chosen career. But perhaps there are other things about which it is more important to be competent. And if the subject is rewarded for fulfilling his part of the contract, as he does, then we shall have to ask what sort of reward it is to lose career, home, and family? One would hope that the whistle-blower is rewarded with a deeper satisfaction, but it is precisely this that proves so elusive.

Choiceless choice is as close as many whistle-blowers get to evaluating their own narratives.[5] Evaluation is not about stating the moral of the story. Evaluation is about telling the story in such a way that the listener comes to believe that it has a point, that it starts somewhere, stops somewhere else, and that one has learned something along the way. Evaluation, says Labov (1972: 366), is "the means used by the narrator to indicate the point of the narrative, its *raison d'être*: why it was told and what the narrator was getting at. . . . When his narrative is over, it should be unthinkable for a bystander to say, 'So what?'"

The most effective evaluations are not tacked on, but embedded in the story itself. Often this is done by the use of comparators (Labov, 1972: 380-387; Pratt, 1977: 49). Comparators move away from the story line for a moment to consider unrealized possibilities, comparing them with events that did occur, as in "if I hadn't blown the whistle, who knows where I would be today. The boss's office, maybe, or the grave." Comparators give the listener the feeling that humans with choices are involved, that life is a drama, not just a sequence of events. Comparators are the mark of a more fluid inner discourse.

Choiceless choice is a comparator in disguise. It seems to be saying "I had no choice, so comparing alternatives is pointless." In fact, choiceless choice is a strong but undiscursive comparator, letting us know the strength of the sender, compared to which the whistle-blower was powerless, as though he were sent to wrestle an angel, or a devil. Choiceless choice makes whistle-blowing an agony, a struggle between sender and receiver. That may sound a little abstract. Senders and receivers are not yet flesh and blood characters. But sender and receiver are actors, and the struggle between them makes a world. This is more meaningful than the next theme, trapped in chronological time, in which actors become patients, to use Bremond's term (Prince, 1987: 69).

NARRATIVES STUCK IN STATIC TIME

For the first several months that I attended the whistle-blower support group, I thought that most of the men and women there had recently blown the whistle, or had been recently fired. Their recall appears total, their emotional reaction as real as today. In fact, many were talking about events that happened five to ten years ago, and often longer than that. It is not as if nothing happens in the intervening years, but what happens is organized strictly by chronology. First this happened, then that, then that.

My boss did this, the company did that, then they committed this outrage, then they did that, and that, and that. Joseph Chaine put it this way. "First they moved my office to what used to be a broom closet, then they took away my computer, and finally they had me wrapping packages. I came in one day and my desk was piled high with other people's reports, and a note that I was to wrap them and mail them. They even gave me the wrapping paper, and a felt-tip pen. And after I did that. . . . " This from a nuclear physicist at the Department of Energy who blew the whistle on his agency's misuse of computer simulations. Such accounts feel bereft of meaning, one act equivalent to another in an endless chain of abasement.

What makes meaning? In trying to make sense of why chronological accounts feel bereft of meaning, we may learn to better answer this question: What makes some narratives more meaningful than others? In a cheap detective story, meaning inheres in the plot. Who done it? In more complex stories, real human stories, meaning seems to inhere in character development. Or rather, plot and character development are one. The bildungsroman represents their union, but the conjunction of plot and character development is not restricted to that genre. What marks a static narrative, stuck in chronological time, is the way in which it subtly substitutes sequence for plot, including the plot that is character development. The result is a narrative stuck in static time.

Chronology is not an alternative to meaning. The king died, and then the queen died, to use E. M. Forster's (1927) example, is a meaningful story. Chronology is the imposition of a powerful, primordial meaning structure on chaos and fragmentation. Chronology is both the alternative to fragmentation and another form of it, sequential fragmentation, the fragments ordered into line, like a cold and ragged queue of strangers who do not even share the time of day.

Against chronology one wants to oppose plot. The king died, and then the queen died of grief, to use Forster's example again, is the simplest plot, one event causing another. Trouble is, many whistle-blowers swing from chronology to plot with a vengeance, from mere sequence to plots in which everything is meaningfully connected to everything else, a theme that could be called paranoid narrative.

The Paranoid Narrative

If narrative is built on the exploitation of the *post hoc, ergo propter hoc* fallacy, as Barthes (1975) argues, then paranoid narratives are the most narrative of narratives. Nothing just follows, everything is causally connected, and the whistle-blower is the prime mover. Like the better known Prime Mover, the whistle-blower is strangely absent from the chain of events he or she has set in motion. Nominally an internal narrator, the whistle-blower talks more like an external narrator, telling us from a position of vast remove about a world that considers him terribly important.

One gains new respect for paranoia from listening to whistle-blower narratives. Not because "even paranoids have real enemies," as the cliché goes. It is true, but it is not the point. Chronology finds meaning only in sequence, because the flow of experience has been lost. Paranoia finds meaning everywhere. Paranoia is a surfeit of meaning, the world overflowing with meaning. Paranoia is the will to meaning. Or rather, paranoia is a last desperate attempt to flood the world with meaning. Paranoia is a defense against loss of meaning, the same loss of meaning that is the source of dread.

One more element of the paranoid narrative deserves discussion, but it is hard to know how to describe it, except to say that the paranoid whistle-blower is absolutely right. Not about the details, like the manager who may have smashed the windows of the whistle-blower's car. About the details it is hard to know. The paranoid whistle-blower is absolutely right that his organization is not just out to fire him, but to obliterate him or her. The whistle-blower's paranoia is an accurate emotional reading of an emotional reality: the one who has become the scapegoat cannot just be dismissed, but must be destroyed, so that others will know.

Marjorie Gooden put it this way. "After mom got fired from the Department of Agriculture for being a whistle-blower, I think she went a little crazy. Mom thought the car that ran her off the road was from her agency. But, you know, after awhile I realized that they did want to kill her. Not really, but they wanted to make it as if she had never existed, that everything she said had never happened. That's a type of murder too." The worst kind according to George Orwell in *Nineteen Eighty-Four*: to have the record of one's life shoved down the memory hole, as though one had never existed.

It is this aspect of paranoia that is the most difficult of all for an outsider to come to terms with because it represents a truth that is hard to know: that if the organization feels sufficiently threatened by the individual, it will remove him or her. Not just beyond the margins of the organization, but all the way to the margins of society. The average whistle-blower of my experience is a 55-year-old nuclear engineer working behind the counter at Radio Shack. Divorced and in debt to his lawyers, he lives in a two-room rented apartment. He has no retirement plan, and few prospects for advancement.

Because the power to marginalize is so frightening, it is easier to attribute paranoia to the whistle-blower rather than to see the whistle-blower as a prophet: not just in what he or she has to say about waste, fraud, and abuse, but what he or she has learned in crossing that frontier between loyalty and morality. It is not a reality that is easily expressed in words. It is the paranoid form of the narrative that comes closest to this truth.

Scherherazade

In *The Writing of the Disaster*, Maurice Blanchot (1995: 7) is concerned with the way in which the disaster de-scribes, making writing (and telling) about it almost impossible. By disaster, Blanchot means those experiences that disrupt our experience of going on being with the world, so that we cannot put ourselves and the world back together again. The mark of the disaster is that we cannot weave a meaningful story around it. We cannot weave a story because we have lost the place from which to speak. That place is the present.

The narrative voice may speak from past and future, inside the story and outside. The power of narrative stems from the narrator's ability to be there and then, as well as here and now. But the implied author (not the narrator, but the one whose existence is implied from the design of the story) must be present, and feel present, in order for the listener to share the story. This is especially true for spoken narrative, in which speaker and listener are in each other's presence, but it is as true of a 2,000-year-old text.

If, that is, we understand presence in its dual sense of contemporaneous, as well as intellectually or emotionally available, accessible, knowable. The disaster de-scribes because it destroys not chronology, but the meaningful experience of time. Chronology substitutes for the experience of going-on-being, as the psychoanalyst D. W. Winnicott (1958: 304) labels it, one of the authors cited by Blanchot. Chronology is the defense against time that has lost its meaning, probably because life has lost its meaning. Mere chronology takes the place of an experience of time as flow that carries us with it, which is why strictly chronological narratives feel so wooden. Time loses its meaning because the present no longer holds, in the sense of being a place that it is possible to be—because the I is no longer present to be there.

The "presentiment of a something which is nothing" is how Kierkegaard (1957: 38) defines dread. We may think about dread as something terrible, but that is not how dread is experienced. Dread is experienced as no-thing, an experience that is void because we are unable to put it in a story. As Blanchot (1995: 15, 29) puts it, "When the subject becomes absence, then the absence of a subject . . . subverts the whole sequence of existence, causes time to take leave of its order. . . . Time has radically changed its meaning and its flow. Time without present, I without I." Narrative goes all over the place in time and space, speaking in dozens of voices, but it still needs the present presence of an I to tell it.

Narratives that lack presence feel vicarious, somehow unreal, as if the teller were not fully there. *The Stranger*, by Camus, achieves its literary power from the exploitation of this effect, with Meursault strangely absent from his own story. Many whistle-blower narratives have this same quality. The difference is that the whistle-blower is not a character in a novel, so it becomes useful to ask what happened to the whistle-blower so that his story feels unreal.

What has happened is that the whistle-blower has become Scherherazade, desperately keeping the story going lest disaster strike: the disaster of having nothing more to say because the story is finally over. "And then they didn't do anything else because it was over." To say this is to be abandoned by one's persecutors to a faithless world, which is why so few whistle-blowers can say it. As Jim Beam, a long-time member of the whistleblower support group put it, "Any time I'd say something bad about them to the newspapers, they [the company that fired him] used to sic their lawyers on me. Now they don't even respond when I threaten to sue them. I'm starting to think I don't exist."

"The turbulence of stagnant motion" is how another whistle-blower described his years of exile. It is also a good description of narratives stuck in static time, filled with meaningless motion, an endless sequence of events, because the storyteller cannot bear to bring the story to an end and so finally know its meaning.

Stories are defined by their end. Everything that happens before is reinterpreted in light of how it all turns out in the end. Without an ending there can be no plot, and hence no satisfactory meaning. Which is precisely why whistle-blowers cannot bear to end their stories. One could argue that it is because the whistle-blower does not know the meaning of his story that he cannot bring to a stop the endless sequence of events. On the contrary, it is precisely because he does know that he cannot find the end. Then he would have to learn the meaning of what he already knows. That, evidently, is almost unbearable.

"Our ability to gain access to these narratives depends on what we are prepared to forsake to listen to them" observes Langer (1991: 195). He is writing about listening to the narratives of Holocaust survivors, but it applies to whistle-blowers too. Not because whistle-blowers have suffered similarly. The suffering of survivors exceeds that of whistle-blowers by orders of magnitude. Indeed, this is precisely the point.

Not as wounded as the survivor, the whistle-blower is more likely to just keep talking, so that he himself will not have to give up the truths of common narrative, the stock stories we all draw upon to make sense of our lives. The "little man who stood up against the big corporation and won" is a common narrative. Common narratives are not lies. They are more like clichés, worn and out of context truths, insufficiently complex to account for experience.

Knowledge as Disaster

To know what he has already learned, the whistle-blower would have to give up what every right-thinking American believes in. To forsake this is particularly difficult for the largest group of whistle-blowers I listened to: conservative middle-aged men. "Hell, I wasn't against the system," said Bob Warren, a civil engineer and retired naval officer. "I was the system. I just didn't realize there were two systems."

What must the whistle-blower forsake in order to hear his own story?

▸ That the individual matters.

▸ That law and justice can be relied upon.

▸ That the purpose of law is to remove the caprice of powerful individuals.

▸ That ours is a government of laws, not men.

▸ That the individual will not be sacrificed for the sake of the group.

▸ That loyalty is not equivalent to the heard instinct.

▸ That one's friends will remain loyal even if one's colleagues do not.

▸ That the organization is not fundamentally immoral.

▸ That it makes sense to stand up and do the right thing. (Take this literally: that it "makes sense" means that it is a comprehensible activity.)

▸ That someone, somewhere who is in charge knows, cares, and will do the right thing.

▸ That the truth matters, and someone will want to know it.

▸ That if one is right and persistent, things will turn out all right in the end.

▸ That even if they do not, other people will know and understand.

▸ That the family is a haven in a heartless world. Spouses

and children will not abandon you in your hour of need.

▸ That the individual can know the truth about all this and not become merely cynical, cynical unto death.

Not only is it hard to come to come to terms with these truths, but when one finally does, it seems one is left with nothing. "My case is not grievable," Warren noted. He meant that it was not subject to further grievance procedures, but one might think about it another way. Warren could not feel the appropriate grief because to do so he would have to learn too much about what he had already knew.

Or consider the case of Joseph Rose, who exposed the Associated Milk Producer's illegal contributions to President Richard Nixon's reelection campaign. "I believe I can make a contribution to the young people in this country by continuing to respond with a strong warning that all of the public utterances of corporations, and indeed, our own government concerning 'courage, integrity, loyalty, honesty, and duty' are nothing but the sheerest hogwash" (Glazer and Glazer, 1989: 223). How in the world could one want to teach this to schoolchildren and not be possessed by cynicism? Rose would teach a lesson as bitter as his heart.

"Knowledge as disaster" is how Blanchot puts it. Not knowledge of the disaster, but knowledge as disaster, because it cannot be contained within existing frames and forms of experience, including common narrative. The result is that Bob Warren is stuck in chronological time, an oxymoron that isn't once one considers that chronological time may be experienced as a respite from the end of time, or at least the end of the story, when one must finally know its meaning.

"I just can't live with myself knowing what I know," said Amy Brown with a long sigh. "I just have to do something about it." She finally did, but I cannot get beyond the first part of her statement, the one before the sigh-as-caesura. Amy Brown is a psychologist who went to the FBI over Medicaid fraud committed by her previous employer. (Medicaid fraud is probably the single biggest source of whistle-blower complaints, primarily because there is so much of it.) Her boss went to jail, but she could not get a job in the state where she worked. "They were all afraid I might commit the truth," she said. Eventually she moved across the country.

"My new colleagues, the ones who didn't know my story, kept asking me if I'd had been violated in some way. They meant rape or assault. There must be something about the way I carried myself, like I was scared of being intruded upon or something."

Amy Brown was violated by knowledge. The violation is the knowledge, knowledge as violation. Ordinarily we think of knowledge as something gained. But what if the gain implies losses we can hardly bear? The unwanted knowledge of the way the world really works invaded Amy Brown, possessed her, and the only way for her to be free would be to give up the truths of common narrative. She is headed in that direction, but it will take a while.

Being vindicated, as Amy Brown was, is not enough, and now we are in a position to see why. What is the satisfaction in being right if as a consequence once has to give up everything one believed in?

Another whistle-blower, a nurse who reported an extreme case of Medicare fraud at her old job, had to quit her new job when she discovered that the home health care company she went to work for was bending the rules regarding patients' eligibility for Medicare. I told her I thought she quit because she could not stand being a whistle-blower again. No, she said. "That's not it. I could do that. What I can't stand is thinking that everybody cheats."

Or consider the case of Mike Quint, an engineer who exposed defects and cover-ups in the construction of tunnels to be used by Los Angeles Metro Rail. Since Los Angeles is the site of frequent earthquakes, shortcuts in building the tunnels endangered hundreds of lives. Though Quint was eventually fired from the construction management company that oversaw the building of the tunnels, he persisted in his letter-writing campaign. As a result the construction management company was removed from the project, the tunnel contractor performed eight months of remedial work, and several employees of Los Angeles Metro Rail went to jail. Quint takes little satisfaction in his victory. Not only does he say he would not do it again, but he has turned into something of a zombie on his new job. Whistle-blowing "has reduced my trust and faith in people and in our justice system. . . . I [now] expect fewer benefits from work, and perform my duties as directed, with fewer questions of decisions or procedures" (Miethe, 1999: 161-162).

Why does Quint despair? He was right, the *Los Angeles Times* made sure everyone knew it, and he has a job in his field again. It must be his perverse choice to see the glass as half empty when he could just as well see it as half full. Or so the distant observer might think.

What if Quint has lost the glass? What if he has lost the container that held everything he cared about and valued, what he calls his trust and faith in people. Simple words, but what if they really mean something? For some, the earth moves when they discover that people in authority routinely lie, and that those who work for them routinely cover-up. Once one knows this, or rather once one feels this knowledge in one's bones, one lives in a new world. Some people remain aliens in the New World forever. Maybe they like it that way. Maybe they don't have a choice.

What is the meaning of life? To this little question Freud answered love and work, an answer that by now is almost a cliché (Erikson, 1963). What happens when the world becomes unlovable, and our work impossible? One might argue that the world can never become unlovable. We just need to try harder. But this does not seem to be Freud's position. If love is not just a psychic discharge, but a way of being in the world, then that way of being "demands that the world present itself to us as worthy of our love" (Lear, 1990: 153). If love is not just a feeling, but the force that makes the world go around, as Freud speculated in his later works (and as Plato imagined in the *Symposium*), then loving the world and being able to love the world because the world is lovable are two sides of the same coin. We make the world meaningful with our love, and the world makes our lives meaningful by being lovable. When one partner fails, both do. The meaning of life depends upon our ability to remain in a love affair with the world. Like any long-term love affair, this means that the world must love us back, even if this only means remaining worthy of our love.

It will not do to encourage the whistle-blower to try harder. He or she must find alternative sources of meaning—other aspects of the world that remain worthy of the whistle-blower's love.

"LIVING IN THE POSITION OF THE DEAD"

Maybe the whistle-blowers knew more about what they were doing than I did. Maybe there was an unspoken permanent agenda among the whistle-blowers, to which I was not privy. With the term unspoken permanent agenda, Labov (1972: 370) refers to the way in which the context and point of the story are set by the expectations of the listeners, not just the narrator. Among the young men Labov studied, a fight narrative was always on the agenda. It was "felt to be tellable," simply because it was about a fight. One did not have to explain the point; it already had one.

Sometimes it seemed to me that the point of the whistle-blower support group was to experience pleasure in hearing the same old stories, whether told by old members or new, over and over again. I became impatient, wanting to ask "So, what's the point? What's next? What did you learn? How are you doing to use what you learned on the rest of your life's journey?" But, this was my agenda, an instrumental one, albeit in the service of life, or so I believed. Sometimes it seemed to me that the whistle-blowers had another agenda: taking pleasure in the same old stories. There was, in other words, a contract between the whistle-blowers to which I had not signed on. What I took as narrative forms that risked imprisoning the whistle-blowers, they experienced as forms that held and comforted them. Or so I sometimes suspected.

Since this is my story as much as theirs, I will continue with my argument, recognizing the possibility that whistle-blowers might see it differently, because they are operating from a different agenda. One reason I believe that I am right (which does not make the whistle-blowers wrong) is because I occasionally came across a whistle-blower whose narrative did not sound stuck or imprisoned. The difference was striking. Most whistle-blowers' narratives seemed stuck in time, or imprisoned in a closed universe in which everything refers to everything else, with nothing left over for the world. A few whistle-blowers sounded free, but hardly in the conventional sense.

One expression of this freedom was the freedom of one "who lives as already dead," as the Japanese express it (Benedict, 1946: 248-250). Though I never heard an American whistle-blower use this term, I heard the idea several times. To live as if one is already dead is what is said about a Japanese who has suffered a terrible experience of shame, humiliation, and loss and lived through it. The term may also be used as an admonition. When a Japanese student is about to take an exam his friend may say "Be as one already dead." The term implies a supreme release from conflict: between the desire to be free and the desire to fit in and serve. To live as if one were already dead is to live free of self-watchfulness, self-surveillance, and constant concern with what other people think, a concern of us all, and a special concern to some Japanese.

"One day I realized I didn't care what people thought any more. I make barely enough to live on, but I can tell the truth about anything." Joe Wahlreich said this, a lawyer who now cleans the building in whose basement he lives in order to make ends meet. This was as close as I heard a whistle-blower come to living in the position of the dead. His freedom was, I believe, Wahlreich's reward for having fulfilled his contract with the sender. Finally he was free of its terrible power, because its demands could no longer destroy his life. His sender had done its best (or worst), and Joe was still standing.

Wu-wei is a Taoist term meaning nonaction, but better rendered as action that is in accord with nature. Living in the position of the dead is wu-wei. Perhaps it is more akin to mimesis, becoming the disaster in order not to be destroyed by it. I believe this is what Blanchot (1995: 41) means when he says "the danger [is] that the disaster acquire meaning instead of body." To become disaster's body is to live in the position of the dead.

To know the truth behind the veil, the truth that not only is concealed by common narrative but antithetical to it, is already to be in the position of the dead. To know it is already to be socially dead—that is, unable fully to be present with those who do not know it. For it is to know that most of the things people value about society are already dead, lost illusions.

"You know what's different now?" Joe Wahlreich asked. "It's a funny thing, a little thing really, but if feels like a big one. I can't make small talk anymore. When I hear someone saying the little things people say everyday I get impatient. I want to say to them 'Look, open your eyes. People around you are living in hell, and you don't even notice.' I was in hell and no one noticed. I didn't either, not for years. You can't get out of hell until you know you're there."

Where are you now?

"Purgatory, I guess. And you know what? That's as good as it's going to get for me. I know too much to ever get into heaven."

For Joe, getting into purgatory meant living in the position of the dead.

For another whistle-blower, Martin Edwin Andersen, getting into purgatory has meant accepting that he had accomplished something very different from what he set out to do with his life.[6]

> I've always wanted to be somebody, but I guess I should
> have been more specific. . . . Integrity—what should be a
> minimum requisite for public service—has become instead
> your specific, and perhaps only real, memorable contribu-
> tion to the workplace. Forget your years of professional
> preparation for greater challenges and greater recognition;
> forget the sacrifices you and your parents have made to get
> where you are, and forget your fondest dreams of advance-
> ment. The bottom line is that when you look around, your
> career is stalled, and you feel alone.

One is reminded of Polemarchus, a character in Plato's *Republic* (331d-334c), who learns from Socrates that justice is not just one profession among many, but a just man's only true calling. In this world that knowledge can feel cold as ice.

CONCLUSION

Is living in the position of the dead a coda or a resolution? If we see it as a coda, then we will emphasize the way it serves to bring the story back to the present, the purpose of the coda (Labov, 1972: 365-66). If we see it as a resolution, then we will see it as the whistle-blower's successful attempt to escape the prison of static time, albeit in a way that is most ironic. By living in the position of the dead, the whistle-blower's life becomes subject to infinity—that is, endless time. This, though, may be taking the phrase too literally. Because living in the position of the dead is the way in which Joe Wahlreich has found new meaning in his life, it is probably most accurate to see it as a resolution, through which he returns to the world of meaningful experience, albeit in a way he had never imagined, as a passionate bystander.

Most whistle-blower narratives lack a resolution. They just go and on. Not because the whistle-blower lacks the narrative skills to bring his story to an end, but because the resources of common narrative are insufficient. The stories that most of us tell are too superficial, too dedicated to not looking, to be of much help to the whistle-blower who has seen what one is not supposed to know.

So many Americans hate their government and distrust big corporations one would think that whistle-blowers would find more understanding for their stories. After all, some whistle-blowers become heroes, at least to a large segment of the public. A movie, *The Insider*, was made a few years ago about a cigarette company executive who became a whistle-blower (though even the movie devoted most of its attention to the television personality who interviewed him). A few years ago, *Time* magazine put three women whistle-blowers on its cover as "Persons of the Year" (December 30, 2002). "The little man who stood up against the big corporation and won" is a type of folk hero. But that is just the problem. He is a type of folk hero, which is a stereotype. Everyone wants to hear about the stereotype, no one wants to know how vulnerable we are to power, and how much it can take from us, including the meaning of our lives. It is this that the whistle-blower has to teach, but no one wants to learn.

We may tell our own stories, but we cannot tell them to ourselves. We can tell them only if others are prepared to hear them in something resembling the terms they are told. (In the language of narratology, one can tell one's story only if the narratee is on the same diegetic level, which means shares the terms of the fiction.[7]) What happens when the terms we most value, the terms of the sender, are not recognized by the world? What happens when principles for which one has ruined one's life are regarded by others as mere words?

The ignorant reaction of the world to the whistle-blower becomes a part of the whistle-blower. The whistle-blower becomes less at home in the world, because the world is not an understanding place to be. It is this homelessness that is the present absence in narratives structured strictly by time, or flooded with paranoid meaning, that last desperate alternative to no meaning at all.

The suffering the whistle-blower experiences has the quality of what Michel Foucault (1979) calls discipline. "Nuts and sluts" is the term many whistle-blowers use to describe this disciplinary process, referring to the way those who raise ethical issues are treated as disturbed or morally suspect. About this discipline one cannot tell a story. Or at least one cannot tell a human story, about a protagonist engaged in a quest. Discipline works through the language of science and medicine, in which actors become patients. In other words, discipline operates at a different diegetic level, its subjects transformed into objects.

Joe Klein struggled for years to make sense of what happened to him. An accountant for a large corporation, he had gone to his boss about his suspicion that they were overcharging the government on a contract they were working on. "First thing, they sent me to the doctor, then they put me on medical leave, and when I tried to go back to work they told me I was too sick. Before I knew it they gave me early retirement, made me take it. Don't get me wrong, I got great benefits, better than if I'd kept my mouth shut, but it's not what I wanted. I wanted to do the right thing, save the government some money. Now I'm the one with the money and no job." Joe Klein does not know if he's a victim, a hero, or a co-conspirator.

The failure of common narrative is not just a cultural failure. It is also a political failure, the failure of our society to address the isolation and sacrifice of the moral individual in this evidently most individualistic of societies. Narrative analysis can help us see this, and richer narrative forms can help us make sense of this experience. But such forms are dependent on the forces of power and production, just as culture is dependent, even as it is no mere superstructure. New narrative forms are unlikely to be forthcoming, at least on a large scale, in the absence of social and political change.

Neither the whistle-blower nor the rest of us lives in a world of wall-to-wall narrative, to paraphrase the late Edward Said. The whistle-blower's narrative is not arrested because all narratives are arrested. The whistle-blower's narrative is arrested because the whistle-blower has had experiences that cannot be framed and formed within the resources of common narrative. These last remarks may seem obvious. They are aimed at those few academics who occasionally write as if narratives lived a life of their own.

NOTES

* Most of the research for this article, as well as the methodology involved, is discussed in my book (Alford, 2001). Several interviews were conducted in the intervening years.

1. In theory, anyone who speaks out in the name of the public good within the organization is a whistle-blower. In practice, the whistle-blower is defined by the retaliation he or she receives. No retaliation, and the whistle-blower is just a responsible employee doing her job to protect the company's interest. This almost certainly results in overstating the amount of retaliation whistle-blowers receive.

2. One study (Miceli and Near, 1992: 226-227) found significantly less retaliation. Most of the difference depends on who and how one counts. Miethe's (1999) remains the most empirically extensive published study of whistle-blowers and bystanders. I (Alford, 2001) listened for over 100 hours to over two dozen whistle-blowers. The profile of these whistle-blowers fits that of the average whistle-blower

described by Miethe remarkably well, with one exception. Among the whistle-blowers to whom I listened, over two-thirds lost their jobs.

3. I have turned to the theory of narrative in order to think more systematically about whistle-blower narratives. Most helpful was the work of William Labov (1972), a structural linguist, whose most famous work, *Language in the Inner City*, is a study of black English vernacular. I also turned to several narratologists, as they are called. Here I include the works of Roland Barthes (1975), Gerald Prince (1987), Gérard Genette (1988), Algirdas Greimas (1983), and Mieke Bal (1997). The best definition of narratology is that of Genette (1988: 8), who says that narratology is distinguished by "respect for mechanisms of the text." This includes verbal texts, tales, and stories. One of the achievements of narratology is to demonstrate the sophistication of everyday narratives, which share almost every mechanism of the classic text. I turn to narratology as an adjunct to interpretation, not for the sake of the text, but for the sake of understanding.

4. A fully developed narrative has the following elements according to Labov (1972: 362-370) and Pratt (1977: 45-46):

   a. Abstract (establishes the relationship to the listener)
   b. Orientation (sets the context, time, place, persons)
   c. Complicating action (then what happened)
   d. Evaluation (what it all means, the point of the story)
   e. Resolution (the ending)
   f. Coda (closes the sequence of events, often returning to present)

   No whistle-blower narrative has all these elements, and there is no reason it should. Some elements are more important than others. The resolution is essential, the coda is not. Many whistle-blower narratives have more the quality of anecdotes, and that too is fine. What is missing is evaluation and resolution. Even an anecdote has to have a point. What is missing, in other words, is the meaning of the story as framed by its ending.

5. One could argue that the experience of being stuck in static time

is itself an evaluation by whistle-blowers. Several whistle-blower comments, such as the one by the whistle-blower who spoke of his life as "the turbulence of stagnant motion," support this claim. Overall, however, it was my experience that the dominance of chronology over plot that marks this theme was itself an alternative to evaluation, a way for the whistle-blower to put off evaluating the narrative. One sees this, for example, in the way in which narratives organized strictly by chronological time rarely change tense. Time travels only in one direction: from the past slowly forward into an ever receding present. This makes it more difficult to gain even a little perspective on events.

6. Martin Edwin Andersen asked that I use his real name, as did several other whistle-blowers. The quotation is from an e-mail titled "The Zen of Whistle-blowing (Notes from 4:30 in the morning, one Sunday)."

7. Diegesis refers to the fictional world in which the situations and events that are narrated occur. It is fictional only in the sense that it stems from the subjective experience of the narrator. All worlds are fictional in this sense.

REFERENCES

Alford, C. Fred. *Whistle-Blowers: Broken Lives and Organizational Power*. Ithaca, N.Y.: Cornell University Press, 2001.

Arendt, Hannah. "What Is Freedom?" *Between Past and Future: Eight Exercises in Political Thought*. Enlarged ed. Harmondsworth, England: Penguin Books, 1956: 143-172.

Bal, Mieke. *Narratology: Introduction to the Theory of Narrative*. 2nd ed. Toronto: University of Toronto Press, 1997.

Barthes, Roland. "An Introduction to the Structural Analysis of Narrative." *New Literary History* 6 (1975): 237-262.

Benedict, Ruth. *The Chrysanthemum and the Sword: Patterns of Japanese Culture*. Boston: Houghton Mifflin, 1946.

Blanchot, Maurice. *The Writing of the Disaster*. Trans. Ann Smock. Lincoln: University of Nebraska Press, 1995.

Erikson, Erik. *Childhood and Society*. 2nd ed. New York: Norton, 1963.

Forster, E. M. *Aspects of the Novel*. London: Methuen, 1927.

Foucault, Michel. *Discipline and Punish: The Birth of the Prison*. Trans. Alan Sheridan. New York: Vintage Books, 1979.

Genette, Gérard. *Narrative Discourse Revisited*. Trans. Jane Lewin. Ithaca, N.Y.: Cornell University Press, 1988.

Glazer, Myron Peretz, and Penina Migdal Glazer. *The Whistle-Blowers*. New York: Basic Books, 1989

Greimas, Algirdas. *Structural Semantics: An Attempt at Method*. Trans. Daniele McDowell et al. Lincoln: University of Nebraska Press, 1983.

Kierkegaard, Søren. *The Concept of Dread*. Trans. Walter Lowrie. Princeton: Princeton University Press, 1957.

Labov, William. *Language in the Inner City: Studies in the Black English Vernacular*. Philadelphia: University of Pennsylvania Press, 1972.

Langer, Lawrence. *Holocaust Testimonies: The Ruins of Memory*. New Haven: Yale University Press, 1991.

Lear, Jonathan. *Love and Its Place in Nature: A Philosophical Interpretation of Freudian Psychoanalysis*. New Haven: Yale University Press, 1990.

Levi, Primo. *The Drowned and the Saved*. Trans. Raymond Rosenthal. New York: Vintage Books, 1988.

Miceli, Marcia, and Janet Near. *Blowing the Whistle: The Organizational and Legal Implications for Companies and Employees*. New York: Lexington Books, 1992.

Miethe, Terance. *Whistle-blowing at Work: Tough Choices in Exposing Fraud, Waste, and Abuse on the Job*. Boulder, Colo.: Westview Press, 1999.

Pratt, Mary Louise. *Toward a Speech Act Theory of Literary Discourse*. Bloomington: Indiana University Press, 1977.

Prince, Gerald. *A Dictionary of Narratology*. Lincoln: University of Nebraska Press, 1987.

Rothschild, Joyce, and Terance Miethe. "Keeping Organizations True to Their Purposes: The Role of Whistle-blowing in Organizational Accountability and Effectiveness." *Final Report to the Aspen Institute*, 1996.

Winnicott, D. W. "Primary Maternal Preoccupation." *Collected Papers: Through Paediatrics to Psycho-Analysis*. New York: Basic Books, 1958: 300-305.

Ethics

an international journal of social political and legal philosophy

Editor: John Deigh

Subscribe today!

About the Journal

Founded in 1890, *Ethics* publishes scholarly work in moral, political, and legal philosophy from a variety of intellectual perspectives, including social and political theory, law, and economics. In addition to major articles, *Ethics* also publishes review essays, discussion articles, and book notes.

Quarterly.
ISSN: 0014-1704

For more information, E-TOC alerts, RSS feeds, and a free sample issue, visit us online:
www.journals.uchicago.edu/ET

Individual Subscription Prices:
Rates valid through December 31, 2007. Additional shipping and taxes applied to international orders.

Print and electronic, $48
Electronic only, $42
Print only, $42
Students (electronic only), $24
(photocopy of current student ID required)

To Subscribe:
Phone: (877) 705-1878 (USA/Canada)
         (773) 753-3347 (International)
Fax: (877) 705-1879 (USA/Canada)
         (773) 753-0811 (International)
Online: www.journals.uchicago.edu

3/07

Notes on Contributors

C. FRED ALFORD is Professor of Government and Distinguished Scholar-Teacher at the University of Maryland, College Park. He is author of *Whistleblowing: Broken Lives and Organizational Power* (2001) and, more recently, *Psychology and the Natural Law of Reparation* (2006).

MARY B. ANDERSON, Executive Director of CDA Collaborative Learning Projects, has worked in international development and humanitarian assistance for over 40 years. She is author of *Do No Harm: How Aid Supports Peace--or War* (1999), a book that helps aid workers deal with some of the complications of working in conflict zones.

DAN W. BROCK is the Frances Glessner Lee Professor of Medical Ethics in the Department of Social Medicine and Director of the Division of Medical Ethics at the Harvard Medical School. He is also Director of the Harvard Program in Ethics and Health. His books include *From Chance to Choice: Genetics and Justice* (with Buchanan, Daniels and Wikler, 2000).

KENNETH KIPNIS is a Professor of Philosophy at the University of Hawaii at Manoa. He has written extensively on ethics in health care, including disaster medicine, the treatment of low-birth-weight infants, breaching confidentiality, the surgical "normalization" of infants with ambiguous genitalia, and the foundations of professional ethics.

SANFORD LEVINSON is the W. St. John Garwood and W. St. John Garwood Jr. Centennial Chair in Law at the University of Texas Law School and Professor of Government at the University of Texas at Austin. His most recent book is *Our Undemocratic Constitution: Where the Constitution Goes Wrong (and How We the People Can Correct It)* (2006).

ISAAC LEVI is John Dewey Professor of Philosophy Emeritus at Columbia University, where he taught from 1970 until 2003. He is author of eight books, the most recent of which is *Mild Contractions* (2004) and many articles on the rational conduct of scientific and value inquiry.